Academic Library Services for Graduate Students

Academic Library Services for Graduate Students

Supporting Future Academics and Professionals

Carrie Forbes and Peggy Keeran, Editors

LIBRARIES UNLIMITED®

An Imprint of ABC-CLIO, LLC

Santa Barbara, California • Denver, Colorado

Library of Congress Cataloging-in-Publication Data

Names: Forbes, Carrie, 1975– editor. | Keeran, Peggy, 1959– editor.
Title: Academic library services for graduate students : supporting future
   academics and professionals / Carrie Forbes and Peggy Keeran, Editors.
Description: Santa Barbara, California : Libraries Unlimited, [2020] |
   Includes bibliographical references and index.
Identifiers: LCCN 2020000426 (print) | LCCN 2020000427 (ebook) |
   ISBN 9781440869532 (paperback) | ISBN 9781440869549 (ebook)
Subjects: LCSH: Academic libraries—Services to graduate students. |
   Academic libraries—Relations with faculty and curriculum. | Academic libraries.
Classification: LCC Z711.92.G73 A23 2020 (print) | LCC Z711.92.G73 (ebook) |
   DDC 027.7—dc23
LC record available at https://lccn.loc.gov/2020000426
LC ebook record available at https://lccn.loc.gov/2020000427

ISBN: 978-1-4408-6953-2 (paperback)
      978-1-4408-6954-9 (ebook)

24 23 22 21 20   1 2 3 4 5

This book is also available as an eBook.

Libraries Unlimited
An Imprint of ABC-CLIO, LLC

ABC-CLIO, LLC
147 Castilian Drive
Santa Barbara, California 93117
www.abc-clio.com

This book is printed on acid-free paper ∞

Manufactured in the United States of America

Contents

**Part Four   Rethinking Library Spaces for Graduate Populations:
Collaborative Design for Academic and Affective Needs**

Acknowledgments

We would like to thank Jessica Gribble, our editor at Libraries Unlimited, for her support, thoughtful guidance, and insightful recommendations. We would also like to thank Dr. Daniel J. Callison for his invitation to submit a proposal for this book to Libraries Unlimited. The library world is indeed small: Dr. Callison was Carrie Forbes' professor in her master's LIS program. Finally, we wish to acknowledge our contributors' hard work, dedication, and valuable expertise, which made the editing of this volume a pleasure. Their commitment to supporting graduate students' success and their innovative approaches to academic library services are inspiring!

Introduction

Carrie Forbes and Peggy Keeran

Graduate students were once seen simply as an extension of their undergraduate counterparts. It was assumed that because they were mature, well-focused, goal oriented, and college graduates, they were capable of handling the responsibilities of graduate study without needing special services (Blummer, 2009). High graduate student attrition rates have challenged that assumption and stimulated a reexamination of how institutions might better serve their graduate student clientele (Gilmore, Wofford, & Maher, 2016).

The graduate student population has changed much more than the programs that serve it. Today's graduate programs are much more likely to enroll adult students who are employed full-time, who commute to and from campus, and who enroll on a part-time basis. Although some students enroll in a graduate program immediately after completing their undergraduate program, many others enroll only after a gap of several years. Such students find themselves without peers with whom they can relate easily; most have responsibilities that strain their time and their finances. In addition, underrepresented graduate students (e.g., students of color, first-generation students) often must deal with these same pressures while also facing issues of discrimination, marginalization, and isolation (Gay, 2004).

These changes necessitate the rethinking and restructuring of student services. The premises on which these services were originally based no longer apply. For example, it has been assumed that the responsibility for addressing graduate student needs belonged to academic departments or to the institution's graduate division. As demonstrated in the chapters, today's graduate students have such diverse needs that multiple service providers must be involved, including individual advisors, departments, colleges or graduate studies offices housed within colleges, university-wide graduate schools, and other campus student service units, such as libraries.

Academic library services and instructional programming has tended to target undergraduates, who are generally perceived to be the group who require the most assistance in navigating the complexities of the academic library, but as more and more students attend graduate programs, either at the master's or doctoral level, many academic libraries have established professional development programs to help ensure that graduate students learn the wide range of skills to be successful as both students and as future professionals or academics (Baruzzi & Calcagno, 2015; Blummer, 2009). To presuppose that graduate students are proficient library users, conscious of the full spectrum of library services, is a mistake (Baruzzi & Calcagno, 2015). As noted in a recent ACRL publication, *Transforming Libraries to Serve Graduate Students* by Renfro and Stiles (2018), graduate students do need and want help, and many libraries are now offering specialized services for this diverse population.

In order to enhance academic library services for graduate students to better equip them for the realities and complexities of 21st-century academic and professional environments, librarians and information professionals must understand and be able to support graduate students based on their differing identities and roles. Preparing graduate students for the rigors of academic work, teaching them the skills and resources they will be required to have as either future faculty members or practitioners, and addressing other social and emotional needs though the development of life skills, are all emerging areas of graduate student services in higher education.

This edited volume contains 15 chapters of case studies, grouped into four sections, corresponding to the different roles and needs of graduate students. Because the diverse roles and identities of graduate students tend to intersect in a variety of ways, discussions on creating inclusive services for international students, students of color, students with different learning styles, first-generation students, low-income students, distance learners, and more, are covered throughout. The volume offers academic librarians a convenient compilation of timely issues and service models at comparable institutions. As academic libraries shift from functioning primarily as collections repositories to collaborating as key players in discovery and knowledge creation, value-added services for graduate students are even more central to libraries' changing missions.

Supporting Graduate Students as Students: From Foundational Research Skills to Co-Curricular Programming

In Part 1, chapters cover library services and resources for graduate students aimed at enhancing their academic experience, from library instruction workshops on research and writing to outreach and promotion of databases and tools to effective collaborations across campus. Brantley, Corrigan, and Duffin describe a series of seminars developed at Eastern Illinois University in response to the Graduate Student Advisory Council's request that librarians teach graduate students to navigate, understand, and appreciate the scholarly landscape, both as researchers and as content creators. The three seminars help students build skills to be successful throughout the thesis process, by focusing on the research methods and academic scholarly communication, organization of sources, and the afterlife of the thesis in the open access environment. Becksford, DeBose, Lener, Pannabecker, and Saylor discuss the evolution over the years of the for-credit graduate student information literacy course offered at Virginia Tech. The online course, arranged into modules by broad disciplinary subsections, benefits both traditional and distance graduate students, and the authors relate what worked, what didn't, and how they were able to grow this course successfully. Rosenstein employs an andragogical framework for her work with students in the Doctor of Nursing Practice (DNP) at Pace University, to alleviate the information anxiety of these students who are returning to graduate school after years of working in the profession. Building mutual trust and respect are core to developing relationships with the students as they conduct in-depth research on the systematic reviews that are the culmination of their degree program. The Syracuse University program became an R1 institution in 2015, and the graduate student population is growing because of the more robust research agenda. Anantachai and Hart relate how the library began to reach out proactively to graduate students by collaborating with graduate student services and graduate student organizations to develop and fund a variety of programing that would meet the differing levels of library research skills, and the diverse interests of that expanding population, including international students.

Preparing Future Academics: Professional Expectations of the Academy

Part 2 focuses on professional development for graduate students, particularly how academic librarians can assist with the preparation of future faculty members or academic researchers. Opening the section, Shaw, Milewicz, Madden, and Boers review how their assessment of graduate student research needs led to a redesign of the instructional services at Duke University. Working in a cross-disciplinary instructional group, they have developed a robust series of workshops, which mirror the research life cycle, to enhance students' digital literacies and to provide them with the skills for future academic careers. Chapter 6 also examines the interdisciplinary nature of research and emphasizes the importance of building community for effective student support. De Forest, Dowson, Moore, and White describe how Simon Fraser University fosters community among graduate students through three distinct programming efforts as part of their Research Commons: a graduate peer program, a "Thesis Boot Camp," and communities of practice. In particular, the authors document the dramatic expansion of their Research Commons, which has grown from a small department of two librarians to a comprehensive research support team of eight librarians and two paraprofessionals, offering data services, digital scholarship assistance, and outreach and programming for graduate students and postdoctoral fellows. Community and collaboration is also an important element in teaching graduate students about publishing. In "The Nuts and Bolts of Scholarly Publishing," Hon and Lundy note that graduate programs typically lack explicit instruction in scholarly communication, even though it is an essential element to professoriate or other academic work. Their chapter provides details on the University of Washington Libraries' publishing workshop series, which teaches students how to select publication venues, details the typical steps in the journal publication process, explains journal publication contracts, and finally gives practical advice concerning author rights and open access. Chapter 8, the closing chapter of the section, written by Shirazi and Cirasella, discusses how the librarians at the City University of New York (CUNY) have transformed the "institutional ritual" of students submitting a dissertation or thesis for deposit into an opportunity for advanced information literacy instruction on scholarly communications practices. Centering on the "process" of dissertating rather than simply preservation and access of documents, they have expanded the role of the library to include teaching concepts related to scholarship, such as manuscript preparation, rights clearance, and approval and submission systems—all important knowledge for graduate students entering academia.

Focusing on Future Professionals: Professional Expectations of the "Real World"

Chapters in Part 3 detail how librarians are fostering the development of skills graduate students will need beyond their academic lives. Bowers states why evidence-based practice is important in the careers of future social workers, and how faculty and librarians are collaboratively integrating this essential professional skill into the curriculum. She describes her own experiences working with doctoral students on systematic reviews as a model, and the steps taken to teach students to conduct solid research. Ding and Rassibi relate how they have partnered with instruction designers at Tseng College at California State University Northridge, a program that provides graduate degrees and certificate programs that prepare midlife adults for career advancement. Using a combination of andragogy theory, Universal Design for Learning, and knowledge about the three networks of neural systems (affective, recognition, and strategic), the team works to ensure learner variability and multiple means of engagement in order to make the online information literacy modules accessible, relevant, and beneficial to the success of the students in their professional lives. Farrell details her work with graduate student workers staffing the reference desk in the libraries at two academic institutions, one public and the other private. Using mentoring principles to guide her supervisory style, she seeks to make the work experience in the library meaningful and empowering to students' success in both their current and future lives, by offering opportunities for learning that are tied to both academic success and career goals, and by addressing often unspoken barriers to success, such as imposter syndrome and microaggressions. At Oklahoma State University, the library took the lead in establishing a digital badge program for their 360° program, in which student services across campus began collaborating to help sustain graduate students outside the classroom, from library resources to writing to career services to wellness to community building. Baeza and Ippoliti explain why digital badges are effective in allowing individuals to develop skills, to build relationships they deem necessary to their own success, and to control their own narratives.

Rethinking Library Spaces for Graduate Populations: Collaborative Design for Academic and Affective Needs

Conventional wisdom often regards library spaces as being primarily used by undergraduate students, while graduate students are perceived as users of services and collections. In stark contrast to the usual discussion of graduate students and space, Part 4 highlights how academic librarians are rethinking library spaces through collaborative design processes to meet the unique needs of graduate students, who are not only students and scholars from diverse backgrounds, but often parents, spouses, caretakers, and working adults. All of the authors in this section describe the important ways that physical space can meet graduate students' intellectual, social, and affective needs. This section begins with Courtney and Courtney detailing how Indiana University Bloomington Libraries has designed two spaces, the Grad Commons and Scholars' Commons, to serve both students' academic demands, as well as providing space for more informal networking and studying. An important element of the space renovations was the participatory design process that involved extensive graduate student feedback on the services, resources, and furniture they desired. In addition, Paiva and Pankl explain why the demographics on the University of Utah campus necessitated the creation of a space for families and a graduate-only study room. With a strong motivation to target affective learning outcomes, the authors emphatically point out the importance of productive work space in helping graduate students become acclimated to the demands of intensive graduate study. Finally, the section ends with Cardoso describing an innovative approach to space design for both virtual and physical spaces. Working collaboratively with graduate students, she created three "immersive professional experiences" allowing student groups to redesign the new graduate student orientation and the physical study space in the reference area. A key component of the revised student orientation included a virtual tour, and the student researchers noted the importance of getting to know a space virtually before they could feel comfortable taking advantage of in-person study and resource options.

Conclusion

The chapters in this book represent multiple ways in which librarians at academic institutions are engaging with graduate students, both inside and outside the curriculum, in order to provide this population with the knowledge and skills necessary to be successful within their programs of study and beyond. Much of this work is done collaboratively with faculty, with graduate student organizations, and with other campus services. The graduate programs and institutions discussed differ widely in terms of the locations, size, demographics, and graduate degrees conferred. Some of the case studies described are well established, but continue to evolve due to ongoing assessment of what works and what doesn't, while others are more exploratory, identifying gaps in the graduate student experience and investigating additional ways to provide support. Themes that run throughout this book include being proactive in understanding and addressing the academic, occupational, and affective needs of graduate students; thinking holistically about the students and the variety of roles they play and responsibilities they have; communicating and collaborating directly with graduate students; seeking ways to have graduate students interact and build community, whether in library spaces designed for them, through workshops, online classes, etc.; and assessing the programming to ensure students' expectations are being met. The diversity of demographics, experience, and hard and soft skills of the graduate student population offer librarians both challenges and opportunities to assess their unique needs, and to refocus resources and services that can assure these members of academic communities are as central in library and institutional strategic planning and decision making as those of undergraduates. The chapters in this book model the ways in which library programming and outreach, targeted specifically to graduate students, can bolster foundational skills vital to increasing their retention and overall academic accomplishments. As graduate programs prepare both practitioners and scholars, their academic achievements are crucial to the long-term success of, not only the professional world, but also to higher education institutions as a whole.

References

Baruzzi, A., & Calcagno, T. (2015). Academic librarians and graduate students: An exploratory study. *portal: Libraries and the Academy, 15*(3), 393–407. doi:10.1353/pla.2015.0034

Blummer, B. (2009). Providing library instruction to graduate students: A review of the literature. *Public Services Quarterly, 5*(1), 15–39. doi:10.1080/15228950802507525

Gay, G. (2004). Navigating marginality en route to the professoriate: Graduate students of color learning and living in academia. *International Journal of Qualitative Studies in Education, 17*(2), 265–288.

Gilmore, J., Wofford, A. M., & Maher, M. A. (2016). The flip side of the attrition coin: Faculty perceptions of factors supporting graduate student success. *International Journal of Doctoral Studies, 11,* 419–439.

Renfro, C., & Stiles, C. (Eds.). (2018). *Transforming libraries to serve graduate students.* Chicago, IL: Association of College and Research Libraries.

PART 1

Supporting Graduate Students as Students: From Foundational Research Skills to Co-Curricular Programming

Thesis Research 101: Cultivating Relationships with Graduate Student Scholars beyond Course-Based Instruction

Steve Brantley, Ellen K. Corrigan, and Kirstin I. Duffin

Introduction

Academic librarians at many institutions work to promote information literacy through partnerships with the teaching faculty, discussing with faculty the importance and need for graduate students to be exposed to ideas surrounding researching the literature, organizing their sources, and presenting their scholarship in the online environment. Sometimes graduate students will recognize where their knowledge falls short and seek assistance from their university. This is what occurred at Eastern Illinois University (EIU), the authors' institution. Graduate students of the Graduate Student Advisory Council (GSAC) reached out to librarians to advance their awareness of the scholarly landscape. These students were seeking guidance in learning how to conduct effective literature reviews and manage the growing list of articles they were collecting through their coursework and thesis research. These foundational skills allow graduate students to develop as scholars in their chosen field. Both EIU faculty librarians and master's graduate students felt a need to address research methods more substantively than possible at the traditional general orientations and one-shot library instruction sessions. To that end, with the support of the GSAC, a small group of librarians developed an outreach initiative to promote library use and research skills to graduate students. The "Thesis Research 101" seminar series was launched in the spring of 2016 and has been offered each fall and spring semester since then.

"Thesis Research 101" consists of three seminars, all one hour in length, designed to help graduate students as their scholarship progresses by bridging undergraduate knowledge with the more rigorous demands of graduate research programs. The first seminar, "Researching the Literature," led by Steve Brantley, frames the research process and teaches advanced research strategies and techniques. The second seminar, "Organizing Your References," led by Kirstin Duffin, introduces citation management software and scholars' networks. The third seminar, "Presenting Your Thesis," led by Ellen Corrigan, draws attention to how students' scholarship may be discovered once their theses are deposited in The Keep, EIU's institutional repository. These core research skills, while seen as valuable by the graduate students who approached the library for collaboration, are not taught in the core curricula of many graduate programs. Librarians, who aren't bound by curricular constructions, are able to adapt library services to meet students' expressed needs.

By blending concepts from the Association of College and Research Libraries' (ACRL) *Framework for Information Literacy for Higher Education* (2015) with scholarly communication service models, these seminars help graduate students to understand their role within the scholarly conversation. The seminars have also improved the frequency and quality of librarian engagement with graduate students. Librarians seeking to offer adaptable instruction sessions for their graduate students will find that the "Thesis Research 101" program can easily be tailored to their institutions.

Background

Located in Charleston, Illinois, EIU is a regional, public university with 1,514 graduate students, many of whom are international students and distance learners. EIU graduate enrollment includes full-time (45%) and part-time (55%) students and a 1:2 male to female ratio, with racial and ethnic demographics reported as white (68.7%), African American (6.4%), Hispanic (2.7%), multiethnic (2.3%), Asian (1.7%), American Indian or Alaska Native (0.1%), Native Hawaiian or other Pacific Islander (0.1%), not reporting (0.6%), and international (17.2%). EIU's Graduate School offers nearly 40 master's degrees, two specialist's degrees, and seven postbaccalaureate certificates. Many of these programs require a thesis for degree completion. To support the university's teaching and research needs, Booth Library, EIU's sole library, makes available research and educational resources in print and online (including more than 1 million books as well as journals, government documents, maps, microforms, audio and video recordings, and curriculum materials), and also holds governing membership in the Consortium of Academic and Research Libraries in Illinois (CARLI). EIU is in a small, semirural community in East Central Illinois. The university population is approximately half of the town's total population, and larger than most of the surrounding communities within several miles. Booth Library is a major area resource for educational events and resources. The library includes 13 faculty librarians and 19 civil service staff.

Literature Review

Service to graduate students represents a small but growing area in the library literature, and articles can be found reaching back into the 1970s describing instruction in bibliographic research and documentation (Clarke, 1972; Cornick & Ishaq, 1978; Shapiro & Hill, 1979). We have made strategic selections from this body of work for our review and concentrated on the current decade, though some earlier work is mentioned.

With the rapid and ongoing change to the scholarly information landscape, its forms of communication and modes of access to published research continually shifting, the graduate student—a primary consumer of this information—has become the focus of attention for academic librarians seeking to support this key stakeholder of university library collections. "The accelerated rate at which library resource providers merge and re-package journal content and update interface displays creates a condition where many graduate students approach library databases as novices to the search process semester to semester" (Allen & Weber, 2012, p. 130). Given the increasing complexity of the information environment coupled with the diverse demographic of students seeking graduate degrees, monographs devoted to the support of research students, such as U.K. researcher Allan's *Supporting Research Students* (2010), have emerged in the literature for at least the last 10 years. Edited volumes, as well, bring together a wide variety of case studies and other essays examining online graduate programs, student readiness, the value of credit-bearing courses, and different approaches to the range of master's and doctoral level degrees now offered across higher education (Renfro & Stiles, 2018; Siegel, 2009).

Two themes of note in the literature supporting graduate student services are collaboration and community building (Green & Bowser, 2002; Havert, 2018). Ince (2018) analyzes academic library websites for the evidence and depth of support for graduate students and provides a valuable review of recent literature. While many articles document the educational programs and spaces provided by academic librarians for graduate students (Colvin, 2010; Fleming-May & Yuro, 2009; Gupta, Salisbury, & Bailey, 1995; Morrissey & Given, 2006; Switzer & Perdue, 2011; Wilson & Chu, 2014), other studies examine graduate student proficiencies and information-seeking behaviors, and survey or assess graduate student research practices (Allen & Weber, 2012; Gibbs, Boettcher, Hollingsworth, & Slania, 2012; Rempel, 2010; Sadler & Given, 2007; Washington-Hoagland & Clougherty, 2002). A survey performed at the University of Notre Dame measures graduate students' frequency of library use, type of material, and whether that use was for their own benefit or for a professor (Kayongo & Helm, 2010). At the University of Idaho, *LibQUAL+* results enabled librarians to "define [the library's] strengths and weaknesses and prioritize service and collection improvements. . . . Analyzing [graduate student] survey data . . . increased institutional awareness of which library services and resources they value most highly" (Jankowska, Hertel, & Young, 2006, p. 75).

The longitudinal study by Rempel (2010) on the effectiveness of information literacy instruction to graduate students stands out for its focus on assessing long-term value: the study emphasizes the imperative for successful graduate students to "become rooted within their disciplinary communities" (p. 533). She argues that this process of becoming rooted often happens as the student writes an extensive literature review. Through longitudinal interviews with graduate students who participated in a literature review workshop, Rempel is able to make several targeted recommendations to colleagues developing similar interventions and conclude that the one-shot literature review workshop did indeed have lasting benefits to students, despite personal and disciplinary distinctions in how research was conducted.

Outreach, Promotion, and Marketing

Being a program that emerged from the grassroots of GSAC, librarians already had a constituency group with a stake in the success of "Thesis Research 101." Historically, librarians would provide information literacy instruction to graduate populations only at the request of a course professor. The frequency of this opportunity to engage with the graduate student population was dependent on a teaching faculty's understanding of their students' degree of information literacy, or the professor's relationship with a librarian. That the students sought out this opportunity speaks to the complexity of research in the contemporary environment and to the preparedness that graduate students feel they need to perform the scholarly rigor of a graduate education.

At Booth Library, a full-time director of communications and a part-time graphic designer assist with visual communication and print and online delivery of the promotion for the seminars. Each seminar is described in brief, and the librarian teaching the seminar is identified. The seminars are offered once during evening hours and once during the day within the same week, with each subsequent seminar offered at the same times in the following week over the course of three weeks. The seminars are advertised through multiple outlets. Information about "Thesis Research 101" is offered in a general press release to the campus paper and local news outlets. (Being a small community, events at the university are frequently announced in the local newspaper.) Additionally, broad-based social media outlets are employed, including Twitter and Facebook. Our strategy for social media is to post on our own library channels and also to post directly to many departments' and student organizations' presences on Facebook and Twitter, so that our news appears directly in their feeds via @ tags or hashtags, as opposed to relying on the intended audience being followers of the library channels. Our messages are amplified by the GSAC and Graduate College social media outlets.

Although this relatively passive marketing is a necessary element of the promotional strategy, it is reliant on the student being exposed to the information and the student understanding the value of the offering. We employ an alternative method of promotion by using professors, graduate coordinators, department chairs, and advisors to encourage their students' attendance. Staff at the graduate college are helpful in providing the names and e-mail addresses of every graduate coordinator across the university. We send e-mail to graduate coordinators, professors who are thesis advisors, and all chairpersons in departments with graduate programs. Each group receives an e-mail containing the "Thesis Research 101" information and greetings directed to their particular role. In this way we seek to avoid our message being ignored in the recipient's e-mail inbox or sent to the trash unread.

Creating a broad awareness for "Thesis Research 101" was the initial hurdle for us. Ensuring attendance has been the second and perhaps more difficult task. We chose to require registration for the events, believing that the task of completing a web form will help solidify the events in the students' memory and the schedule of busy graduate students' lives, who have many obligations competing for their time and attention. We also agreed that we would not turn away walk-in attendees, space allowing. We created the web form using Machforms, a university-licensed software, in which we ask the students to identify their degree program and provide a brief statement about their thesis topic. On the form we require an attendance response for each seminar event, asking if they will attend the morning or evening seminar, or if they will not attend any of the seminars. The registration link is promoted using our branded short URL tool, YOURLS (Your Own URL Shortener), which prepends any custom text with booth.eiu.edu. For "Thesis Research 101," our short link is booth.eiu.edu/thesisreg.

Session 1: "Researching the Literature"

The first of three seminars, "Researching the Literature" attempts to help the graduate student answer the question, "When do I know if I have enough?" The "Researching the Literature" seminar introduces concepts and tools that extend the student's information literacy beyond finding books and articles on their thesis topic to a more holistic understanding of how research literature is published, described, and disseminated in their discipline. "Researching the Literature" poses several questions to the student at the beginning of the session:

1. What are your online research destinations?
2. What are the key journals in your field?
3. What are the key review articles or published bibliographies that could benefit your work?
4. Do you know the controlled vocabulary for your field?
5. Are library databases enough? What are the alternatives?
6. How do you know when to stop? How do you know when you have enough?
7. Who is your subject librarian?

With the exception of questions six and seven, each of the first five questions assumes some previous understanding of how scholarly work is produced and disseminated; therefore, working with master's degree candidates generally requires some "unpacking" in order to provide a complete answer. Number six allows the librarian to address a common, yet vague and difficult to answer, question. Since there is no short answer to when you know you have enough research for your thesis, this question provides an opportunity for us to give some reassurance and advice to the students, especially since this topic follows a lengthy and detailed description of the contemporary landscape of scholarly communication, most of which is completely new to the student. The last question, "Who is your subject librarian?," emphasizes that the library faculty are available to them and capable of providing knowledgeable support. Often the fact that there is a specialist librarian in their field comes as new information to the graduate student.

Posing the question, "What are your research destinations?," suggests to the student, perhaps for the first time, that researching the scholarly literature in their discipline requires a strategy. The search process is not, as has been so aptly put by Boyd-Byrnes and Rosenthal (2005), "a purely mechanical transaction, putting in terms and getting a product" (p. 219). Suggesting online searching as beginning with a considered destination and requiring more than one search tool, as opposed to a single open-web Google search, helps dismantle the "misperception that the research process is a simple delivery transaction rather than a complex cognitive activity" (Boyd-Byrnes & Rosenthal, 2005, p. 223). In the seminar, we discuss such destinations as the local library catalog, consortial catalog, and *WorldCat*, in iteratively searching larger collections of content. Then we discuss the concepts of subject specific article databases and how they are presented on our local library website. This allows the introduction of concepts like licensing, subscription, paywalls, and authentication into the discussion, underscoring the ACRL frame "Information Has Value" (ACRL, 2015). During the discussion of general and subject-specific library databases, we also talk about the differences between abstracting and indexing databases and full-text databases, as well as technologies such as link resolvers that allow for external linking to subscription content.

In answering the question, "What are the key journals in your field?," we are able to introduce formal tools for searching and browsing journals by subject or title on the library website. We direct students to journal ranking tools and explain impact factor ratings, and point them to the list of periodicals indexed by the article databases in their fields. Finally, we suggest indirect methods, like exploring the professional or scholarly associations and, perhaps most valuable for their immediate needs, reviewing their professors' curriculum vitae to identify where their professors are sending their work to be published.

By referring students to review articles within a discipline and introducing them to book-length bibliographies, we help the students see that, while they may not be able to fully comprehend the entire research literature of a discipline, they can begin to understand the contours of the current and historical debates in their specialized area. This question also allows us to introduce the many subject-specific reference tools at their disposal: dictionaries, manuals, and encyclopedias that can be invaluable in clarifying theory or bolstering a basic understanding of a topic.

Introducing the idea of controlled vocabularies is almost always an eye opener for students, undergraduate and graduate alike. They are frequently astounded at the power of strategically selecting subject headings for searching, and this concept allows us to talk about the powerful searching that can be done by designating terms to be searched within specific database fields. In this conversation, we discuss the fluid and changing nature of disciplinary understanding through the continual exchange between authors, whether the understanding is based on empirical data, debate, or both. By referring to outdated terminology, that is, "See" and "See Also" references within a thesaurus, students begin to understand the ACRL (2015) frame "Scholarship as

Conversation," and their emergent place within that conversation. Librarians often point to the rigorous use of citations and the list of works cited within academic discourse as an example of the "conversation" occurring between scholars. Pointing out the way controlled vocabulary changes over time also demonstrates that even "official" knowledge is subject to changes or expansions in how experts understand and wish to represent a concept.

When posing the question, "What are some alternative research resources?," we have the opportunity to introduce the open access (OA) publishing model and issues surrounding its emergence and growth. These ideas, perhaps more so than discussions of licensing and subscriptions, emphasize the ACRL (2015) frame "Information Has Value" when considering the big business of scholarly publishing and its sustainability in an era of disinvestment in higher education. Setting aside a debate about OA's importance for the health of the research communication environment, introducing OA as an option for discovering and accessing scholarly information allows us to bring into the discussion institutional repositories, subject repositories, aggregators like *OpenDOAR: Directory of Open Access Repositories*, *Directory of Open Access Journals (DOAJ)*, and *COnnecting REpositories (CORE)*, and scholars' networks, such as *Digital Commons*, *ResearchGate*, and *Social Science Research Network (SSRN)*.

At the conclusion of the "Researching the Literature" seminar, students leave having been introduced to a broad array of tools and ideas. The seminar will help them do better graduate work, understand more about what is available to them (and why), and appreciate the various methods by which information can be accessed.

Session 2: "Organizing Your References"

The goal of the "Organizing Your References" seminar is practical in nature: to introduce students to these specialized tools and to orient students to their use. In working with graduate students one-on-one with their research, the librarians learned that graduate students generally aren't aware of citation management software. This seminar developed out of this unmet research need on campus. After attending this seminar, the students' overwhelming response is that they wished they had known about the software earlier in their academic career and that they will assuredly use it in their thesis work.

Graduate students who attend this seminar have little to no experience in using citation management software. As such, the session offers an introduction to these tools. The content of the session comprises what citation management software is; why students will want to use it; what platforms are available; what the interfaces look like; and how to use the software—that is, how to add and organize citations within one's library, how to use the word processor plug-in to format in-text citations and reference lists, and how to use the collaborative and networking components of these tools. We also discuss where to get support, including from the tools' online guides and from their librarians.

This seminar can be led in a few ways. One option is the lecture format, by presenting the software, highlighting features, and demonstrating workflows. A second option is to make the session a hands-on experience, allowing students to practice saving citations to their library within the software, organizing their library, and using the word processor plug-in to format citations. A third option is the flipped format, asking students to view a tutorial video and create their account prior to attending the seminar in order to delve more deeply into the tools' advanced features during the session. The advantage of the lecture is that the librarian can give a canned presentation and ensure that all software features are demonstrated. This style may work well with larger classes, and especially if computer access is not available to students. The advantage of the hands-on experience is the potential for improved learning and retention. Since many learners enhance their understanding of a concept through performing a task, this hands-on style is preferred when students have access to computers during the session. The third option, that of the flipped classroom, is most useful for dedicated learners who want a more thorough understanding of citation management tools. Students should be encouraged to bring their own laptops with them to this seminar in whatever format it is led, but especially with the active learning and flipped classroom styles. It should be noted that small devices, such as tablets and smartphones, do not offer the full functionality of citation management tools at this time.

The first time we offered this seminar, we used the lecture format, allowing students to ask questions throughout the session. We provided a hands-on exercise, which we had created, for students to gain practical experience with the software after attending the hour-long seminar. Students who attended that session agreed that hands-on work during the seminar would be more beneficial, so all subsequent seminars have been structured around active learning. We do not use flipped-style learning for this session, since graduate students already have many demands on their time. Focusing the learning to occur during the seminar removes any extra burden of time that advanced preparation of a flipped class would require. Less content can be covered in the hands-on session as compared to the lecture format, since time must be allotted for students to create their account and download and set up the software, and technical troubleshooting issues arise in this process. The advantage to this active learning format is that participants benefit from hearing the questions that arise in using the software, and the presenter is able to demonstrate how to resolve these types of obstacles during the seminar. Students get to see the librarian struggle through the troubleshooting process, which helps students pick up skills to work through resolving issues on their own. When necessary, the presenter can follow up with attendees, when attendance sheets are kept, with answers to questions that are asked during the seminar.

The citation management seminar incorporates two frames of the ACRL *Framework* (2015): "Information Has Value" and "Scholarship as Conversation." "Information Has Value" emphasizes the importance of proper attribution when citing sources. "Scholarship as Conversation" is discussed while demonstrating the networking component of these tools. Users can view scholar profiles, and some tools (e.g., Zotero) allow a user to message another user through their scholar profile. The simple act of viewing a scholar's photograph in their profile can help to humanize the research process. Scholar profiles in some tools (e.g., Mendeley) display a scholar's coauthors, which allows graduate students to explore related research.

This seminar also covers accessibility, which is one component of the ACRL Advocacy and Issues topic "Scholarly Communication" (ACRL, n.d.) in support of the ACRL strategic plan (ACRL, 2018). During the session, we have discussed proprietary and open source tools and how some tools may start as open source and later become proprietary. Students are encouraged to use tools that will remain available to them after graduation. Librarians should note that these tools have a cap on their free storage space, but this storage is preponderantly sufficient for writing a master's thesis. Students can choose whether to store PDFs with each of their citations, which helps in managing storage space.

For students unable to attend the face-to-face seminar, supporting material has been made available in a library research guide. Just as for the first and third seminars, the presentation slides are embedded into the guide and available for download and include presenter notes. An exercise for Seminar 2 that orients the learner to using citation management software is also available for download. This exercise walks the learner through using the software, from account creation to importing and organizing citations in one's library to using the word processor plug-in for generating formatted citations. A five-part video tutorial of the session is also available from this guide. The videos are focused on a particular aspect of the seminar in order for learners to select what components they want to view: "What Is Citation Management Software," "Organize Your Sources," "Cite Your Sources," "Advanced Functionality," and "For Additional Help." The videos range from 39 seconds to 3 minutes in length, with the entire series lasting just over 10 minutes. Making these materials openly available ensures that distance education learners and students whose schedules make it difficult to attend in person still have access to these learning objects.

It should be noted that undergraduate students have also attended this seminar. Although librarians do not actively recruit undergraduate attendance like we do graduate students, the promotional materials for the "Thesis Research 101" seminars are posted to the library website, public computer screensavers, and social media. Since many undergraduate students are working on research papers, we encourage their attendance. Graduate and undergraduate students have voiced their appreciation for this session. Some attendees have met with the librarians later in the semester as they progress with their research for a refresher, or to ask advanced questions about using citation management tools.

Session 3: "Presenting Your Thesis"

The "Presenting Your Thesis" seminar resulted from serendipitous networking: Ellen Corrigan happened to be at the reference desk when the Graduate Student Advisory Council (GSAC) president at the time stopped by to discuss the seminar idea with another librarian. Having been exposed to thousands of master's theses—creating MARC bibliographic records for newly deposited theses, as well as inputting metadata and uploading files to The Keep, EIU's institutional repository, for retrospectively digitized theses—Corrigan had seen just about everything imaginable, and she offhandedly mentioned to the GSAC president that perhaps graduate students could benefit from a few practical tips.

The goal of this lecture-style seminar is to assist students in producing their theses, the culmination of their academic careers to date, as flawlessly as possible. Although the subject matter for this seminar takes more of a pragmatic approach to details, attendees are challenged to reflect on how they search for information and how they evaluate the results retrieved by their searches.

The seminar title alludes to one idea we emphasize in this session: students will be presenting their theses not only to their committees, but to the world at large. Digital copies are made available through the EIU library catalog, the CARLI statewide consortium catalog and *WorldCat*, as well through The Keep, from which they are indexed by *Google Scholar*. The availability of a digital version supports the ACRL (n.d.) Scholarly Communication principle of open access to scholarship, providing not only an opportunity to discuss open access (as mandated by university policy and Illinois state law) along with the big picture on scholarly communication, but also offering a reminder that their theses may be viewed by prospective employers, doctoral programs, and similar audiences.

To demonstrate that EIU master's theses are accessible to anyone, anywhere in the world with an Internet connection, we show statistics and infographics derived from *Digital Commons*. As of this writing, The Keep contains 4,241 theses, 85% of which have been downloaded at least once and 1% of which have been downloaded more than 1,000 times. At present, the most downloads for a single thesis—*A Quantitative Study of the Source of Stress for First Generation Freshman Female College Students*—is 10,973, with a grand total of 386,202 downloads for the entire thesis collection. EIU theses have been downloaded in 212 countries, literally all around the world.

We also call attention to the fact that theses are submitted not to the Graduate School, but to the library. Employees who accept theses may check for paper quality and margins to address the library concerns of binding and long-term preservation, but when the thesis committee members sign off, that's the final approval of the work—therefore, any changes to the thesis itself need to take place before this happens.

During the seminar, we focus on the metadata—obtained from information supplied by the students themselves—that are key to making their theses discoverable, as well as potential pitfalls to avoid when supplying that data. We indicate the official Graduate School thesis title page, the only form required of all theses, as the source of this information. Because we have observed that this form often seems to be filled out in a rush, almost as an afterthought, we caution that even those who are not normally error-prone might make a mistake.

Much of the presentation is rooted in common sense. For example, "no typos in the title" is an obvious tip, as misspelled words may affect where (or even if) the thesis appears in the results retrieved by a search. On the other hand, consistently using the same form of their own name throughout the thesis is less likely to be something students have considered. We also review how best to identify their degree, graduate program, advisor, and year of degree conferral. We further address the importance of using a standard font for optical character recognition (OCR), spelling out abbreviations at first use, describing local or regional topics in some depth, and other such details that might be overlooked. Each point is illustrated by real examples from the EIU thesis collection. We explain that information will be entered as metadata "as found," so that the surrogate records represent the submitted theses as accurately as possible—meaning that, as a matter of ethics, any inaccuracies or errors will be transcribed.

Overall, we try to stress the usefulness of copyediting and proofreading. Human error aside, technology can be great, but it can also be glitchy. As an example of the formatting oddities that can occur, Booth Library once received a thesis in which the pagination jumped from the 13 pages of preliminary matter (up to Roman numeral xiii) to page 14 (Arabic numeral) of the body of the thesis—in other words, the first 13 pages of the thesis text proper were missing.

During the session attendees demonstrate their engagement by asking questions or offering comments. International students (approximately half the audience at these seminars) often indicate that they have learned about different cultural expectations of which they were previously unaware. As with the other seminars in the "Thesis Research 101" series, an abridged version of the presentation slides is available in an online research guide for those unable to attend the live session. Contact information is also provided, should students opt to follow up with additional questions at a later date.

Conclusion and Recommendations

Graduate students are developing scholars. They may begin their graduate studies with a limited understanding of the research process and have a resolute interest in cultivating this knowledge. These research skills include power searching the library databases and free online resources for increasingly complex types of information; knowing how to effectively and efficiently search, refine, and evaluate results; organizing found sources; using a citation management tool to streamline the attribution process; and considering how their work will be searched for and accessed by others. Librarians can address this need of building foundational research skills among graduate students through the creation of a "Thesis Research 101" seminar series, which can be easily adapted to the needs of graduate students at other institutions.

"Thesis Research 101" seminars can be made available for students in person and online, using a variety of presentation formats, such as presentation slides, hands-on activities, video tutorials, and research guides. Once developed, sessions can be extended to include undergraduate and doctoral students, depending on the relevance of the sessions' topics to these audiences. Sessions can be offered to the campus-wide community as drop-in classes or integrated into a departmental graduate student orientation or curriculum. The series can be expanded to contain more seminars depending on students' needs. Librarians at other institutions can reach out to their GSAC or its equivalent to survey graduate students for their interests to address gaps in the curricula.

"Thesis Research 101" empowers graduate students as scholars by acknowledging them as content creators. This series of seminars introduces graduate students to issues of access to the scholarly literature and research tools and features components of the ACRL (2015) *Framework for Information Literacy for Higher Education* and the ACRL (n.d.) Scholarly Communication advocacy issue. Within the seminars, librarians suggest methods of expanding their research expertise as scholars. Librarians also encourage graduate students to consider how their research will be discovered by the broader research community. As graduate students possess a maturing appreciation for scholarship, librarians are able to engage in conversations with these learners in a way that advances the students' knowledge and expresses awareness of the skills they have already acquired.

The "Thesis Research 101" series serves as a platform from which librarians can directly interact with graduate students, rather than having to communicate through a faculty member teaching a course. This seminar series allows librarians to take a proactive role in providing services to graduate students, since the librarian is freed from the subordinate partnership with the teaching faculty, which is often reactive to the demands of the teaching faculty. By responding expressly to the needs of graduate students, librarians can take on a leadership role in guiding graduate students along their path as emerging scholars.

References

Allan, B. (2010). *Supporting research students*. London, England: Facet Publishing.

Allen, E. J., & Weber, R. K. (2012). Graduate student searching proficiencies in the selection of qualitative and quantitative journal references. *The Journal of Academic Librarianship, 38*(3), 130–134.

Association of College and Research Libraries (ACRL). (2015). *Framework for information literacy for higher education*. Retrieved from http://www.ala.org/acrl/standards/ilframework

Association of College and Research Libraries (ACRL). (2018). *ACRL plan for excellence*. Retrieved from http://www.ala.org/acrl/aboutacrl/strategicplan/stratplan

Association of College and Research Libraries (ACRL). (n.d.). *Scholarly communication*. Retrieved from http://www.ala.org/acrl/issues/scholcomm

Boyd-Byrnes, M. K., & Rosenthal, M. (2005). Remote access revisited: Disintermediation and its discontents. *The Journal of Academic Librarianship, 31*(3), 216–224.

Clarke, J. A. (1972). Orientation and instruction of graduate students in the use of the university library: A survey. *College & Research Libraries, 33*(6), 467–472.

Colvin, G. (2010). The scholars commons: Spaces and services for faculty and graduate students. *Florida Libraries, 53*(1), 6–8.

Cornick, D. P., & Ishaq, M. R. (1978). Library and research consultations (LaRC): A service for graduate students. *RQ, 18*(2), 168–176.

Fleming-May, R. A., & Yuro, L. (2009). From student to scholar: The academic library and social sciences PhD students' transformation. *portal: Libraries and the Academy, 9*(2), 199–221.

Gibbs, D., Boettcher, J., Hollingsworth, J., & Slania, H. (2012). Assessing the research needs of graduate students at Georgetown University. *Journal of Academic Librarianship, 38*(5), 268–276.

Green, R., & Bowser, M. (2002). Managing thesis anxiety: A faculty-librarian partnership to guide off-campus graduate education students through the thesis process. *Journal of Library Administration, 37*(3/4), 341–354.

Gupta, U., Salisbury, L., & Bailey, A. S. (1995). SuperService: Reshaping information services for graduate students. *Research Strategies, 13*, 209–218.

Havert, M. L. (2018). Building boot camp success: Graduate dissertation and thesis programs at the University of Notre Dame. In P. Keeran & C. Forbes (Eds.), *Successful campus outreach for academic libraries: Building community through collaboration* (pp. 49–66). Lanham, MD: Rowman & Littlefield.

Ince, S. (2018). Trends in academic libraries graduate student services: A case study. *Journal of Academic Librarianship, 44*(3), 426–429.

Jankowska, M. A., Hertel, K., & Young, N. J. (2006). Improving library service quality to graduate students: LibQual+ survey results in a practical setting. *portal: Libraries and the Academy, 6*(1), 59–77.

Kayongo, J., & Helm, C. (2010). Graduate students and the library: A survey of research practices and library use at the University of Notre Dame. *Reference & User Services Quarterly, 49*(4), 341–349.

Morrissey, R., & Given, L. M. (2006). International students and the academic library: A case study. *Canadian Journal of Information & Library Sciences, 30*(3/4), 221–239.

Rempel, H. G. (2010). A longitudinal assessment of graduate student research behavior and the impact of attending a library literature review workshop. *College & Research Libraries, 71*(6), 532–547.

Renfro, C., & Stiles, C. (Eds.). (2018). *Transforming libraries to serve graduate students.* Chicago, IL: Association of College and Research Libraries.

Sadler, E., & Given, L. M. (2007). Affordance theory: A framework for graduate students' information behavior. *Journal of Documentation, 63*(1), 115–141.

Shapiro, B. J., & Hill, R. C. (1979). Teaching sociology graduate students bibliographic methods for document research. *Journal of Academic Librarianship, 5*(2), 75.

Siegel, G. (Ed.). (2009). *Libraries and graduate students: Building connections.* New York, NY: Routledge.

Switzer, A., & Perdue, S. W. (2011). Dissertation 101: A research and writing intervention for education graduate students. *Education Libraries, 34*(1), 4–14.

Washington-Hoagland, C., & Clougherty, L. (2002). Identifying the resource and service needs of graduate and professional students: The University of Iowa user needs of graduate professional series. *portal: Libraries and the Academy, 2*(1), 125–143.

Wilson, L. J., & Chu, A. N. (2014). Navigating the information highway: A multilayered approach for first-year graduate students. *Christian Librarian, 57*(2), 146–153.

CHAPTER TWO

Sustaining Graduate Information Literacy Instruction: A Case Study of Best Practices

Lisa Becksford, Kyrille DeBose, Edward F. Lener,
Virginia Pannabecker, and Kodi Saylor

Introduction

Sustaining instructional programs can be difficult in higher education, especially in support units serving the entire university, such as the library. Although credit-bearing library courses have become more common, contexts can change, key personnel may leave, and programs can fizzle out despite the best intentions of those involved. Even with these challenges, the University Libraries at Virginia Tech have successfully offered a one-credit, pass/fail, elective course, GRAD 5124: Research Skills for Graduate Students, for over a decade. The course was first offered in 2006 as an in-person special seminar, and, with the graduate school's support, has evolved into an online course with multiple discipline-specific sections. This course focuses on helping graduate students develop the foundational research skills they need to succeed in graduate school and beyond, from database searching and information evaluation to considering their roles as potential creators of scholarly work.

Background

Virginia Tech is a large public research university located in Blacksburg, Virginia. The University Libraries at Virginia Tech are comprised of over 90 faculty, 50 staff, and many hourly and student employees who provide services and resources both online and at library locations in Blacksburg, Roanoke, and the National Capital Region. In the fall of 2018, Virginia Tech's total enrollment was 34,850 students, with 6,370 graduate students. Of fall 2018 graduate students, 49% were white, 31% were international students, 6% were Asian, 5% were black or African American, 4% were Hispanic of any race, less than 1% were Native Hawaiian or Pacific Islander, 3% were of two or more races, and 2% did not report this demographic; 41% were female, 59% were male, and less than 1% did not report gender (Virginia Polytechnic Institute and State University, 2018, 2019). Approximately 30% of fall 2018 graduate students took classes online or at one of the university's multiple extended campus locations (Virginia Polytechnic Institute and State University, 2019). The University Libraries support graduate students in a variety of ways, including a liaison program through which relationships are developed between the library and all academic areas and several co-curricular areas.

Literature Review

Graduate students can sometimes be neglected in library instruction. Many instruction programs target undergraduates, particularly first-year students, and thus much of the literature focuses on this population. In addition, some may assume that graduate students are already information literate, demonstrated by their acceptance to graduate school (Harkins, Rodrigues, & Orlov, 2011). Although some do possess the skills to conduct graduate-level research (Green, 2010), many do not. Graduate students also have unique information literacy–related requirements. Beyond learning how to use library resources and search for information, graduate students, especially those planning careers in academia, need to develop what McClellan, Detmering, Martinez, and Johnson (2017) called "scholarly publishing literacy" (p. 544). Other topics that may be optional for undergraduates, such as citation managers and advanced searching, are crucial for graduate students (Zhao, 2015).

Graduate students differ from undergraduates in other ways as well. For instance, graduate students are more likely than undergraduates to be enrolled in online programs (United States Department of Education, n.d.) and may be working adults who have been away from school for several years. International graduate students who are non-native English speakers may struggle as they navigate both the culture of American higher education and conducting research in English (Click, 2018).

Finally, due to their "unique social position" in higher education, graduate students may be more likely than undergraduates to deal with feelings of social and academic isolation (Grady, La Touche, Oslawski-Lopez, Powers, & Simacek, 2014, p. 5), with international and distance education students being two groups particularly at risk (Erichsen & Bollinger, 2011; Irani, Barbour Wilson, Slough, & Rieger, 2014). To maximize community and combat isolation in graduate online courses, it is important for instructors to intentionally build community through support of participants (Phirangee & Malec, 2017) and through engagement strategies for learner-learner and learner-instructor interactions (Martin & Bolliger, 2018).

To reach students beyond the typical one-shot library instruction, some institutions have turned to credit-bearing undergraduate and graduate information literacy courses, though these courses are the least common format for instruction. In Cohen et al.'s (2016) survey of a variety of institutions, 19% of respondents offered for-credit courses (p. 566). There are many benefits to credit-based courses. Research is more than just knowing the mechanics of database searching, and credit-bearing courses provide students with the opportunity to learn to navigate a challenging information landscape (Badke, 2008). In addition, students have a chance to develop a wide range and breadth of research skills (Mery, Newby, & Peng, 2012). Beilin and Leonard (2013) noted the potential for credit-bearing courses to teach critical information literacy to further empower students. The literature describes both in-person and online courses, with some libraries beginning with in-person classes and transitioning to online classes (Frank & MacDonald, 2016). Although much of the literature about credit-bearing courses focuses on those for undergraduates, others have described classes for graduate students in particular departments (O'Clair, 2013; Tunon & Ramirez, 2010) and also for students across disciplines (Hintikka & Paasio, 2015).

History of GRAD 5124

The course that later became GRAD 5124 was first taught in the spring of 2006 as a special seminar open to all graduate students. This seminar was inspired by a one-credit, semester-long, in-person, library instruction course offered through Biomedical and Veterinary Sciences and focused on such topics as using the library's website and catalog, citation management software, literature searching, subject-specific databases, and other online information resources. In partnership with the graduate school, a course proposal was created to convert the seminar into a formal university course. After receiving approval through university governance, the first iteration of GRAD 5124 was taught in the fall of 2006.

This initial course featured the same basic lectures and assignments as the seminar and was taught in both the fall and spring. With only a single course listing in the catalog, students from any discipline could sign up for GRAD 5124. To provide subject-specific instruction, students were then divided into groups by discipline. This format proved problematic as there was not always a good match between available subject librarians' expertise and the number of students in each discipline.

In the fall of 2007, GRAD 5124 course listings were divided in the course catalog to include general subject areas (e.g., physical sciences, social sciences, and life sciences) so students could see available subjects and choose the most applicable section. The change to subject-based sections also allowed individual librarians to be listed as the instructor of record for each separate section, thereby reducing confusion among students and providing instructors direct access to class rosters and grade information. This model remains the format still in use over a decade later.

Changes were made to the course over time. In 2008, GRAD 5124 transitioned to being delivered completely online so that distance learners could enroll and all students could work at their own pace to better accommodate their schedules. By 2012, students increasingly complained about some assignments' simplicity and repetitiveness, and librarians indicated burnout from needing to update content for each module every semester. In response, two librarians made significant modifications to the content of their section and ran it as a pilot course in the fall of 2013. New modules, developed in conjunction with expert colleagues, were created to address changes to the scholarly communication landscape, and repetitive modules were combined to streamline development of those skill sets. Based on positive feedback, the changes were taken through university governance for approval in 2014.

In addition, in 2014, course instructors moved to a team-based approach to address updates. To maintain consistency across the courses and ensure each section met a common set of learning outcomes, a course shell with a master set of modules was created, with room for instructors to add relevant disciplinary examples. Using enrollment data, instructors were given the choice of which semester to offer the course depending on student interest. This team-based approach eased the transition when Virginia Tech switched to the Canvas learning management system (LMS) from a version of Sakai. The team used the LMS change as an opportunity to streamline shared course content and focus on best practices for online learning.

Feedback from students since the last major course redesign has generally been positive. Content continues to evolve and comments from students are often incorporated into the next iteration. Since students who took the course toward the end of their academic programs often indicated the skills covered and developed would have been more beneficial to them earlier in their programs, marketing and promotion of the course is now targeted toward new graduate students.

Philosophy and Structure

Common Threads

Although each section has been tailored to a discipline, there are several common threads. International students who are non-native speakers frequently take GRAD 5124. It's also common to have some students taking classes at the main campus and others who are in online programs or at an extended campus. Although some students have begun graduate school immediately after completing their undergraduate programs, others have been away from higher education for a while. Each class also contains a mix of students who plan to go into academia and those who do not.

Student-Centered Pedagogy

The content and assignments of each section have been crafted to be student centered. Within the LMS, a master course shell consisting of 12 modules and a final project is customized by the instructor to suit each section's discipline. The structure of the course shell will be described in more detail later in the chapter. The course consists of a variety of content and assessment types, giving students multiple opportunities to practice selecting and evaluating relevant resources, constructing effective search strategies, ethically using information, and utilizing library resources and services. Interim deadlines make sure students stay on track and allow the instructors time to provide them with feedback as they progress. Giving students choices within assignments, such as research topic, database, discipline, medium of submission, and tools utilized, ensures that each assignment is relevant and useful to the individual student's field of study, enriches students' engagement with the course, and allows them to apply the course content to their context. Although deadlines offer guidance on the pace of the course, students have some level of flexibility to accommodate their schedules and workload, a benefit especially for those juggling work responsibilities as well (Phirangee & Malec, 2017). To alleviate students' costs, no textbook is used, and all course materials and readings are open educational resources or available through the library.

Creating opportunities for peer-to-peer discussion is another core tenet. To combat graduate students' potential isolation, this course builds in learner-learner opportunities for communication and collaboration, as recommended in Martin and Bolliger (2018), that allow students to share their disciplinary expertise while learning from each other. This component is essential to creating a sense of classroom community. Although the course does cover advanced research skills, it also touches on an array of topics from scholarly communication, copyright, scholarly and personal information management, data management, and curation of scholarly identity (see syllabus in supplemental materials in Becksford, DeBose, Lener, Pannabecker, & Saylor, 2019). Student interest, understanding, and competence with these topics varies. Prereflection assignments are often used at the start of a module to encourage students to consider their current knowledge of a topic or use of tools and how it may differ from that of their classmates. Postreflection assignments, in which students are asked how they might apply what they are learning to their graduate work, offer opportunities to evaluate what students already know, what they are learning, and what they see as valuable for their context. These reflective assignments help students challenge their own assumptions about what they are learning and its value (Becksford et al., 2019). This aspect is important given the beliefs that many people have about graduate students' research/information literacy abilities and the difficulties graduate students may have in assessing their own skills (Michalak, Rysavy, & Wessel, 2017). Required content and assignments are also kept to a reasonable weekly amount for a one-credit course, listed in the syllabus as about three hours a week with the caveat that some modules may be completed more quickly than others.

Disciplinary Subsections

Life Sciences

The life sciences section has been offered continually in the fall semester since the very first course enrollment began. In some years this course has been taught by one librarian, in other years by two. It has attracted students across several departments that relate closely to the life sciences: agriculture, natural resources, environmental sciences, biological sciences, and veterinary medicine. Despite drawing on a large population, it has traditionally maintained lower enrollments than other subject areas. Early sections of the course included two to four students, all from the College of Agriculture and Life Sciences (CALS). It seemed that students from the other colleges saw the phrase "life sciences" and thought it was only for students in CALS programs as there was no mention of their programs. The course name was changed to Agriculture and Natural Sciences, which increased enrollment beyond CALS. Although the course now comprises students from multiple colleges, enrollment still has not exceeded seven students in a given semester. However, this low enrollment has proven to be beneficial, as it has allowed this section to be used as a pilot course to try out new content and delivery methods and to assess the feedback of students in the course before applying those modifications to other sections.

Health Sciences/Biomedical

To address growing research interests and programs focused on health, a health sciences section, built off the life sciences section, was offered starting in 2015. This section is taught by two librarians, one teaching in the fall and the other in the spring. To support the multidisciplinary nature of health sciences research and learning at Virginia Tech, the section targets students in health sciences programs but is also open to students in any discipline interested in the health sciences. Over the last few years, students completing the course have been in a variety of programs: biochemistry; biological sciences; biomedical engineering and mechanics; computer science; human foods, nutrition, and exercise; psychology; public and international affairs; and public health. The course is similar to the life sciences section with the additional objective of applying research skills to support evidence-based practice.

Evidence-based practice (EBP) is fundamental to health research practices. A commonly cited definition (specifically for evidence-based medicine) is "the conscientious, explicit, and judicious use of current best evidence in making decisions about the care of individual patients. The practice of evidence-based medicine means integrating individual clinical expertise with the best available external clinical evidence from systematic research" (Sackett, Rosenberg, Gray, Haynes, & Richardson, 1996, p. 71). EBP uses a five-step approach to (1) ask (a focused research question), (2) acquire (information sources), (3) appraise (information sources), (4) apply (information, knowledge, expertise, and patient/stakeholder values to a problem), and (5) assess (the particular intervention or treatment plan). The health sciences section has addressed EBP with a module that includes completing an EBP tutorial, finding background research sources, and developing a research question. This section also covers systematic and comprehensive searching and critical appraisal. The EBP module has taken the place of the effective searching module in the course shell, with the other unique content added to relevant course modules.

Social and Behavioral Sciences

The social and behavioral sciences section attracts students from a wide range of departments, such as education, public and international affairs, psychology, urban and regional planning, and political science, with a mix of doctoral and master's students. In addition to differences in background and long-term goals, some are attending graduate school full-time, while others, particularly education students, are working full-time and taking graduate classes part-time. With this diversity in student population, it is difficult to create assignments that will fit perfectly for all. For these reasons, students have options in this course: how the assignments are completed (for instance, a written reflection or a video reflection); the databases searched; and optional readings. To help with time management, the instructor uses a reading time estimator and lists that information at the beginning of each module to give students a sense of how long each reading might take. Additionally, some of the content from the course shell, particularly that covering research impact and data management, is not as helpful for these students. These sections have been modified significantly from the course shell to focus more on the aspects of the topic that are relevant to these students.

Engineering and Physical Sciences

The engineering and physical sciences section has one of the largest enrollments of any section and has been regularly offered since the course's launch. Most students come from the dozen departments in the College of Engineering, while most of the rest are from the College of Science. In addition, the content is flexible enough that this section can accommodate a small number of students whose course of study may not fit in well with any of the other existing subject-based sections. There are a mix of master's and PhD students, though the latter predominates. Many who enroll are international students or nontraditional students returning to academia after time in the workplace who can benefit from learning more about the range of scholarly resources available at a research university.

Two instructors coteach this section. Responsibilities have been divided roughly equally, with one instructor taking the lead on and grading the first two units while the other teaches the remaining two units. In addition, one instructor handles the logistics of making the content available online while the other excels at editing and reviewing materials for accuracy. The course content in the section has closely followed the overall layout in the course shell, with database requirements and search examples adjusted to reflect the subject background of the course participants. Engineers are not known for being prolific writers, so additional information such as minimum word count is often added to assignments to clearly communicate expectations. All students must complete modules related to searching *Engineering Village* and *Web of Science*, with additional databases selected and assigned based on individual student needs. Students are encouraged to research a topic of relevance to them so that they leave the course with a useful product in the form of a research log and bibliography of resources.

English

Because the English section is limited to the creative writing or English literature programs and is required, the curriculum deviates slightly from the other sections. Although the core learning outcomes remain the same, the content, tools, and examples match the needs of arts and humanities graduate students. A core aspect of GRAD 5124 is familiarizing students with subject-specific resources. For literature research, databases such as *MLA International Bibliography*, *Literature Resource Center*, and *Humanities International Complete* are valuable resources that are covered, but the focus on literature research has left out those who are studying creative writing. Although knowledge of these databases is important to MFA students, as they often take graduate literature courses, these databases are not seen by students as a core aspect of the way they produce knowledge. To address these concerns, the English section contains an assignment called "Research as a Mode of Creative Production" (Becksford et al., 2019), which can be completed in two ways, depending on the discipline or interest of the student. This assignment has asked students to think about how creative people, particularly writers, use information in their work. Students can choose either to look at the creative work of a writer and attempt to analyze how the writer is using information sources in their work or to create their own creative work utilizing information/research as part of the writing process. In this way, the section has maintained the course's core learning outcomes while also addressing the context of the discipline.

To support MFA students, this section emphasizes creative writers' use of information as part of the creative process and encourages the use of information literacy skills for creative writing, in addition to engaging critically with literature. It is also important to note that nearly all the students in this course will teach first-year writing as part of their graduate assistantship. This fact makes their understanding of the research process and basic information literacy key to their success as future instructors. In order to facilitate this understanding, this section asks students to use the research skills and knowledge they have acquired during the course to design an assignment that addresses research and information literacy skills.

Using archives and primary sources is another example of a topic extremely relevant to students studying literature and creative writing. Although this topic is mentioned briefly in other sections of this course, this section features an entire archives and primary sources module. This module asks students to identify general features of physical and digital archives, make use of relevant resources for finding primary source materials, and locate and compose a response to an item or group of items in an archive collection of personal, scholarly, or creative interest (Becksford et al., 2019).

Although grants, data management, citation managers, and authorship are still pertinent to English graduate students, these topics can be difficult to tailor to their learning needs. For example, how and why a poet applies for a grant is very different from how grants are approached in other disciplines. Further development of new data- and grant-related content that supports the learning outcomes of the course and is relevant to graduate students in the English department is a current goal.

Best Practices

Sustainability

Regular updates, use of a common master shell, and shared instructor workload have been key factors in the sustainability of this course over time. By distributing the responsibilities for maintaining the course, no one instructor bears an overwhelming portion of the work, and each can contribute in their areas of expertise. This approach also helps ensure that each instructor has sufficient time to make disciplinary-specific revisions for their section prior to releasing the material to students. Another benefit to this shared-responsibility approach is that as personnel changes, the course can continue to be offered since one expert is not relied on to provide the content.

Coordinator

Another helpful practice to clarify responsibilities among instructors and ensure continuity from year to year is having one person serve as the coordinator of the class. The coordinator communicates with the graduate school to schedule classes, works with the library marketing team to promote the course, and convenes and leads meetings of all GRAD 5124 instructors throughout the year. Since the course began in 2006, five people have served as the coordinator; the current coordinator has been in this role since 2016.

Annual Course Review Cycle

Making updates for the following year begins with a meeting in mid-to-late spring to discuss ideas for the next iteration. Although instructor self-assessment is included, instructors also share summary student feedback. Such feedback is received via direct communications, comments, and questions from students during the course; student course evaluations (when available); and student comments from the reflection component of their final project. No personally identifying information is shared, and the feedback is used only to identify needed updates for the next course offering.

Modifications both large and small are considered each year to improve the course. Necessary revisions such as checking links and incorporating new library resources are always addressed. A seemingly simple shift may require revisions not only to module text but also to any associated assignments, tutorials, and videos. Based on student feedback and updates to topics covered, modules may also be reordered, revised, or replaced. These larger scale changes must include regular input and communication from instructors during the revision process.

Prior to the end of each spring semester, initial publicity for the upcoming fall course sections is distributed through various communication points so that students may register ahead of leaving for summer work or breaks. At the beginning of the summer, the course coordinator creates a new GRAD 5124 course shell and shares it with all instructors. The final version of the previous year's course shell is imported and used as a starting point for revisions. In order to equally distribute the work, each instructor is assigned one or more modules to update. From May to mid-July instructors often work independently on their assigned updates, sharing a log to track changes. Several weeks ahead of the start of the fall semester, the instructors meet to check in again as needed on updates and to finalize decisions. It is important to have all work on the master course shell completed early to allow time for customizations to be made for each of the sections.

When the semester begins, all course materials should be in place. Each section instructor reaches out to students with a welcome e-mail that includes the syllabus, contact information, and general structure of the course. Instructors then send out regular updates as the course progresses. Students may work at their own pace, and each weekly module has one or more assignments for them to complete. Instructors generally grade assignments as they come in as subsequent modules may build on the prior weeks' content. Each instructor continues to make minor updates to their own course materials during the fall and notes any changes that may be required for the master course shell during the next cycle. The instructors also communicate regularly with the course coordinator about their respective sections and any issues that arise concerning students or course content.

Making time to complete updates is always a challenge. Since each section is customized, instructors require at least two weeks before the class start date to make changes. Although the coordinator's primary role is to keep everyone on track, instructors also recognize their interdependence and the need for all to stay accountable and complete assigned updates in a timely manner to ensure a good start for everyone.

Course Shell Structure in Canvas

A shared Canvas course structure is another consistent component among GRAD 5124 course sections. Each course begins with a Home page with information about the instructor (at minimum a biography, photo, and contact information, with some instructors adding an introductory video as well). The Home page also links to the syllabus and describes important course navigation elements. The course content is defined by modules, with one module per week and three modules per unit. Each module begins with a "Module at a Glance" page that briefly introduces the module's topic and lists the module's learning objectives, readings and materials (required and optional), assignments, due dates (for week and for unit), and navigation instructions. All modules have one or more content pages, links to openly available readings, and links to appropriate items (images, documents) in the course files. Instructors may modify content to focus on examples from their disciplinary area. The modules contain discussions and other assignments that can be used as they are or with modifications by discipline. To create a logical structure for both students and instructors, every module contains an assignment group. Similarly, the files are organized into a folder for each week that contains images, documents, and other files for that week's content. The course syllabus and general images are contained in appropriately named folders as well to keep things organized for students and instructors.

Accessibility

Since the class is delivered online, accessibility of the LMS and instructional materials is a concern that has grown in recent years. In addition to using Canvas's built-in accessibility tools, instructors are encouraged to use only captioned videos and provide alt-text for images. Instructors are expanding their skills and understanding in this area in order to ensure that their courses are accessible for all learners.

Marketing

Since only the English department requires the course, other instructors rely on their relationships within their liaison areas to help grow enrollment. In addition to sending information about GRAD 5124 to their own liaison areas, instructors typically ask other liaisons to promote the course as applicable for their subject areas. Whole-campus marketing is also used; the coordinator works with the library's marketing team to develop flyers and social media/website content promoting the course both campus-wide and in the library. Information about the course is sent via the graduate school's listserv multiple times during the enrollment period, and flyers are hung on bulletin boards in the graduate student center. GRAD 5124 is also promoted in the graduate student library orientation workshops offered at the beginning of each fall semester.

Beyond GRAD 5124

With an increase in requests for developing data management skills, the format used in GRAD 5124 was applied to the development of another library-led credit course, GRAD 5024: Data Management Skills. The first iteration of this course was taught in the fall of 2017. Using the successful format of GRAD

5124, the instructor of record created the master shell and partnered with experts in the library who contributed their knowledge to specific modules and provided updates to those sections in future renditions of the course. Several of these experts did not formally teach, but their work resulted in greater depth and skills development within the course (DeBose, 2018).

Conclusion

In looking back over more than a decade of GRAD 5124, several lessons emerge. One important lesson is the need to adapt: GRAD 5124 moved from in-person to online, from one section to many, and from one LMS to another, and additional modules were also added based on students' emerging needs. Without instructors' flexibility, the course may have been derailed by any one of these changes. This potential for change extends to personnel; although some instructors have been involved since the course's beginning, others have not. Having a workflow that isn't reliant on a single person helps maintain consistency from year to year. Finally, it's important to make adjustments as needed to ensure that the course meets the needs of the students for which it's intended. Though GRAD 5124 has always focused on building students' foundational research skills, the course content was adjusted to make room for additional topics when it became clear that the concept of foundational skills needed to expand. Although the course and the needs of its students will undoubtedly continue to evolve, the team looks forward to continuing to build on the strong foundation already laid.

References

Badke, W. (2008). A rationale for information literacy as a credit-bearing discipline. *Journal of Information Literacy, 2*(1), 1–22.

Becksford, L., DeBose, K., Lener, E. F., Pannabecker, V., & Saylor, K. (2019). *Supplementary materials for "Sustaining graduate information literacy instruction: A case study of best practices,"* University Libraries, Virginia Tech. Retrieved from http://hdl.handle.net/10919/89332

Beilin, I., & Leonard, A. E. (2013). Teaching the skills to question: A credit-course approach to critical information literacy. *Urban Library Journal, 19,* 1–10.

Click, A. B. (2018). International graduate students in the United States: Research processes and challenges. *Library & Information Science Research, 40*(2), 153–162.

Cohen, N., Holdsworth, L., Prechtel, J. M., Newby, J., Mery, Y., Pfander, J., & Eagleson, L. (2016). A survey of information literacy credit courses in US academic libraries: Prevalence and characteristics. *Reference Services Review, 44*(4), 564–582.

DeBose, K. (2018). Teaching data management skills in a one credit course: A case study. In C. Renfro & C. Stiles (Eds.), *Transforming libraries to serve graduate students* (pp. 301–304). Chicago, IL: Association of College and Research Libraries.

Erichsen, E. A., & Bolliger, D. U. (2011). Towards understanding international graduate student isolation in traditional and online environments. *Educational Technology Research and Development, 59*(3), 309–326.

Frank, E. P., & MacDonald, A. B. (2016). Eyes toward the future: Framing for-credit information literacy instruction. *Codex: The Journal of the Louisiana Chapter of the ACRL, 4*(4), 8–21.

Grady, R. K., La Touche, R., Oslawski-Lopez, J., Powers, A., & Simacek, K. (2014). Betwixt and between: The social position and stress experiences of graduate students. *Teaching Sociology, 42*(1), 5–16.

Green, R. (2010). Information illiteracy: Examining our assumptions. *Journal of Academic Librarianship, 36*(4), 313–319.

Harkins, M. J., Rodrigues, D. B., & Orlov, S. (2011). "Where to start?": Considerations for faculty and librarians in delivering information literacy instruction for graduate students. *Practical Academic Librarianship: The International Journal of the SLA, 1*(1), 28–50.

Hintikka, K., & Paasio, A. L. (2015). An information literacy course for doctoral students: Information resources and tools for research. *Nordic Journal of Information Literacy in Higher Education, 7*(1), 38–47.

Irani, T. A., Barbour Wilson, S., Slough, D. L., & Rieger, M. (2014). Graduate student experiences on- and off-campus: Social connectedness and perceived isolation. *International Journal of E-Learning & Distance Education, 28*(1), 1–16.

Martin, F., & Bolliger, D. U. (2018). Engagement matters: Student perceptions on the importance of engagement strategies in the online learning environment. *Online Learning, 22*(1), 205–222.

McClellan, S., Detmering, R., Martinez, G., & Johnson, A. M. (2017). Raising the library's impact factor: A case study in scholarly publishing literacy for graduate students. *portal: Libraries & the Academy, 17*(3), 543–568.

Mery, Y., Newby, J., & Peng, K. (2012). Why one-shot information literacy sessions are not the future of instruction: A case for online credit courses. *College & Research Libraries, 73*(4), 366–377.

Michalak, R., Rysavy, M. D. T., & Wessel, A. (2017). Students' perceptions of their information literacy skills: The confidence gap between male and female international graduate students. *Journal of Academic Librarianship, 43*(2), 100–104.

O'Clair, K. (2013). Preparing graduate students for graduate-level study and research. *Reference Services Review, 41*(2), 336–350.

Phirangee, K., & Malec, A. (2017). Othering in online learning: An examination of social presence, identity, and sense of community. *Distance Education, 38*(2), 160–172.

Sackett, D. L., Rosenberg, W. M., Gray, J. A., Haynes, R. B., & Richardson, W. S. (1996). Evidence based medicine: What it is and what it isn't. *BMJ: British Medical Journal, 312*(7023), 71–72.

Tunon, J., & Ramirez, L. (2010). ABD or EdD? A model of library training for distance doctoral students. *Journal of Library Administration, 50*(7/8), 989–996.

United States Department of Education. (n.d.). *Fast facts—Distance learning.* Retrieved from https://nces.ed.gov/fastfacts/display.asp?id=80

Virginia Polytechnic Institute and State University. (2018). *International students.* Retrieved from https://graduateschool.vt.edu/content/graduateschool_vt_edu/en/international-students.html

Virginia Polytechnic Institute and State University. (2019). *University wide enrollment.* Retrieved from https://irweb.ir.vt.edu/webtest/Rollcall.aspx

Zhao, J. C. (2015). Making information literacy instruction relevant: A needs assessment approach at McGill University. *Science & Technology Libraries, 34*(3), 241–256.

CHAPTER THREE

Here When You Need Me: Supporting Doctoral Nursing Students

Jennifer Rosenstein

Introduction

The Doctor of Nursing Practice (DNP) degree at Pace University is "designed for nurses seeking a terminal degree in nursing practice and offers an alternative to research-focused doctoral programs" (Rosseter, 2018). DNP students enter their doctoral program with a wealth of practical work experience, and a significant gap between completing their master's degree and starting the DNP program. These students need foundational research skills in order to complete their degree and to serve as clinical leaders promoting evidence-based practice in a wide variety of health care settings.

This chapter will discuss the intensive library support provided to the DNP program at Pace University, focusing on the importance of understanding key characteristics of this group of students. DNP students are experienced clinicians but often lack research skills and facility with subject-specific databases. Many of the students also struggle with unfamiliar technology. In order to create an inclusive space for these students, librarians must be flexible—both practically in terms of scheduling research consultations outside of regular work hours, and emotionally in order to mitigate students' information anxiety.

The research for this chapter consisted of an online survey sent to all current DNP students and DNP alumni (see Appendix 3.1) and of a small focus group with DNP faculty (see Appendix 3.2) who are themselves alumni of the program. The focus group yielded valuable insight from the professors' dual perspective as former students and current faculty. Quotations that follow in this chapter from DNP faculty were elicited during the focus group. The survey was approved by Pace University's Internal Review Board and distributed via e-mail. The aim of the survey was to better understand students' personal and professional backgrounds, and the effectiveness of the library support provided during their doctoral program.

Background

Pace University was founded in 1906 in lower Manhattan as an accounting school, and has steadily grown into a university that currently has nearly 13,000 graduate and undergraduate students at campuses in Manhattan and Westchester County, New York. Currently, the Lienhard School of Nursing runs undergraduate and graduate programs on both main campuses. Students in the DNP program come from a wide range of backgrounds; approximately 6% identify as Hispanic, 14% identify as Asian or Asian American, 32% identify as black, and 37% identify as white.

The DNP program was the second such program to be approved in New York State, and the first cohort of students entered the program in 2008. The most recent group, which began the program in the fall of 2018, is cohort 11, and the program has been shortened to two years with an evidence summary as the final project. Previously, the DNP program lasted three years with a required systematic review as the capstone project. The systematic reviews were published by the Joanna Briggs Institute and therefore had to meet the institute's strict guidelines. This chapter will focus on the library support for systematic reviews; however, students need very similar research skills to complete their evidence summaries.

A systematic review "attempts to collate all empirical evidence that fits prespecified eligibility criteria in order to answer a specific research question" (Higgins & Green, 2011, 1.2.2). One of the hallmarks of such a review is "a systematic search that attempts to identify all studies that would meet the eligibility criteria" (Higgins & Green, 2011, 1.2.2). This type of search requires an in-depth knowledge of medical database searching, including the difference between subject headings and keywords. Students have needed to understand how to build a thorough yet targeted search that will uncover all relevant studies without picking up too many irrelevant results. The students also have needed to document their search strategy in detail, so that it can be reported in their systematic review.

The level of database searching required for a systematic review proved to be far beyond the knowledge level of most DNP students and necessitated significant support from the library. Luckily, one of the instruction librarians working at Pace in 2008, Shannon Kealey, had extensive experience as a health sciences librarian and understood the literature search process required for a systematic review. However, Kealey did not understand the unique characteristics of DNP students—specifically that most of them had been out of school for a significant period of time and were unfamiliar with much of the technology they would need to use (S. Kealey, personal communication, November 15, 2018).

Most DNP students enter the program with substantial clinical experience working as nurse practitioners. Kealey stressed the importance of acknowledging with students the difference between their approaches to a medical question as clinicians versus the approach needed to build a successful literature search. She emphasized that it is crucial to explicitly recognize students' expertise and experience and make connections between their prior knowledge and the new skills they need to acquire (S. Kealey, personal communication, November 15, 2018).

Currently, I handle nearly all of the library support for the DNP program. I was hired at Pace in the fall of 2011 as first year outreach services librarian. I had no academic library experience before starting at Pace, having previously worked in secondary schools. Although much of my work has focused on undergraduates, there has been a need for all the instructional librarians to be flexible and work with a wide variety of disciplines and student levels. In order to meet the increasing demand from the DNP program, Kealey trained me on supporting systematic reviews, and I sought out other professional development opportunities. When Kealey left Pace in the spring of 2012, I became the main liaison between the library and the graduate nursing program.

Over time, the role of librarian support in the DNP program became more codified. In 2015, Dr. Jason Slyer became the director of the program. Slyer is himself an alumnus of the DNP program; he graduated from the first cohort of students. He has required students to meet with the librarian in the early stages of developing their systematic review. Each group of students has had to meet with me at least once as they refine the clinical question for their systematic review and begin to write the systematic review protocol. In this first meeting, I have consulted with the students on the scope of their clinical question in order to help them begin to create a concept map of search terms and to suggest important databases and sources of grey literature to search.

Literature Review

My approach to working with DNP students is based on two theoretical concepts, andragogy and information anxiety. The andragogical model is most associated with Knowles (1968); throughout his career, he articulated the differences between pedagogy (the teaching of children) and andragogy (the teaching of adults). The andragogical model is based on a set of assumptions about adult learners:

1. "Adults need to know why they need to learn something before undertaking to learn it" (Knowles, Holton, & Swanson, 2005, p. 64).
2. "Adults have a self-concept of being responsible for their own decisions, for their own lives" (Knowles et al., 2005, p. 65).
3. "Adults come into an educational activity with both a greater volume and a different quality of experience from that of youths" (Knowles et al., 2005, p. 65).
4. "Adults become ready to learn those things they need to know and be able to do in order to cope effectively with their real-life situations" (Knowles et al., 2005, p. 66).
5. "Adults are life-centered (or task-centered or problem-centered) in their orientation to learning" (Knowles et al., 2005, p. 67).
6. "Adults are responsive to some external motivators . . . but the most potent motivators are internal pressures" (Knowles et al., 2005, p. 68).

All of these assumptions of the andragogical model resonate greatly with my experience of working with DNP students. Knowles emphasizes the importance of creating a climate of mutual trust, respect, and collaboration that is crucial for a productive working relationship between librarians and DNP students. The other key concept that informs my work with DNP students is that of information anxiety. The idea of information anxiety evolved out of earlier work on library anxiety. Mellon (1986) first articulated a theory of library anxiety in the 1980s. She found that "75 to 85 percent of students in each class described their initial response to the library in terms of fear or anxiety" (Mellon, 1986, p. 162).

As research moves online and out of the physical space of the library, there is a need for a broader understanding of library anxiety. Katopol (2012) articulated the concept of information anxiety, which:

> focuses on what students are actually doing, fulfilling an information need, rather than *where* they do it. The mental stress surrounding information activities and filling information needs should be labeled as such, since the goal is obtaining information, which may or may not include visiting the library. (p. 9)

I operate on the understanding that DNP students experience significant information anxiety and that one of the primary aims of my work as a librarian is not just to teach practical research skills, but to allay information anxiety.

There is a notable lack of research on library services for graduate nursing students, and nothing available on the particular needs of doctoral nursing students. There is, however, some research on doctoral students in other fields that has relevance for doctoral nursing students as well. Green and Macauley (2007) conducted interviews with American and Australian doctoral students and academic librarians. They write, "doctoral education students, and especially those who enroll in the EdD, are motivated by an imperative to improve their field's professional practice . . . they are skilled in negotiating multiple commitments and blending them when necessary" (Green & Macauley, 2007, p. 322). In my experience, this is equally true for DNP students. The DNP, as opposed to a PhD in nursing, is a degree centered on clinical practice; students are highly focused on improving patient care and skilled at juggling the multiple demands of their professional and personal lives.

Green and Macauley (2007) go on to say,

> . . . delivery of instruction and consultation should be planned to accommodate multiple learning styles and incorporate scaffolded training and instruction. Instruction should be delivered at the time of need and appropriately support candidates' requirements to accumulate, critique, manage, synthesize, and distribute information and knowledge. (p. 324)

All of the qualities they describe are crucial for the library instruction and consultations provided to the DNP program. As one of the DNP faculty members put it, "you (the librarian) listen to them before you tell them what to do . . . and then you synthesize information. And you don't give them the answer, you help them find the answer."

Library Support for the DNP Program

The DNP program is a hybrid program. Most of the work is conducted online using the Blackboard learning management system, but students spend one full day on campus a month. I have initially met students during their summer orientation, where I have done a brief presentation as an introduction to database searching and some of the library services. The most important aspect of that orientation has been simply to introduce myself to the students, let them know that there is a librarian dedicated to the DNP program, and hopefully present myself as approachable and helpful.

DNP students have had multiple points of contact with me before they begin formal work on their systematic reviews. I created a detailed LibGuide for a health policy class that is part of the DNP program, and I have usually visited that class in-person to present the guide. DNP faculty members will invite me to visit their classes during one of the monthly on-campus days to help students with a specific research task, or do an introductory lesson on database searching.

As mentioned earlier, once students begin formal work on their systematic review they have been required to meet with me at least once. The DNP students work on their systematic reviews in small groups of three to four students. These initial meetings are usually conducted in-person, but I always offer to speak with students online. After the initial required meeting, students may contact me for ongoing group and individual consultations as needed. The number of sessions per group and per student varies widely. Some groups do not schedule any follow-up consultations after the required meeting. With other groups I sometimes meet weekly or biweekly, especially over the summer while students are working intensively on their systematic reviews. The number of sessions has been determined by individual students and their comfort level with technology and database searching.

There are advantages and disadvantages to both in-person and online meetings. I find that students are better able to absorb information when meeting in-person, and we can cover more ground more quickly. However, it is up to students to take notes in order to remember the details of what we discussed. One of the big advantages of online meetings is that we can record the meeting. Knowing that the recording is available allays students' anxieties. With this level of complex database searching there are many little steps to remember, and I have always told students I don't expect them to remember every step. They can always refer back to the recording.

I have realized over time that it is important to give students opportunities for self-directed learning, as consistent with andragogical principles. With this aim in mind, I created a series of video tutorials that students can watch independently. The videos are posted publicly on YouTube, and I also embed them in the Nursing Research LibGuide that I manage. I initially started with a series of four videos: "Understanding Controlled Vocabulary," "Concept Mapping," "Creating a Systematic Review Search in PubMed," and "CINAHL." I have since added videos on searching the *Cochrane Library* and *PsycINFO.* As of April 2019, the first video on understanding controlled vocabulary has been viewed almost 1,900 times.

Students have reported to me that they have found the videos incredibly helpful. Having the videos available relieves student anxiety because they know they can always refer back to them. It can be difficult for students to admit publicly that they are struggling with new concepts and skills, adding another layer to their information anxiety. They can watch the videos as many times as they need without fear, shame, or stigma from classmates. A DNP faculty member also stressed the value of the videos, "you can go through those step-by-step and they're very clear and then you follow that up with a meeting with you (the librarian) where you got stuck. That combination is really pretty powerful."

Flexible scheduling and being able to meet online is crucial in order to effectively work with DNP students. Most of the students work full-time during their doctoral program, and many work 12-hour shifts in hospitals. It is often impossible for students to meet during business hours or physically travel to the library. Due to the hybrid nature of the program, students are also geographically distant and live throughout the greater New York City metropolitan area, many at a significant distance from the university's lower Manhattan campus.

I am always willing to meet with students online outside of regular business hours, usually around 8 p.m. on weeknights, less commonly on the weekend. Since I'm usually meeting with three to four students and sometimes their faculty advisors, this allows each person to join the meeting from their home without the time and difficulty of traveling to a central location. There are, of course, challenges to offering this service. I need to work around my own family and child care demands and use my personal laptop for these meetings. This also requires institutional support from the library for flexible scheduling. I have been allowed in the past to take any hours spent holding evening or weekend meetings with students as compensatory time. Without that ability, I would not be able to offer online meetings outside of business hours. For some librarians it may be difficult to convince their supervisors or library administrators to allow this kind of flexible schedule. I have found it absolutely necessary, however, to be able to support students who are working and struggling to manage busy professional and personal schedules.

Perhaps the most important characteristic of the library support for the DNP program is the most difficult to quantify—the interpersonal aspect. As one of the DNP faculty members put it:

> I've noticed with the DNP work and our systematic review, when they get to the database search and they have to build a strategy this is a very new, kind of raw concept and it challenges their weaknesses and maybe their lack of knowledge . . . But they get through it and because you (Jennifer) have always been neutral, and sticking to the points, I think that's helped them stay polite and not push back . . . or spin out of control in a different direction. I know my teams and myself have always valued your input because of the neutrality and your expertise in getting the task done.

One of the most important interpersonal characteristics of a librarian working with this kind of student population is to acknowledge students' wealth of professional knowledge. I strive in the initial meeting with students to defer to their professional knowledge as much as possible. This is both an andragogical and a practical strategy. It is andragogical in that by doing so I acknowledge students' expertise and help them feel valued and confident. It is also practical because I have no formal educational background in health sciences, and I quite often don't understand the specifics of the clinical question students are exploring. I need them to explain the research question to me, but by doing so I also demonstrate my own willingness to learn and acknowledge gaps in my own knowledge. This helps students feel more comfortable acknowledging the areas in which they struggle with new research skills.

It's common for students to say, as I lead them through a complex database search, "I never would have known how to do this." I have a standard response that I've come to use with every cohort over the years, which is, "we all have our different areas of expertise. No one expects you to know how to do this kind of database searching, and no one wants me putting in a catheter." It always elicits a laugh, and demonstrates to students that we are equal partners with different realms of expertise and their wealth of clinical knowledge is highly valuable.

Dr. Joanne Singleton, the founding director of the DNP program, also sees intellectual curiosity as a key characteristic of any librarian supporting this group of students. She described the importance of the librarian responding enthusiastically to student research topics and always demonstrating an interest in learning more about the topic. She said, "if the person from the library staff is not embracing the energy and the curiosity around it then it's just going to be very black and white" (J. Singleton, personal communication, January 16, 2019). This intellectual curiosity and enthusiasm helps students stay energized throughout their literature search and understand that it is a complex and nuanced process.

Another important interpersonal characteristic is acknowledging the challenges of the DNP program. The program is academically rigorous and requires students to take on many new areas of knowledge, including quantitative and research skills. Most students continue to work while completing their doctoral degree and have to manage very busy schedules. I openly express to students how much I admire them and I understand that it is incredibly difficult to complete a doctoral program while working and managing family obligations. I am in awe of the strength and resilience of these students. As examples: students have had babies during the DNP program; one student suffered a concussion; a student injured her ankle and was on bed rest for months; another student was the primary caretaker of an elderly parent with dementia; and many students are working parents. All of the DNP students are nurse practitioners and, as previously mentioned, many of them work 12-hour shifts—sometimes overnight—on busy hospital floors, while trying to juggle school and family. Acknowledging these difficulties is important for gaining students' trust and demonstrating that I, the librarian, see them as capable and resilient. Another faculty member, who is also an alumna of the DNP program, said:

> I always struggled with writing and so turning in papers made me feel very vulnerable. But I think the design of our program where we work from day one in groups and it was easy to see that everyone felt vulnerable and we

all had different strengths and skills and we supported each other. That helped a lot. It was not an easy transition from being the expert to being the student.

It is also important to cultivate a friendly relationship with students by being open about my own life. I tell students that I need to schedule online meetings after my children's bedtime. I've swapped parenting advice with students and discussed some of my own family life where it intersects with students' experiences. I hope that this helps students feel more comfortable approaching me with questions and being honest about their own struggles, without violating professional boundaries. All of these interpersonal aspects create the atmosphere of mutual trust and respect that is necessary for adult learners.

Student and Alumni Survey

In the spring of 2019 I sent an online survey to 38 current DNP students and about 100 alumni, using the Qualtrics survey platform. The survey was distributed via e-mail. The director of the graduate nursing programs sent the survey to all current students, and the Office of Development and Alumni Relations e-mailed all DNP alumni. Unfortunately, response rates were quite low; only about 15% of recipients completed the survey. However, I still found the data helpful for reflecting on the library's role in the DNP program. The survey shows that most respondents found library support necessary to complete their systematic review. As mentioned earlier, DNP students are nurse practitioners who often have a wealth of clinical experience. About half of the respondents reported more than seven years elapsing between finishing their master's degree and starting the DNP program. The majority of respondents also reported feeling extremely or moderately competent as nurse practitioners. Respecting this wealth of clinical knowledge and experience is an important aspect of my interactions with DNP students.

Nearly all of the students and alumni reported that they worked full-time while completing their doctorate, and nearly half reported that they were the primary caretaker of a child or other family member at the same time. Seventy-eight percent reported feeling anxious about balancing school, work, and family obligations during the DNP program. The same percentage felt anxious about completing the literature search for their systematic review. This aligns with Katopol's (2012) concept of information anxiety. Students felt anxiety about an information need for which they lacked the foundational research skills, and meeting with a librarian helped allay that anxiety.

The survey data also shows how intensively DNP students utilize library support. Half of respondents met with the librarian more than four times, and nearly all of those individuals met with the librarian online most of the time. As discussed earlier, being able to meet with students online outside of business hours is crucial to adequately support this population. Half of the survey respondents said they usually met with the librarian during the evening, and another third met with the librarian on the weekend. If anything, I need to be available more often during evenings and weekends. One student wrote, "I reached out to the librarian a few times last semester to schedule time to meet. She was unable to meet every suggested time I gave her . . . I gave up and stopped asking." Another student stated, "I wish the librarian was available to meet more often in the evening and on the weekend."

A majority of respondents, 61%, also used the video tutorials and found them helpful. One student wrote, "they [videos] were very helpful because I was able to re-watch them several times on my own." However, students found meeting with the librarian even more helpful. One student agreed that the videos were useful, "although direct communication and demonstration was even more helpful." Online learning objects can only supplement, not replace, individual attention from a knowledgeable librarian.

The survey data suggests that the interpersonal aspects of library support described above are, in fact, meeting the needs of DNP students. The overwhelming majority of respondents agreed that the librarian was approachable and supportive and helped them feel less anxious. They also reported that the librarian understood their needs and respected their professional knowledge. One respondent wrote, "The librarians are knowledgeable and skilled experts in providing access to information and retrieving information. They are excellent teachers in reference management, academic writing and research." Another respondent stated, "The librarians were critical resources and support for my academic success."

The survey data suggest that my anecdotal observations of DNP students are correct in terms of seeing the students as knowledgeable clinicians who struggle with the transition to graduate school. The survey data and comments also suggest that overall the library is meeting students' needs for support that is focused on specific research skills, and attuned to the students' emotional needs. However, even with the flexible scheduling I offer, there is a need for even more availability outside of regular business hours.

Conclusions and Recommendations

DNP students have characteristics that are common to many other graduate students: they are experienced professionals returning to school in order to further their career goals; they are deeply committed to their field; and they have complex lives with a multitude of academic, professional, and personal responsibilities. Therefore, there are two crucial structural components to library support for similar graduate students: offering online meetings and appointment times outside of regular business hours and creating online learning objects, such as videos, that allow individualized learning.

Along with these structural components, it is important for librarians to understand the affective dimension of working with comparable students. Librarians need to acknowledge the wealth of professional knowledge and experience that students bring with them, and help students make connections between their prior knowledge and the new skills they're gaining as doctoral students. Working from an andragogical framework can help allay student's information anxiety so that students feel their experience is valued, they are solving real-life problems, and there is an atmosphere of mutual trust and collaboration. Librarians need to demonstrate enthusiasm, intellectual curiosity, and understanding. Although the librarian needs to remain neutral and separate from any intragroup conflicts, it is important to acknowledge the emotional demands of graduate school and demonstrate respect for the many hurdles students must negotiate in order to complete their degree.

It can be challenging but also immensely rewarding working with DNP students, who need many hours with a librarian in order to fully grasp the necessary research skills. However, in my experience the students are also incredibly grateful for the library support and are vocal in their appreciation. Working with graduate students in general is exciting because we as librarians get a glimpse into the real-world problems students are working to solve, and we are a key part of these efforts.

References

Green, R., & Macauley, P. (2007). Doctoral students' engagement with information: An American-Australian perspective. *portal: Libraries and the Academy, 7*(3), 317–332. https://doi.org/10.1353/pla.2007.0031

Higgins, J. P., & Green, S. (Eds.). (2011). *Cochrane handbook for systematic reviews of interventions* (5.1.0). The Cochrane Collaboration. Retrieved from http://handbook-5-1.cochrane.org

Katopol, P. F. (2012). Information anxiety and African-American students in a graduate education program. *Education Libraries, 35*, 5–14.

Knowles, M. S. (1968). Andragogy, not pedagogy. *Adult Leadership, 16*(10), 350–352.

Knowles, M. S., Holton, E. F., III, & Swanson, R. A. (2005). *The adult learner: The definitive classic in adult education and human resource development.* Burlington, VT: Routledge. Retrieved from http://ebookcentral.proquest.com/lib/pace/detail.action?docID=232125

Mellon, C. A. (1986). Library anxiety: A grounded theory and its development. *College & Research Libraries, 47*(2), 160–165. https://doi.org/10.5860/crl_47_02_160

Rosseter, R. (2018, October). *DNP fact sheet.* Retrieved from https://www.aacnnursing.org/News-Information/Fact-Sheets/DNP-Fact-Sheet

Appendix 3.1: Online Survey for DNP Students and Alumni

The purpose of this survey is to collect responses from current and former DNP students, to be used as part of the research for a chapter of the book *Academic Library Services for Graduate Students,* forthcoming from Libraries Unlimited.

You are invited to participate in a research study using the Qualtrics online survey platform. Participation is completely voluntary. Please read the information below and ask questions about anything that you do not understand. A researcher listed below will be available to answer your questions.

Introduction and Purpose My name is Jennifer Rosenstein. I am the assistant university librarian for graduate services at Pace University. I would like to invite you to take part in my research study, which concerns the library support provided to the Doctor of Nursing Practice (DNP) program.

Procedures If you agree to participate in my research, I will ask you to complete the following online survey. The survey will involve questions about your experience as a DNP student, and should take about 20 minutes to complete.

Benefits There is no direct benefit to you from taking part in this study. It is hoped that the research will help other academic librarians serving graduate student populations.

Risks/Discomforts There are no risks associated with this study. If any of the research questions make you uncomfortable or upset you, you are free to decline to answer any questions you don't wish to, or to stop participating at any time. As with all research, there is a chance that confidentiality could be compromised; however, we are taking precautions to minimize this risk.

Confidentiality Your study data will be handled as confidentially as possible. No individual names or other personally identifiable information will be collected, and all survey responses are anonymous. When the research is completed, I may save the data for use in future research done by myself or others. I will retain these records for up to 10 years after the study is over. The same measures described above will be taken to protect confidentiality of this study data.

Compensation You will not be paid for taking part in this study.

Rights *Participation in research is completely voluntary.* You are free to decline to take part in the project. You can decline to answer any questions and are free to stop taking part in the project at any time. Whether or not you choose to participate, to answer any particular question, or continue participating in the project, there will be no penalty to you or loss of benefits to which you are otherwise entitled.

Questions If you have any questions about this research, please feel free to contact me. If you have any questions about your rights or treatment as a research participant in this study, please contact the Office of Sponsored Research.

If you agree to take part in the research, print a copy of this page to keep for future reference, then fill in the "Agree" button below.

Clicking on the "Agree" button indicates that

- You have read the above information
- You voluntarily agree to participate
  - ○ Agree
  - ○ Disagree

Which of the following best describes you?

- ○ Current DNP student
- ○ Graduate of the DNP program

How many years elapsed between obtaining your master's degree and starting the DNP program?

- ○ 1–3
- ○ 4–6
- ○ 7–10
- ○ More than 10

Prior to starting the DNP program, how did you feel about your work as a nurse practitioner?

- ○ Extremely competent
- ○ Moderately competent
- ○ Slightly competent
- ○ Neither competent nor incompetent
- ○ Slightly incompetent
- ○ Moderately incompetent
- ○ Extremely incompetent

Which of the following describe you? (select all that apply)

	Yes	No
Veteran or active military	○	○
English is not my first language	○	○
I worked full-time while completing the DNP program	○	○
I worked part-time while completing the DNP program	○	○
I was a primary caretaker of children or other family members while completing the DNP program	○	○

Did any of the following aspects of the DNP program make you feel anxious? (select all that apply)

☐ Using new technology (e.g., Blackboard)
☐ Balancing school, work, and family obligations
☐ Academic writing
☐ Conducting the systematic review search
☐ Learning statistics
☐ None of the above
☐ Other

What other aspects of the DNP program created anxiety for you?

____

Approximately how many times did you meet with the librarian during the DNP program?

○ 0
○ 1
○ 2
○ 3

○ 4
○ More than 4

How did you meet with the librarian (most of the time)?

○ Online
○ In-person
○ I didn't meet with the librarian

Skip to Q15 if How did you meet with the librarian (most of the time)? = I didn't meet with the librarian.
When did you usually meet with the librarian? (select all that apply)

☐ Morning
☐ Afternoon
☐ Evening (after 5 p.m.)
☐ Weekend

It was important to me to be able to meet with the librarian online at night.

○ Strongly agree
○ Somewhat agree
○ Neither agree nor disagree
○ Somewhat disagree
○ Strongly disagree

Meeting with the librarian . . .

	Strongly agree	Agree	Somewhat agree	Neither agree nor disagree	Somewhat disagree	Disagree	Strongly disagree
helped me understand the process of conducting the literature search for my systematic review.	○	○	○	○	○	○	○

	Strongly agree	Agree	Somewhat agree	Neither agree nor disagree	Somewhat disagree	Disagree	Strongly disagree
helped me organize and document my searches.	O	O	O	O	O	O	O
taught me how to navigate medical databases.	O	O	O	O	O	O	O
helped me find relevant articles for my systematic review.	O	O	O	O	O	O	O

Please share any comments about your experience meeting with the librarian.

Did you use the videos created by the librarian for the DNP program? (*the video series that explains concept mapping, controlled vocabulary, and PubMed and CINAHL searching*)

- O   Yes
- O   No
- O   Don't remember

Did you find the videos helpful? Why or why not?

In my experience, the librarian . . .

	Strongly agree	Agree	Somewhat agree	Neither agree nor disagree	Somewhat disagree	Disagree	Strongly disagree
was approachable.	O	O	O	O	O	O	O
was supportive.	O	O	O	O	O	O	O
understood my needs.	O	O	O	O	O	O	O

	Strongly agree	Agree	Somewhat agree	Neither agree nor disagree	Somewhat disagree	Disagree	Strongly disagree
helped me feel less anxious.	O	O	O	O	O	O	O
respected my professional knowledge.	O	O	O	O	O	O	O

Is there anything else you'd like to share about the support provided by the library during the DNP program?

____

Appendix 3.2: Faculty Focus Group Questions

1. What drew you to the DNP program?

2. How many years elapsed between finishing your master's degree and starting the DNP program?

3. When you started the DNP program, were you interested in teaching?

4. Prior to starting the DNP program, did you feel competent as a nurse practitioner?

5. One of my hypotheses is that it's very challenging for students to go from being experts in their clinical practice, to being novices as doctoral students and systematic reviewers. Is that true in your experience?

6. Once you started the DNP program, were there aspects of the program that made you feel anxious?

7. From your perspective as a faculty member, what causes the most anxiety for DNP students?

8. Did you meet with the librarian while you were a DNP student?

9. Can you describe your interactions with the librarian as a student? Did you find the librarian helpful and approachable?

10. Can you discuss your experience as a faculty member with the library support provided to the DNP program? Does it seem like the librarian is effective in mitigating students' anxieties?

11. Should librarians get involved where there are conflicts within student groups or refer the issue to faculty?

12. Have you used the videos created by the library for the DNP program? Have students discussed with you their experience of using the videos?

13. What do you think are the characteristics of effective library support for the DNP program, both in terms of interpersonal characteristics and structural (e.g., online videos, flexible meeting times)?

CHAPTER FOUR

Capitalizing on Connections: Developing Holistic Co-Curricular Graduate Programming

Tarida Anantachai and Emily K. Hart

Introduction

Developing outreach and co-curricular program initiatives for graduate students presents a host of unique challenges. A few of these challenges include students entering their programs with widely diverse baseline skill sets in research, varying awareness of the library resources and services available to support their burgeoning graduate careers, and a lack of clear curricular touch points for libraries to connect systematically with them. At the undergraduate level, higher education institutions devote significant resources toward developing unified experiences such as general education requirements, learning communities, and first-year or capstone courses. However, at the graduate level, programs are typically more decentralized, with fewer co-curricular initiatives aimed at building core skills and a sense of community. In addition to having fewer pathways to connect with each other, graduate students face the daunting task of navigating the transition to graduate study, which often requires in-depth subject knowledge and the pursuit of a demanding research agenda (Fleming-May & Yuro, 2009). Adding to these challenges are faculty members' inflated views of the students' baseline skill sets (Rempel & Davidson, 2008), a lack of programmatic support (perhaps as a result of these erroneous expectations), and being siloed within their degree programs, often contributing to feelings of isolation (Goldenberg-Hart, 2008).

This can be especially true for the increasing number of international graduate students on university campuses, who in 2017–2018 represented 43% of new international student enrollments in the United States (Institute of International Education, 2018). Previous studies reveal that graduate international students, similar to their U.S. classmates, struggle not only with adjusting to the added emphasis on research output, but with simultaneously navigating the U.S. higher education system and their libraries (Click, 2018). As highlighted by Baruzzi and Calcagno (2015), "International students often have limited knowledge about what is available to them through the library and may have experienced a very different type of library system at home" (p. 403). Although our goal is to summatively support the graduate student population at our institution, accounting for the unique challenges and baseline needs of graduate international students is key to the success of our programs.

Library and information literacy instruction can be an effective approach toward reaching and helping students develop foundational research skills and an awareness of essential library resources. However, lacking a more unified experience and curriculum, library instruction for graduate students is often limited to one-off presentations and other nonregularized interactions. Although still valuable, these stand-alone opportunities often take place early on in graduate students' programs, and not at their point of need. Furthermore, this approach does not scale to provide meaningful support for our already large and rapidly expanding graduate student populations; it does not accommodate the diverse needs of distinctive graduate programs (such as PhD students versus master's students in nonthesis degree programs), nor does it address the unique challenges faced by international students orienting to a new culture and the rigors of the U.S. higher education system.

In an attempt to better meet the demands of a rapidly expanding graduate student population at Syracuse University, our Libraries initiated a co-curricular graduate program. In establishing the program, our Libraries sought partnerships with graduate student groups and offices who frequently offer services to graduate students. Through these collaborations, we have leveraged funding and expertise to develop a recurring co-curricular graduate events series. The series combines more informal networking and relationship-building events, with a number of smaller roundtable events aimed at taking a deeper dive into specific skills and topics. Our ultimate goal was to support graduate students' holistic success as scholars, from expanding their baseline research competencies to encouraging networking across degree programs, and helping to equip them with the professional skills they would need in both their graduate careers and beyond. This chapter details our efforts to launch this graduate co-curricular program at our university, including relevant background details on our institution; a review of literature on graduate student outreach initiatives; details on the creation and planning process of our event series; assessment and feedback gathered from participants and colleagues; and recommendations for starting similar programming based on our personal experiences. Finally, we will reflect on insights gained from other institutions' efforts, as well as our future plans for continually updating and cultivating our co-curricular graduate program.

Background

Institutional Background

A private research university located in upstate New York, Syracuse University's (SU) total student enrollment was over 22,800 in 2018—with graduate students making up almost 7,000, or approximately 30% of total enrollment (Syracuse University Office of Institutional Research, 2019). As with many U.S. higher education institutions, SU's international student population has seen a steady increase in recent years. Of particular note, international student enrollment makes up a significant portion of our graduate student population. International students, hailing from over 126 countries, constitute approximately 19% of total enrollment, and, at 32%, nearly a third of the total graduate student population (Syracuse University, 2019; Syracuse University Office of Institutional Research, 2019). Although our focus is on developing holistic co-curricular graduate programming, we have noted enthusiastic participation from international graduate students, and thus recognize the importance of accounting for the unique needs and growing presence of this group. Syracuse is a mid- to large-sized university, comprising 13 schools and colleges and over 200 graduate degree programs. The university's size and diverse scope presents challenges in creating a unified student experience and sense of community. Although initiatives are underway to establish more integrated undergraduate experiences, the graduate experience remains fragmented.

In recent years, SU underwent a significant institutional change that directly impacted the size of the graduate student population. In 2015, the university was awarded a Research 1 (R1) designation from the Carnegie Classification of Institutions of Higher Education (Boll, 2016). This status reflects a major increase in SU's research activity, and indicates the need to continue growing our research output going forward. This more aggressive research agenda not only perpetuates the need to bring in higher numbers of graduate and postdoctoral scholars, but also has implications for the skill sets these students will need in order to produce high-quality research. This shift in focus is further evident in the university's Academic Strategic Plan (Syracuse University, 2015); it specifically references the necessity to enhance support for graduate and doctoral programs, by equipping graduate students with the skills needed to succeed in their programs and future careers—in turn bolstering SU's profile as an R1 research institution. This plan also notably contains a section dedicated to internationalization—underscoring the campus-wide need to increase advising, support services, and co-curricular opportunities for this population.

Prior Library Outreach to Graduate Students

In response to the new R1 designation and the university's Academic Strategic Plan, our Libraries formulated a corresponding Strategic Plan and a new information literacy program with strategically aligned outcomes. In particular, the outcomes that most closely related to our graduate programming initiatives include expanding the Libraries' engagement and outreach efforts through the development of extracurricular events and programming (Syracuse University Libraries, 2018b), and creating opportunities to deliver and cultivate information literacy skills in order to support the lifelong learning of the university community (Syracuse University Libraries, 2018a). Similar to the university's, the Libraries' Strategic Plan also calls attention to the broader need to support international students and programs, particularly by improving their awareness of library resources and services. These efforts have not only enabled our Libraries to better align our activities with those of the university at large, but have served as a driving force in building a more comprehensive graduate outreach program.

Efforts to organize this program were motivated by the recognition that our Libraries' outreach and information literacy efforts to date were concentrated almost exclusively on undergraduate students. An examination of our internal data showed that our primary contact with the graduate population was through one-shot instruction sessions and departmental orientations. Other interactions included graduate international information fairs, one-to-one research consultations, and targeted presentations for faculty research groups. In 2016–2017, we estimated that the number of graduate students who received some type of formal presentation from a librarian was only about 1,100, making it clear that our current efforts were largely failing to reach the majority of the graduate student population. Additionally, we conducted some library instruction for graduate international students enrolled at our English Language Institute, a unit offering preacademic preparation courses for a subset of international students before their official enrollment in university graduate programs. In other words, prior to proactively establishing our co-curricular graduate programming, many of our previous encounters with graduate students were driven by individual faculty and student requests. This reactionary approach largely comprised more preparatory content, such as library orientations, or sessions focused on highly individualized standalone research assignments. These encounters provided neither the opportunity to engage meaningfully with students on the many specialized library resources and services valuable to their academic and research careers, nor a mechanism to holistically examine their skill development. Furthermore, this approach limited our ability to connect with students at pivotal points throughout their research and graduate careers. The nature of these exchanges also dictated a more formal and less collaborative experience, not allowing us an appropriate setting for establishing more sustained, professional relationships with these students. As a whole, our Libraries needed a more systematic approach to connect with and assist graduate students in hopes of bolstering their academic, research, and professional success.

Literature Review

Prior to launching our graduate outreach initiatives, we consulted the literature to look for insights and best practices for program development. Our review showed that in the past, less emphasis was placed on instructional outreach to graduate students (Rempel & Davidson, 2008; Roszkowski & Reynolds, 2013); however, in recent years, there has been an uptick in interest on this topic among academic librarians. The burgeoning discourse in graduate student outreach suggests a greater recognition of the need to more actively support this population, as well as the unique role librarians can play in doing so.

When working with graduate students, it is important to first understand the challenges facing this population and how these can impact their ability to complete their often research-intensive graduate programs. A few of these have included graduate students struggling with the transition from a more course-driven undergraduate curriculum to a more research-intensive graduate program (Rempel, 2010); the implied expectation and misconception that they have been sufficiently prepared to undertake the advanced research and technical skills of their programs (Forbes, Schlesselman-Tarango, & Keeran, 2017; Hoffmann, Antwi-Nsiah, Feng, & Stanley, 2008; Rempel, 2010; Rempel & Davidson, 2008; Renfro & Shields, 2017); and a lack of faculty support and a missing sense of community (Rempel, 2010). In other words, graduate students have found themselves in an uncertain domain placing them somewhere in-between, where they are neither undergraduate nor faculty; many have entered without a clear research focus and lack the knowledge needed to develop a research agenda and the competencies they needed to effectively pursue it (Rempel, 2010).

Similar to our experiences, the literature has shown that librarians face several common challenges working with graduate students. These have included the ineffectiveness of orientations and individual research consultations to comprehensively inform graduate students of basic library resources and services. Such interactions have also been an inadequate delivery method for helping students effectively develop the multifaceted skill sets needed to complete their programs and subsequent careers (Bussell, Hagman, & Guder, 2017; Peacemaker & Roseberry, 2017; Rempel, 2010; Rempel & Davidson, 2008). These challenges have been further complicated by the diverse nature of graduate programs; in their study, Covert-Vail and Collard (2012) noted the vast heterogeneity among graduate students—not only in the structural differences between their master's and doctoral programs, but in the range of stages and skill levels they may occupy in the academic life cycle. Embedded library instruction sessions have helped to address some of these gaps; however, graduate students often have fewer required core courses, reducing the number of instructional outreach opportunities available to librarians. At the same time, faculty have often assumed that library or research instruction is not as necessary for this group, which has further limited librarians from meeting graduate students at their point of need (Hoffmann et al., 2008; Rempel & Davidson, 2008). Compounding this is the reality that graduate students—not recognizing the expertise librarians can provide for them—have been less likely to turn to the library for guidance. Rather, they have relied on themselves or their peers for help (Fleming-May & Yuro, 2009; Fong, Wang, White, & Tipton, 2016; Rempel, 2010; Rempel & Davidson, 2008).

The literature has indicated that libraries have stepped up to help fill graduate students' information gaps. One of the more common solutions has been noncurricular library workshops, which have presented graduate students with opportunities to obtain foundational skills not typically covered in their degree programs, and to delve deeper into scholarly topics, such as data management and analysis, conducting literature reviews, and the publishing process (Fong et al., 2016; Rempel, 2010). Additionally, workshops have helped reach and create connections between graduate students across a variety of disciplines (Rempel & Davidson, 2008), thus offering them a space to engage with other interdisciplinary scholars, tools, and topics, as well as to gain transferable skills outside of their siloed programs.

Going beyond the one-shot library instruction session and the one-off workshop model, another common approach to graduate outreach has been creating a coordinated workshop series—delivering a more regularly scheduled, structured program throughout the year and at different stages of graduate students' academic careers (Rempel & Davidson, 2008; Roszkowski & Reynolds, 2013). Virginia Commonwealth University opted for a more consolidated, conference-like approach with a day-long graduate workshop occurring once per semester. These conference-style events incorporated a handful of consecutive sessions on a variety of topics, as well as a follow-up webinar for those who were unable to attend (Peacemaker & Roseberry, 2017). This approach notably reduced the amount of scheduling and logistical labor in planning several events throughout the academic year. Carving out one dedicated day for this event may also make it easier for graduate students to earmark and reserve time in their schedules, rather than making time to attend several shorter workshops.

Other libraries have approached graduate student outreach with more personalized formats, including sponsored dinners, socials, or reading and writing groups (Budzise-Weaver & Anders, 2016; Scheib & Charles, 2018). Although certainly smaller in scale, these more intimate outreach events have enabled librarians to connect with graduate students who may be neglected—for instance, students from smaller graduate departments whose subject areas may not get the same attention nor receive the same degree of resources as those who belong to larger, more prominent disciplinary programs (Budzise-Weaver & Anders, 2016).

The literature has shown that there is a clear need to create learning opportunities beyond formal graduate courses. As an example, librarians Fong et al. (2016) conducted a study of both graduate students and graduate program directors on what scholarly topics and competencies they felt were most needed. Fong et al.'s (2016) comprehensive review compared responses across the humanities, sciences, and social sciences—allowing them to better identify where topics overlapped and diverged in order to design more subject-specific marketing and targeted instruction efforts.

Other institutions chose topics that would help graduate students develop effective research skills and strategies for keeping up with current literature in their field of study—such as advanced research strategies, how to conduct literature reviews, and citation management (Bussell et al., 2017; Fong et al., 2016; Hoffmann et al., 2008; Rempel, 2010; Rempel & Davidson, 2008; Roszkowski & Reynolds, 2013). Others created data and technology-focused workshops, including topics like data management, data visualization, and digital publishing software (Fong et al., 2016; Peacemaker & Roseberry, 2017; Renfro & Shields, 2017; Roszkowski & Reynolds, 2013). Another major area addressed graduate students' desire to identify the financial means to conduct their research, from grant writing to obtaining travel scholarships to finding research funding opportunities (Bussell et al., 2017; Fong et al., 2016; Forbes et al., 2017). Other workshops addressed students' professional development, such as professional portfolio creation, career research and planning, research poster design, scholarly impact, and the dissertation and publishing process (Bussell et al., 2017; Fong et al., 2016; Helmstutler, 2015; Peacemaker & Roseberry, 2017; Renfro & Shields, 2017; Roszkowski & Reynolds, 2013). Again, as graduate students have often relied on their existing skill sets as opposed to reaching out for help (Rempel, 2010), workshops like these can introduce them to alternative methods and tools at key stages in their graduate careers, helping them go beyond what has become routinized.

Though libraries and graduate students alike may agree that building such skills are valuable for their academic and professional success, libraries continue to face challenges in effectively connecting with and encouraging student attendance at noncurricular events. However, through our programming and outreach efforts, and our consultation of the literature, we have found that partnering with other graduate student-supporting groups on campus is essential to a program's success. These could involve units such as campus offices for research, career services, or writing, learning, and technology centers (Fong et al., 2016; Peacemaker & Roseberry, 2017; Rempel, 2010). These collaborations have helped not only to inform other units on campus of the types of services and expertise offered by libraries, but also to reduce duplication of efforts and encourage a more comprehensive view of graduate programming across the university. Some institutions have taken these efforts further and established formal campus-wide graduate student services committees that have incorporated librarians. Within libraries, some have created their own graduate-focused committees, or have appointed graduate student service librarians or coordinators to oversee outreach efforts (Fong et al., 2016; Rempel, 2010; Rempel & Davidson, 2008; Renfro & Shields, 2017).

The body of literature and momentum around developing graduate student library services continues to grow. In 2017, the Association of College and Research Libraries Board of Directors approved the creation of the Academic Library Services for Graduate Students Interest Group (Association of College & Research Libraries, 2019). One year prior, librarians from Kennesaw State University launched the first "Transforming Libraries for Graduate Students" conference, which garnered attendees from R1 to R3 institutions from across the country (Renfro & Shields, 2017) and has since seen its third iteration (Kennesaw State University, 2020). Additionally, Renfro and Stiles (2018) released *Transforming Libraries to Serve Graduate Students*, offering further insights into graduate student programming and outreach activities. Indeed, the academic library community appears to be gathering momentum on this topic—perhaps signifying future resources, initiatives, and areas of research worth monitoring for further exploration.

Developing Co-Curricular Graduate Student Programming

Until recently, our Libraries typical interactions with graduate students took the form of stand-alone presentations and research consultations. Through these limited interactions, mainly driven by student and faculty requests, our Libraries failed to connect with a large percentage of the graduate student population. In devising a more systematic co-curricular approach to supporting these students, we established an outreach and programming plan with the goal of introducing them to pertinent library resources and services, research skills, and professional competencies at key stages during their graduate careers.

Forming Key Partnerships

In launching these more formalized outreach and programming efforts, our Libraries first formed key partnerships with campus offices regularly serving the graduate population, as well as a variety of graduate student groups. In particular, the science and engineering librarian developed close working relationships with graduate groups in her liaison areas, such as the American Society for Engineering Education at Syracuse University (ASEE@SU) and the College of Engineering and Computer Science Graduate Student Organization (ECS-GSO). These groups were natural partners because they were already actively engaged in designing educational workshops focused on improving graduate students' soft skills, and the librarian had already helped them with programming in the past. These student groups also fell within graduate programs that are predominantly comprised of international students—a core population of interest within both the university's and the Libraries' larger strategic goals. In the fall of 2017, the science and engineering librarian approached these groups to propose jointly hosting a graduate student event series, largely organized by our Libraries with input and cosponsorship from the graduate groups. Historically, our Libraries have been severely limited in pursuing larger outreach initiatives due to the lack of an established funding source for regularized programming and outreach. Having sponsored funding when hosting noncurricular events is crucial for offering incentives, such as food or giveaways, and for reserving venues of different sizes and settings outside the Libraries that could further entice graduate student attendance. It is also a well-known fact that graduate students love free food!

To gain additional funding for these events, ASEE@SU and ECS-GSO, along with our science and engineering librarian, reached out to the Syracuse University Graduate Student Organization (GSO). This student-run governing body focuses on supporting the voices and concerns of the graduate student population at SU (Syracuse University Graduate Student Organization, 2019), and serves as the primary funder of noncurricular graduate programming on campus. In the absence of a more centralized sense of community and cohesive curricular program, this group plays a critical role in bringing otherwise disparate groups together. Within its governing structure, the GSO encompasses dozens of registered graduate student organizations, including ASEE@SU and ECO-GSO, which are given small stipends annually to host events and/or administer services for graduate students. The GSO has also established partnerships with key, nongraduate student groups on campus, such as the

Office of Graduate Career Services, the international student services office, and, as a result of our collaborations with ASEE@SU and ECS-GSO, the Libraries. It offers opportunities for these campus units to apply to become "Service Providers"—that is, other recognized university groups that directly support the graduate student experience. The campus units that earn this designation benefit by gaining access to annual funds, as awarded by the GSO. Submitting an application to become a GSO Service Provider each spring has become part of our ongoing planning process; in doing so, we map out all of our events and an itemized budget for each of them in the coming fiscal year. Our graduate programming is directly contingent on the GSO funds we receive. In addition to receiving funding through this group, we quickly realized the benefits of a Libraries-GSO partnership, including helping us connect with other graduate student groups and GSO-recognized service providers, and creating communication channels for marketing our events to graduate students. After forming these fundamental connections and a more consistent funding source, this opened the door for us to create more regularized, library-initiated graduate programming throughout the year.

Prior to establishing this co-curricular initiative, our librarians participated in an annual Dissertation Boot Camp, organized by the director of graduate programs. Held prior to the start of the spring semester, Dissertation Boot Camp is a weeklong workshop, encompassing full days of writing with invited lunchtime speakers who discuss professional development topics. Hosted in spaces within the Libraries, librarians are available throughout the week for on-call research appointments. This type of intensive programming geared toward doctoral candidates is a natural place for librarians to embed their services. Our librarians have also sporadically participated in graduate student events hosted by the Office of Research, the international student services office, and the Office of Graduate Programs, but these interactions have largely been initiated and organized by other offices, and not from within the Libraries. In order to systematically expose graduate students to the many specialized library resources, services, and personnel encompassed within our Libraries, we recognized the need for us to play a more active role in graduate program planning and development.

The Graduate Research Roundtables

Combining the ideas we found in the literature and feedback garnered through our interactions with graduate students, in the spring of 2018, we launched the Graduate Research Roundtables, an event series focused on library and research services in collaboration with ASEE@SU and the ECS-GSO. During the planning, the graduate student groups assisted with event logistics, such as reserving a location, securing additional funds from the GSO, and arranging food orders through campus catering services. The graduate groups also provided valuable insights on how to more effectively promote the series, from strategies on framing the program topics and marketing the events to selecting dates and event locations that would garner a higher turnout. For example, we held the first kickoff event at a campus bar and grill that caters to graduate students by giving discounts on food and drinks. We also discovered that each Thursday during the semester, the GSO sponsored a trivia night at this location. To capitalize on this popular event, we scheduled our programs immediately prior to trivia to help boost attendance, using the advertising catchphrase, "Come to learn, stay for trivia!"

Our event series opened with a more informal, kickoff speed-dating style event that introduced graduate students to key individuals and resources at our Libraries in a social setting, followed by three smaller Graduate Research Roundtables that concentrated on specific needs as gathered through online registration forms and feedback surveys. The first event, marketed as "Speed Dating the Research Experts," was designed to allow librarians and large numbers of graduate students to get to know each other in a casual environment. A number of our librarians who do not typically interact with students on a regular basis, such as our data librarian and open publishing and copyright librarian, participated and opened our graduate students' eyes to a range of services they may not have normally associated with our Libraries. Additionally, our subject librarians shared information on topics ranging from citation management to research reputation to core databases and research guides, along with other specialized library resources and services for graduate students. The event also served as a method for collecting valuable graduate student input and generating buzz for the subsequent roundtables.

Following this kickoff, we offered a series of more intimate seminar and discussion-style events. These Graduate Research Roundtables were designed to be more personalized, with an attendance cap of 35 graduate students, allowing for a deeper dive into specific resources and skills. Event topics included an introduction to graduate-specific library resources and services, geared toward newer and international graduate students or those who were previously not exposed to our graduate library services; an event on data services and citation management, relevant for students at all levels; a workshop covering support services and submission processes for theses and dissertations, targeted to master's and PhD students who were further along in their graduate careers; and an event focused on career research and funding opportunities. For each of these events, we invited presenters with relevant expertise. The final roundtable on career research featured a presentation from our business and entrepreneurship librarian on finding valuable company information to prepare for interviews; information from our open publishing and copyright librarian on the benefits of publishing in open access resources to make works more accessible and discoverable; a presentation from the science and engineering librarian on finding grants and funding opportunities; and a presentation from the director of the Office of Graduate Career Services on a variety of resources and services provided through their office. This final roundtable helped to establish a relationship between our Libraries and the Office of Graduate Career Services; both the librarians and director of Graduate Career Services responded positively to learning about valuable resources they each offered and recognized great potential for future collaborations. As one of the most well-attended events, this final roundtable is also an example of how reframing library resources in different ways, or advertising them in conjunction with a topic like career preparedness, can help boost attendance. Each roundtable was also structured to allow ample time at the beginning for the students and presenters to casually interact with each other over free dinner and refreshments, thus allowing all participants to build rapport among each other prior to the more formal presentations. Subsequent iterations of the roundtables series have covered finding funding opportunities, jointly presented with the Office of Research; citation management programs; data tools and services; and advanced research strategies, including forward and reverse citation searching, journal metrics, and creating search alerts.

Although we do not typically design programs for specific graduate student populations, such as international students or teaching assistants, we strive to provide an array of recurring workshops that appeal to different baseline skill sets and varying levels of prior knowledge. We discovered early on in our programming that even the most basic information literacy skills are not common knowledge for many graduate students, and thus scaffolded our events accordingly. With this in mind, we have also found that providing information for specific populations within our recurring workshops has been beneficial. For example, demonstrating how to find information on both U.S. and foreign companies in our career research roundtable has allowed us to reflect the interests of our international student attendees.

Needs Assessment and Planning

At each event during this series, participant data were collected through registration and feedback forms. We found that using electronic registration forms was beneficial because it generated a list of e-mail addresses for sending reminders, distributing surveys, and advertising future events. Questions in the registration and feedback forms captured demographic information from participants, such as home department and major; type of program (master's, PhD, etc.); accessibility needs; desired topics of interest; event takeaways; and preferred time, location, and event format. Although the forms did not specifically ask for students' countries of origin, a question regarding students' prior interactions with the Libraries contained options such as attendance at international graduate student information fairs. This allowed us to gather further insights about the reach of our current and past programming to international students.

Data collected from event registration and feedback surveys have been pivotal in making decisions about future program directions. After our speed-dating style event, we found that the majority of attendees were satisfied overall, having made new connections with our staff and gaining an enhanced awareness of our Libraries' resources and services. In feedback captured across all four events, participants responded overwhelmingly that they preferred to attend evening programs. We also gathered some significant qualitative data that spoke to the impact of this series; for instance, one student commented that they would have missed a significant part of university study if they had not participated, and that the events helped them navigate life outside of the isolated course bubbles in which graduate students typically occupy. Notably, international students made up a sizable portion of our attendees, and were especially grateful for the multiple opportunities to learn more about our Libraries' functional areas of expertise and to connect with other academic support systems on campus. Our survey responses indicated that graduate students not only responded approvingly to the roundtable topics we had chosen, but also expressed interest in the other topics we had flagged in our literature review. A few of the topics they were most interested in included an introduction to library resources and services; tips for starting a research project; advanced research techniques; data tools and sources; citations and citation management programs; career resources; resources for self-paced learning; writing help; and finding grants and funding resources.

Having successfully launched the first round of our series, our focus shifted toward thinking about the sustainability and longevity of our graduate outreach and programming efforts. Our goals going forward were to create a co-curricular series focused on developing graduate students' research and professional skill sets that would span across an entire year and continually build on knowledge gained throughout. In addition to feedback gathered from our attendees, we also consulted with other librarians about their prior and current outreach efforts with graduate students to ensure we had a complete picture of our historic and current interactions. We gathered their insights on which topics they deemed most relevant to graduate student academic, research, and professional success. Many of these topics overlapped with those we received in event feedback surveys; additional librarian-suggested topics ranged from support for submitting dissertations and theses, to open access and copyright, to archival research, to research reproducibility and reputation.

After analyzing these comments, we selected topics we felt would be most applicable to students across different disciplines and program types (for instance, master's nonthesis versus doctoral). These topics included citations and citation management tools, an overview of library resources and services, advanced research techniques, data tools and services, and copyright and fair use. Additionally, although these topics would have limited appeal to graduate students in professional, nonthesis degree programs, we decided to cover research reputation, creating research profiles, and the process of submitting dissertations and theses. All of our chosen topics would recur on an annual basis, while other more specialized topics, such as open access and archival research, would be featured in programming occasionally, or if applicable, built into the other topical sessions.

Conclusions, Lessons Learned, and a Call to Action

Since launching this series in the spring of 2018, we have continued to experiment and adjust our program in subsequent semesters. In addition to creating recurring events centered on the core topics discerned from librarian and student feedback, we plan to offer rotating "elective" topics, keeping the program fresh and allowing it to flex with our graduate students' evolving needs. For instance, though we had originally planned our events for Thursday nights to coincide with trivia, in later series we have rotated days and locations in order to accommodate varying student schedules. We found that the mixture of event types—from the larger and more social speed-dating style event to the intimate seminar and discussion-style roundtables—were beneficial in presenting students a dynamic range of formats for information exchange. More recently, we incorporated a Saturday, full-day conference-style weekend event into our programming to provide more intensive workshops in a condensed period of time, with a goal of reaching graduate students focused intently on research and writing, and those with schedules prohibiting them from attending during the week.

Overall, the graduate student response to our programs has been positive, with students inquiring about future series' offerings and our growing list of event partners showing continued interest in future collaborations. A few of the greatest benefits realized through our programming initiatives include the stronger relationships built with graduate students and the development of a valuable network of campus collaborators—from student-run organizations, such as the GSO and its affiliated student groups, to other graduate student-serving units on campus, such as the Office of Research and Graduate Career Services. Through this process we have become acutely aware that campus units providing services to graduate students were largely disconnected, planning events independently of each other, and failing to look holistically at how the campus as a whole could best meet graduate student needs. This inadvertently contributes to the siloed and decentralized nature of the graduate student experience. Going forward, it is our intention to maintain an active role in the planning of graduate programming and outreach, and to be recognized on campus as an influential player in enhancing the graduate experience.

As our Libraries are now a firmly established GSO service provider, we will use GSO funding to support regularized graduate student programming. In planning for the future, we will also look to the GSO for their valuable support and communications network to market and advertise our events. Furthermore, we will maintain our relationships with graduate student groups such as ASEE@SU, who are natural partners because they receive annual funds to host events and are often looking for programming ideas. Partnerships with graduate student groups are also essential for gaining insights on topics and how to best present or "spin" those ideas in ways that appeal to the broader graduate population. Although we have collaborated with our international student services office and English Language Institute on other programs—such as through graduate international information fairs, orientations, and library instruction—given the high number of international students that have participated in our graduate events, there may be further opportunities to strengthen our partnerships with these units. For instance, our international student services office has also been a frequent GSO-recognized service provider; such relationships could potentially open doors to cosponsor and mutually enhance each of our own GSO-sponsored activities in the future.

Our graduate programming efforts have created internal gains as well. They have allowed our subject librarians and functional specialists the opportunity to develop relationships with graduate and international students outside of their subject areas, helping them better understand the specialized needs of graduate students. They have also learned from each other through collaborative presentations at the graduate research roundtable events, ultimately broadening the range of expertise among our colleagues. It has also generated discussions around expanding the scope of our information literacy program to establish graduate information literacy and research competencies, allowing us to more closely align graduate outreach efforts with the Libraries' larger strategic goals.

Already we are seeing how our graduate programming efforts have fostered a culture shift on campus; it has brought together multiple groups both within and outside of our Libraries to have conversations about how to best support the diverse needs of graduate students. With a rapidly expanding university research agenda and plans to bring more graduate students to campus, it is imperative that conversations and collaborations around supporting graduate students remain at the forefront. Libraries are strategically positioned to help in these efforts. As the conversation surrounding libraries and graduate student services continues to gather momentum, will you be there?

References

Association of College & Research Libraries. (2019). *Academic library services for graduate students interest group.* Retrieved from http://www.ala.org/acrl /aboutacrl/directoryofleadership/interestgroups/acr-igalsgs

Baruzzi, A., & Calcagno, T. (2015). Academic libraries and graduate students: An exploratory study. *portal: Libraries and the Academy, 15*(3), 393–407. https://doi.org/10.1353/pla.2015.0034

Boll, C. (2016, February 8). Syracuse University jumps into top research tier in new Carnegie Classifications. *Syracuse University News.* Retrieved from https://news.syr.edu/blog/2016/02/08/syracuse-university-jumps-into -top-research-tier-in-new-carnegie-classifications-51145

Budzise-Weaver, T., & Anders, K. C. (2016). Be our guest: Engaging graduate students through specialized outreach events. *Endnotes: The Journal of the New Members Round Table, 7*(1), 1–12. Retrieved from http://www.ala.org/rt/sites /ala.org.rt/files/content/oversightgroups/comm/schres/endnotesvol7no1 /Article_Be_Our_Guest.pdf

Bussell, H., Hagman, J., & Guder, C. S. (2017). Research needs and learning format preferences of graduate students at a large public university: An exploratory study. *College & Research Libraries, 78*(7), 978–998. https:// doi.org/10.5860/crl.78.7.978

Click, A. B. (2018). International graduate students in the United States: Research processes and challenges. *Library & Information Science Research, 40*(2), 153–162. https://doi.org/10.1016/j.lisr.2018.05.004

Covert-Vail, L., & Collard, S. (2012). *New roles for new times: Research library services for graduate students.* Retrieved from https://www.arl.org/storage /documents/publications/nrnt-grad-roles-20dec12.pdf

Fleming-May, R., & Yuro, L. (2009). From student to scholar: The academic library and social sciences PhD students' transformation. *portal: Libraries and the Academy, 9*(2), 199–221. http://doi.org/10.1353/pla.0.0040

Fong, B. L., Wang, M., White, K., & Tipton, R. (2016). Assessing and serving the workshop needs of graduate students. *The Journal of Academic Librarianship, 42*(5), 569–580. https://doi.org/10.1016/j.acalib.2016.06.003

Forbes, C., Schlesselman-Tarango, G., & Keeran, P. (2017). Expanding support for graduate students: Library workshops on research funding opportunities. *College & Research Libraries, 78*(3), 297–313. https://doi.org/10 .5860/crl.78.3.297

Goldenberg-Hart, D. (2008). Enhancing graduate education: A fresh look at library engagement. *ARL: A Bimonthly Report, 256,* 1–8. Retrieved from https:// www.cni.org/wp-content/uploads/2010/11/arl-br-256.pdf

Helmstutler, B. (2015). Taking research services to the next level: A case study of implementing a scholarly impact outreach program for faculty and graduate students. *Journal of Library Innovation, 6*(2), 96–104.

Hoffmann, K., Antwi-Nsiah, F., Feng, V., & Stanley, M. (2008). Library research skills: A needs assessment for graduate student workshops. *Issues in Science and Technology Librarianship, 53.* http://doi.org/10.5062/F48P5XFC

Institute of International Education. (2018). *Open Doors report on international educational exchange: International student enrollment trends, 1948/49– 2017/18.* Retrieved from https://www.iie.org/Research-and-Insights/Open -Doors/Data/International-Students/Enrollment

Kennesaw State University. (2020). *Transforming Libraries for Graduate Students— Conferences, workshops, and lectures.* Retrieved from https://digitalcom mons.kennesaw.edu/gradlibconf

Peacemaker, B., & Roseberry, M. (2017). Creating a sustainable graduate student workshop series. *Reference Service Review, 45*(4), 562–574. https://doi.org /10.1108/RSR-04-2017-0010

Rempel, H. G. (2010). A longitudinal assessment of graduate student research behavior and the impact of attending a library literature review workshop. *College & Research Libraries, 71*(6), 532–547. https://doi.org/10.5860/crl -79

Rempel, H. G., & Davidson, J. (2008). Providing information literacy instruction to graduate students through literature review workshops. *Issues in Science and Technology Librarianship, 53.* http://doi.org/10.5062/F44X55RG

Renfro, C., & Shields, E. (2017). Transforming libraries to serve graduate students. *College & Research Libraries News, 78*(4), 202–205. https://doi.org/10 .5860/crln.78.4.9649

Renfro, C., & Stiles, C. (2018). *Transforming libraries to serve graduate students.* Chicago, IL: Association of College and Research Libraries.

Roszkowski, B., & Reynolds, G. (2013). Assessing, analyzing, and adapting: Improving a graduate student instruction program through needs assessment. *Behavioral & Social Sciences Librarian, 32*(4), 224–239. http://doi.org /10.1080/01639269.2013.837798

Scheib, S., & Charles, A. (2018). Reading-writing groups for chemistry graduate students: A three-year experiment in finding the interesting thing. In C. Renfro & C. Stiles (Eds.), *Transforming libraries to serve graduate students* (pp. 125–138). Chicago, IL: Association of College and Research Libraries.

Syracuse University. (2015). *Academic strategic plan: Trajectory to excellence.* Retrieved from http://asp.syr.edu/wp-content/uploads/2018/01/ASP_web .pdf

Syracuse University. (2019). *Facts, figures, and rankings—Syracuse University.* Retrieved from https://www.syracuse.edu/about/facts-figures-rankings

Syracuse University Graduate Student Organization. (2019). *Graduate student organization—Syracuse University.* Retrieved from http://gradorg.syr.edu

Syracuse University Libraries. (2018a). *Information literacy—Syracuse University Libraries.* Retrieved from https://library.syr.edu/departments/infolit.php

Syracuse University Libraries. (2018b). *Strategic plan 2018–2022*. Retrieved from https://library.syr.edu/about/documents/sul-strategic-plan-2018–2022 .pdf

Syracuse University Office of Institutional Research. (2019). *Student enrollment by career and ethnicity—Fall 2018 census*. Retrieved from http://institutional research.syr.edu/wp-content/uploads/2019/02/02-Syracuse-University -Student-Enrollment-by-Career-and-Ethnicity-Fall-2018-Census.pdf

PART 2

Preparing Future Academics: Professional Expectations of the Academy

CHAPTER FIVE

Beyond Disciplines: Training Students for 21st-Century Research

*Will Shaw, Liz Milewicz,
Heidi Madden, and Greta Boers*

Introduction

Research practices across disciplines are evolving: scholarship is increasingly collaborative, interdisciplinary, digital, and designed to reach multiple audiences. Yet the mismatch between such expansive research methods (e.g., those found in the digital humanities and data science) and the narrow disciplinary focus of graduate programs creates a problem for students, who may be tacitly expected to know emergent methods or acquire such knowledge on their own. This problem is most obvious with new research practices but is evident elsewhere, too; sometimes, it exists even with well-established methods (e.g., conducting archival research). Who is training graduate students in research methods that span disciplinary boundaries?

The library literature amply documents emerging information and service needs for doctoral students (Baruzzi & Calcagno, 2015; Bussell, Hagman, & Guder, 2017; Covert-Vail & Collard, 2012; Fong, Wang, White, & Tipton, 2016; Peacemaker & Roseberry, 2017; Tancheva et al., 2016). Despite these changes, library and university structures remain organized around disciplines and do not always align with practices and programs that would actually benefit graduate students. How can library staff best help doctoral students in this environment? Libraries are uniquely situated to offer training that crosses disciplinary boundaries and answers developing needs. To do so, we must collaborate with each other while also aligning our work with that of other entities on campus. We must adapt the ways in which we facilitate research, and perhaps more importantly, we must help doctoral students acquire transferable, transdisciplinary skills and critical digital literacies so that they can thrive professionally. These imperatives comprise a pedagogical challenge for libraries in the age of digital scholarship.

The program we describe below is one answer to this challenge. It seeks to identify and meet emerging instructional opportunities while offering an adaptable, reusable model for involving library staff in graduate student education. It understands library staff not as interstitial educators who fill gaps in a curriculum with functional training but as experts who are uniquely positioned to teach graduate students the competencies that build meaningful interdisciplinary work, digital literacies, and professional success.

Background

Duke University is a private research university in Durham, North Carolina. For the 2018–2019 academic year, the university enrolled a total of 8,898 graduate and professional students, and 6,994 undergraduate students. The available demographics identify the total graduate and professional school student body as 44% Caucasian, 30% international, 10% Asian American, 6% African American, 5% Hispanic/Latino, and 6% other backgrounds. The graduate school enrolls 3,273 master's and doctoral students in Biological & Biomedical Sciences, Humanities, Physical Sciences & Engineering, and Social Science; of those students, 1,488 (45%) identify as women.

Like many institutions, Duke is moving toward cross-disciplinary work. It is home to vibrant communities that grow out of—and remain rooted in—traditional disciplines but branch into more expansive research questions and methods. These communities have developed among science, technology, engineering, and mathematics (STEM) programs; our professional schools; and numerous associated centers and institutes (e.g., the Franklin Humanities Institute, Kenan Institute for Ethics, Center for Documentary Studies, and the Social Sciences Research Institute). Alongside these groups and programs, initiatives such as Humanities Futures, Humanities Writ Large, Humanities Unbounded, and Bass Connections encourage scholars to push research and pedagogy beyond traditional forms: scholarship and teaching in these environments is often collaborative, interdisciplinary, digital, and public-facing.

Of course, a larger context surrounds these endeavors, and institutional priorities both inform and reflect local concerns. Recent strategic planning at the university level, in the graduate school, and in Duke Libraries stresses these evolutionary changes in scholarship and graduate education. For example, the university and graduate school plans call for "re-imagining" doctoral education at Duke, with an emphasis on "enhancing the graduate student experience" (Duke University, Graduate School, 2017, p. 22). Such proposals respond to the demands of a rapidly evolving and diversifying job marketplace and a desire to prepare our students to thrive in a variety of careers (Duke University, Office of the Provost, 2017).

As a concrete step toward realizing these goals, the graduate school has added a robust professional development program to its portfolio of student services. Included in the program are a number of initiatives and resources that meet the shifting scholarly and professional needs of graduate students, such as pedagogical seminars; a college teaching certificate program; support for grant writing; a series of Responsible Conduct of Research (RCR) forums across the disciplines; and many other professional development and mentoring opportunities (Duke University, Graduate School, 2019).

Duke Libraries' strategic plan shares many of these priorities. In particular, the Libraries' focus on teaching "emerging literacies" and "bridg[ing] the gaps between these new literacies and those we have traditionally supported" resonates with the aims of several graduate school professional development programs (Duke University Libraries, 2016, pp. 1–2). In this institutional climate, it makes sense to build new graduate instructional programs around work library staff are already well-equipped to undertake: teach information literacy, share and model digital research methods, and facilitate work across disciplines. The Graduate Student Instruction Program (GSIP) working group made this kind of connection with graduate students a priority.

Literature Review

Long before Duke Libraries' 2016 strategic planning cycle, librarians began to change the way they understood research (Dempsey, 2017, p. 338). Instead of analyzing research from a library-centric point of view that emphasizes services and local collections (Cox & Verbaan, 2016, p. 320), librarians began considering the research process from the perspective of researchers themselves. The method behind this reconceptualization is now commonly known as "research life cycle analysis"—the use of ethnographic studies and survey methods to investigate activities in each segment of the research life cycle, allowing libraries to align their services with specific phases of scholarship (Finley & Skarl, 2018, p. 63). Research life cycle analysis emerged as a topic in the library literature around 2010, first in the sciences and then across disciplines (Carlson, Nelson, Johnston, & Koshoffer, 2015; Finley & Skarl, 2018; Fourie & Bakker, 2013; Lucky & Harkema, 2018; Vaughan et al., 2013).

The research life cycle is a model of the research process from conception to preservation. The most cited version of the life cycle is that of the University of Central Florida (UCF) (Finley & Skarl, 2018). In 2013, the UCF Libraries were the first to interactively link research activities with institutional services and resources, creating a visualization of the "Research Lifecycle at UCF" (Dotson, Bishop, & Beile, 2012). This model outlines four key cycles: planning, project, publication, and 21st-century digital scholarship. As scholarship and information literacies have evolved, other institutions have adapted the research life cycle model to reflect emerging needs in such areas as project management (Garwood & Poole, 2018), data management and visualization (Speare, 2018; Whitmire, 2015), 21st-century scholarly communications (Shirazi, 2018), digital publishing (DeMarco & Kyle, 2017; Hansen et al., 2018), and e-preservation and research impact (Day, 2018; Leiss & Gregory, 2016; McClellan, Detmering, Martinez, & Johnson, 2017; Reed, McFarland, & Croft, 2016).

In all of its forms, the research life cycle model is descriptive, not prescriptive: it is a schema for investigating a local context, mapping its idiosyncrasies to general patterns, and thoughtfully aligning library services with research activities. Weiland and others describe the inherent tension between complex local processes and simplified representations of the way research actually takes place: "Inevitably, scholarly practices can belie the structure conveyed by any orderly looking image of the workflow. Segments count more than sequence, and scholarly personality plays as big a role as commitment to the process" (Weiland, 2018, p. 285). Because no abstract model can capture the particularities of every institution, each library that uses research life cycle analysis will come up with a different program of services, one that reflects their institution's research profile and each discipline's distinctive research and information-seeking behaviors.

Any such analysis must also be grounded in an understanding of modern information literacies. Baseline information literacy levels for incoming doctoral students are provided by the *Framework for Information Literacy for Higher Education* (Association of College and Research Libraries, 2016) and the recent six-volume set on teaching with the frameworks, which includes a comprehensive bibliography on pedagogy (Oberlies & Mattson, 2018). Additionally, as Stommel (2014), Alfonzo and Batson (2014), and Russell and Hensley (2017) argue, graduate student library workshops must be infused with critical digital literacies via teaching that goes beyond "buttonology" (i.e., teaching tools instead of concepts) by modeling metacritical approaches to software and process (Russell & Hensley, 2017).

Method

Our team's approach to research life cycle analysis was similar to that described by Vaughan et al. (2013). We were guided by our own expertise and our own knowledge of the local research environment, and we used the established models of the research life cycle segments to walk through research activities comprehensively and systematically. We found, indeed, that research life cycle analysis helped us overcome biases created by our disciplinary or functional perspectives to create a common understanding of doctoral student needs.

We conducted this investigation at Duke in two phases. First, disciplinary groups of subject librarians in the Research and Instructional Services (RIS) department worked together to articulate researcher needs across the research life cycle and explore how they were similar and different in the humanities, social sciences, and sciences and engineering. Second, using the results of this work, a cross-departmental working group identified existing strengths, gaps, and growth areas for graduate student research support and developed instruction based on their analysis.

Building from our Knowledge and Experience

We could have begun our work by creating a survey that asked graduate students what kind of training might help them to undertake their research, create innovative forms of scholarship, or work effectively with archival materials. One foundational assumption underlying this approach is that students will be able to identify and explain their needs (or that we, in creating a survey, will be able to articulate them in ways that resonate with students), even when they exist outside of traditional graduate curricula. Nevertheless, the logic of administering a survey is persuasive: with responses in hand, we could map requests to different parts of the research life cycle, account for disciplinary variance in research processes, and design instruction that demonstrably filled a series of curricular gaps that, while not necessarily unique to our campus, were at least specific to its graduate student population. Having a critical mass of survey responses would also provide clear justification for the effort to develop such a program.

This kind of assessment can be a valuable tool for surfacing patterns or reducing blind spots. In this instance, though, we opted to trust the insight and institutional knowledge our group had already gained from our collective experience partnering with graduate students on digital projects, consulting with them on their research, leading instructional sessions and workshops, and conducting focus groups, as well as all the informal conversations with faculty and students that have helped us understand their research needs. By virtue of our positions at multiple points in the scholarly communication process, library staff have broad insight into researcher behavior. Recognizing the value of this unique experience at the outset helped us build the confidence to imagine new ways of supporting graduate students.

In effect, our approach exemplifies the kind of library innovation model that Brian Mathews (2012) describes as "discontinuous" rather than "continuous" (p. 3). Mathews's formulation, derived from the business literature on research and development (R&D), describes *continuous innovation* as a method of "push[ing] out core services through different channels or new locations"— that is, a process of incremental expansion based on existing services (2012, p. 4). By contrast, *discontinuous innovation* takes a broader view of local needs. In the case of instruction, for example, librarians might pose the general, analytical question, "[W]hat elements are critical for student success? This inquiry opens new paths. Instead of seeking new ways of adapting old services, the intent is to reimagine the role of the library" (Mathews, 2012, p. 4).

Adapting and Applying Research Life Cycle Models

Our approach to understanding Duke Libraries' services for graduate students began as the heads of the Digital Scholarship Services (DSS) and RIS departments discussed how subject librarians might improve support for emerging digital research and publishing activities. They settled on research life cycle analysis as a way to help map researchers' needs to the instructional work librarians were already doing and to identify and incorporate digital scholarship–oriented activities within the Libraries.

During the 2016–2017 academic year, RIS subject librarians worked within their sections to identify common research needs of graduate students and categorized those needs among different phases of the research life cycle (see Figure 5.1). Although there were disciplinary differences in the phases of scholarly work and in specific student tasks, the research life cycle framework made it possible to think about graduate student training opportunities in a common, generalized way. RIS section heads for the humanities, social sciences, and sciences, along with the RIS department head, reviewed these research tasks to identify ones that transcended disciplines and could be used to describe general work undertaken by all graduate students. (See in Appendix 5.1 a complete list of the common research tasks identified through this process.)

In May 2017, the DSS and RIS department heads formed the Graduate Student Instruction Program (GSIP) working group—a group charged with identifying and articulating library-based, cross-disciplinary training for graduate students throughout the research life cycle. Members of GSIP came from multiple departments in the Libraries' Research, Collections, and Scholarly

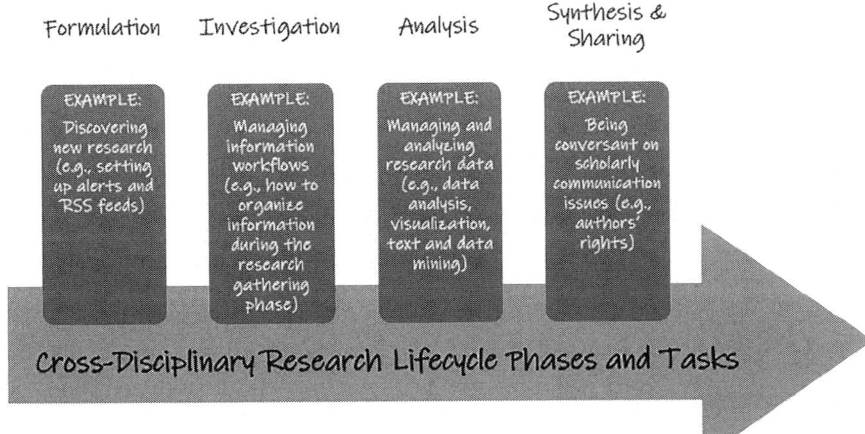

Figure 5.1 Created by Duke librarians, this model of the research life cycle illustrates common tasks across disciplines.

Communication division and represented different disciplinary interests: research and instruction librarians from the sciences, social sciences, and humanities sections; an international and area studies librarian; and staff from digital scholarship services. We saw a cross-departmental, cross-disciplinary team as a critical way to discern patterns and opportunities across our organization, imagine and implement new ways of working across divisions to assist graduate students, and share data and observations on the training graduate students need and desire. The group's first goals were to (1) develop a collective sense of the Libraries' current training for graduate students; (2) assess our existing instructional strengths and expertise in order to better communicate them (both internally and externally); (3) identify gaps in graduate students' training that may point to growth areas in the Libraries or opportunities for partnerships; and (4) develop strategies and programs to support those growth areas in future.

Inventorying Instruction Available to Graduate Students

Having identified common research tasks and potential areas of library instruction across disciplines and phases of the research life cycle, we next sought to inventory what training was already available to graduate students in these areas. This inventory was not merely an effort to identify gaps; instead, we saw it as an opportunity to clarify the Libraries' instructional strengths as well as opportunities for growth. As we mapped common research tasks to instruction and support offered by the Libraries and other campus units, we used the following questions to evaluate the strength, desirability, and feasibility of that support within the Libraries:

- How much do library staff already support this task (e.g., through instruction, one-on-one consultation, and LibGuides)?
- Is this a task that the Libraries would like to better support?
- Is it appropriate for the Libraries to support this task? (i.e., does it fall within the Libraries' mission?)
- Do library staff have sufficient training and expertise to support this task?

Areas of Strength in Research Instruction

If a task was supported, appropriate for the Libraries to support, and aligned with staff expertise and training, we classified it as a strength:

- Searching existing literature for data needed for research (including specialized information such as data sets, engineering standards, images, and primary sources);
- Managing and documenting the research process (e.g., note-taking, citation management);
- Managing and analyzing research data (e.g., data analysis, visualization, text and data mining);
- Using archival and special collections materials (e.g., identifying, accessing, and using relevant special collections and archival materials; capturing and organizing archival research);
- Managing information workflows (e.g., organizing information during the research gathering phase, including selecting tools for interoperability and appropriateness for data; deciding what information to use for different purposes);
- Understanding scholarly communication issues (e.g., authors' rights; publishing options, including open access; assessing impact of scholarship; alternative metrics; embargos); and
- Using Duke and other repositories to preserve and provide access to scholarship.

Potential Growth Areas in Research Instruction

We found it more challenging to categorize tasks that we believed the Libraries *should* support but for which instructional programming is insufficient (e.g., librarians do not have sufficient expertise; support currently offered is limited in scope or format). We identified these tasks as growth areas:

- Discovering new research (e.g., setting up alerts and RSS feeds; consuming social media and other online informal publications; evaluating new media formats);

- Organizing research/data for future use (e.g., file naming; description, including use of metadata schemas; lossless formats; principles for organizing research data for collaboration); and

- Promoting scholarly work through different communication channels (e.g., social media, LinkedIn, conference presentations, professional websites, open access repositories, nontraditional CVs, visualizations).

We also mapped these growth areas to instructional support offered by other units on campus to see whether it might be possible to coordinate or partner with others to offer research training.

This inventory of research instruction revealed that although our instructional support spanned the research life cycle, it skewed toward the earlier stages of research. We realized we could build on our strengths by offering more instruction sessions, partnering with others to address specific topics that might benefit graduate students, and better coordinating this training across our departments. The inventory process also helped us realize where we wanted to train ourselves and work with other departments and campus units in order to teach graduate students effectively. Both strengths and growth areas provided GSIP with clear directions for better communicating our instruction to graduate students and also better adapting our instruction to their needs.

Tailoring Instruction to Meet Graduate Students' Needs

We wanted to develop instruction in a way that allowed us to work across library departments and to create training that would be useful to students in multiple disciplines. We organized workshops around activities in the research life cycle and tried to align those workshops with key moments in graduate students' research—for example, before leaving on summer research trips, after completing a prospectus defense, before preliminary exams, or, in more workaday considerations, during midsemester breaks from coursework or teaching.

The Efficient Archival Researcher Workshop

A good example of this carefully timed instruction is our "Efficient Archival Researcher" workshop, offered at the end of the spring semester and targeted at graduate students preparing to leave for summer trips to archives. In this hands-on workshop, graduate students explored the challenges of working with published and unpublished archival materials, learned to locate appropriate archives around the world for their research, navigated access requirements, and considered different strategies for managing the many digital files and images researchers collect when conducting archival research. Much of the success of this workshop stemmed from partnerships across the library to organize and deliver the content. Several departments contributed to this workshop, including the Rubenstein Rare Book & Manuscript Library, Research and Instructional Services, Data and Visualization Services, and Digital Scholarship Services. Another pivotal partnership was with graduate students themselves: the workshop began with a panel discussion among later career graduate students about their own archival research experiences, providing vivid illustrations of the nature of archival research and the importance of good planning. A graduate student fellow based in the Digital Scholarship Services department led the discussion, helped organize and develop content for the workshop itself, and provided valuable insight for us into topics and examples that would be salient to graduate students.

The goal of this workshop was to help students make the most of their time in an archive. By learning from librarians and archivists who are better positioned than anyone on campus to teach about these subjects, participants developed strategies not only for locating and accessing materials but also for making them usable for future research. The workshop filled quickly, with a substantial waiting list, and feedback from participants suggests that our approach was beneficial. Prompted to share their most valuable takeaways from the workshop, students cited approaches to digital preservation, data management strategies, and "soft" skills such as how to approach archivists in advance of visits. Essentially, students learned how to conduct an archival research trip from start to finish, and they came away with new, broadly useful literacies in information management. The general topic of planning an archive visit is "not something often covered in a course or by an adviser," one participant wrote, underscoring the role of library staff in providing instruction unavailable through traditional graduate curricula or other campus units.

Responsible Conduct of Research (RCR) Days

In addition to developing workshop content from distinctive areas of library expertise and offering instruction at strategic times, we strove to offer instruction that focuses less on the superficial affordances of tools and more on the underlying practices or methodologies that the tools embody. From experience and from sustained contact with graduate students and faculty (including past focus groups and surveys), we know that students across disciplines are not likely to be exposed to some digital scholarly approaches or concepts in the course of their regular studies. For example, the students who may benefit most from learning about automated text analysis—doctoral researchers in English, history, and other humanities fields focused largely on textual research—may have no curricular resources to help them understand, say, topic modeling. In a similar vein, these fields may offer no instruction in the copyright or intellectual property concerns that affect acquisition and reuse of digitized texts and images. But library staff know these topics well and understand their relevance to research: we can draw on our own expertise to offer these kinds of workshops.

This perspective helped us to develop the basic rationale for "RCR Days," an event that took place during the fall semester. At Duke, graduate students must take a certain number of RCR credits; students earn credits by attending RCR Forums, which focus on various ethical dimensions of scholarship (e.g., academic integrity and misconduct, data management, and fiscal responsibility) (Duke University, Graduate School, 2019). Any unit on campus can offer these forums, subject to graduate school approval. Libraries staff offer many of these workshops, drawing from a robust set of established RCR offerings with cross-disciplinary appeal. Because of this collective expertise and experience, we were able to offer a group of RCR Forums during fall break as a two-day event, enabling graduate students to earn several of their RCR requirements at once.

Like the "Efficient Archival Researcher" workshop, the content of our "RCR Days" workshops was driven by both our expertise and our institutional knowledge of student needs. We also considered what workshops had been well attended and favorably received by graduate students in the past; each of the nine RCR workshops listed below was offered during "RCR Days" and had previously been taught (sometimes more than once) by Libraries staff:

- Ethics and Visualization;
- Digital Publishing: Multimodal Storytelling;
- Research Impact Concepts and Tools;
- Digital Publishing: Reaching and Engaging Audiences;
- Image Copyright and Acquisition for Scholars;
- Retractions in Science and Social Science Literature;
- Acquiring and Preparing a Corpus of Texts;
- Topic Modeling and Document Classification with MALLET; and
- Shaping Your Professional Identity Online.

These workshops enlisted staff from several departments of the Libraries, including Research and Instructional Services, Digital Scholarship Services, and Data and Visualization Services. We knew that these workshops had been successful in previous iterations and therefore were likely to engage graduate students when we offered them again; the convenience of "RCR Days"—specifically, the clustering of several cross-disciplinary RCR sessions at a time and place easier for graduate students to attend—would, we hoped, help further engage graduate students in these topics.

Indeed, enrollment and feedback suggested that "RCR Days" were both beneficial and timely. One hundred nine graduate students participated in the sessions, with some students taking multiple workshops. As we had initially hoped, timing was an important driver of student engagement: in our post-workshop surveys, 57% of participants selected "time (fall break)" as a primary reason for attending a given session (fall break sessions "don't interfere with my classes," one participant wrote). More important than timing, though, were specific workshop topics, which nearly 80% of respondents identified as a main reason for attending.

Coupled with the 53% of respondents who indicated that a workshop filled an "academic need," these survey answers help to validate our general approach and underscore the value of library staff expertise in scholarly communication, digital research methods, and emerging literacies. Based on past instructional outcomes and a careful analysis of our local research life cycle, we believed our collective knowledge could both identify and answer some of graduate students' emergent instructional needs. The success of "RCR Days" and the "Efficient Archival Researcher" workshop suggests that we were right.

Conclusion/Recommendations

Benefits to Students

The work of our cross-disciplinary instructional group and its emphasis on supporting graduate students' digital literacies throughout the research life cycle led us to develop programs that offered immediate benefits to students while also encouraging their growth as scholars.

At a practical level, this training was convenient to students' academic schedules. Workshops offered between spring and summer semesters and during fall break, and clustered in the same physical location during those times, didn't compete with typical semester activities, like teaching or attending classes. Having a variety of workshops to choose from, offered at different times of the day, increased the likelihood that students would find a class that was of interest and also fit within their schedule. Offering training in archival research at a time when many students would already be preparing for summer research helped with presenting information when it was most likely to be perceived as useful. This training was also offered in a way that made it more immediately beneficial to meeting their academic goals. By partnering with the graduate school to offer this training for RCR credit, we increased the immediate benefit to students who needed these credits in order to graduate.

Another immediate benefit of the program is its application to the dissertation. By planning instruction that prepares graduate students for common tasks across the research life cycle, we help ensure not only that their current projects are effectively planned but also that future work will be well designed and implemented. Additionally, the workshops we provided fulfilled broad, cross-disciplinary needs in research, ensuring that all students could potentially benefit and receive value from this training, beyond just securing required RCR credits before graduation. This broad, cross-disciplinary appeal is especially valuable for engaging humanities and social sciences students, who have traditionally been underserved by RCR offerings that focus on issues specific to the "hard" sciences. Because we sought to address topics that were independent of any particular disciplinary approach, the resulting workshops emphasized aspects of knowledge creation and sharing that could help students succeed in careers across academia and beyond.

Finally, at more individual levels, library staff saw great benefit from partnering with doctoral students to develop and deliver this training. Graduate students in the later phase of their doctoral work are natural partners in library teaching, and this peer-to-peer teaching creates dynamic exchanges: graduate students get experience teaching alongside library staff, and library staff increase their own knowledge of emerging research practices through close partnerships with students.

Lessons for Library Staff

There are a number of lessons we take from this experience that could be applied by other library staff wishing to provide more convenient, relevant, and beneficial research training for graduate students.

Build a Broad Framework (and Vision) for Library-Based Instruction

Rather than basing instruction entirely on specific requests or previously existing needs, consider the broader research life cycle of graduate students and how emerging instructional opportunities might fit within that framework. Mapping student needs across the research life cycle can help expand possibilities for library-based instruction and potential partnerships with others to develop and deliver that training. Additionally, by thinking beyond disciplines and identifying issues common throughout the research life cycle, library staff can create training that has relevance and value for more students.

Assess the Training Already Available on Campus

Recognizing the full range of training available to graduate students helps library staff create instruction that complements rather than competes with other campus offerings and that highlights and builds on their unique expertise. Simultaneously, greater awareness of other academic support units on campus, their expertise, and their mission can lead to other opportunities, such as offering instruction that supplements their programs or partnering with them to develop and deliver new graduate student training.

Work Closely with Colleagues and Graduate Students

Coteaching with colleagues can improve the quality of pedagogy, from increasing the diversity of content presented to presenting instruction in ways that benefit students' different learning styles. At the same time, coteaching can help staff work toward their own professional development goals, as when library staff work with and learn firsthand from colleagues with functional specialization (e.g., data visualization, digital publishing, copyright and fair use). By teaching with students, or even just working closely with them on different aspects of their research, library staff gained substantial insight into the ways students' research is evolving—and the ways librarians' instructional offerings might evolve with it.

Like other benefits to library staff, this pedagogical improvement and professional development grew from our approach to cross-disciplinary instruction. We recognized, based on both a local research life cycle analysis and our existing knowledge of curricula, disciplinary emphases, and student needs, that it was possible for library staff to play a vital role in educating graduate students at our university. Indeed, we believe libraries are uniquely able to help students cultivate the research practices and competencies that are increasingly necessary for scholarly work in the digital age.

References

Alfonzo, P., & Batson, J. (2014). Utilizing a co-teaching model to enhance digital literacy instruction for doctoral students. *International Journal of Doctoral Studies, 9,* 61–71. doi:10.28945/1973

Association of College and Research Libraries. (2016). *Framework for information literacy for higher education.* Retrieved from http://www.ala.org/acrl/sites/ala.org.acrl/files/content/issues/infolit/Framework_ILHE.pdf

Baruzzi, A., & Calcagno, T. (2015). Academic librarians and graduate students: An exploratory study. *portal: Libraries and the Academy, 15*(3), 393–407. doi:10.1353/pla.2015.0034

Bussell, H., Hagman, J., & Guder, C. (2017). Research needs and learning format preferences of graduate students at a large public university: An exploratory study. *College & Research Libraries, 78*(7), 978–998. doi:10.5860/crl.78.7.978

Carlson, J., Nelson, M. S., Johnston, L. R., & Koshoffer, A. (2015). Developing data literacy programs: Working with faculty, graduate students and undergraduates. *Bulletin of the American Society for Information Science and Technology (Online); Silver Spring, 41*(6), 14–17.

Covert-Vail, L., & Collard, S. (2012). *New roles for new times: Research library services for graduate students.* Retrieved from https://www.arl.org/storage/documents/publications/nrnt-grad-roles-20dec12.pdf

Cox, A. M., & Verbaan, E. (2016). How academic librarians, IT staff and research administrators perceive and relate to research. *Library and Information Science Research, 38,* 319–326.

Day, A. (2018). Research information management: How the library can contribute to the campus conversation. *New Review of Academic Librarianship, 24*(1), 23–34. doi:10.1080/13614533.2017.1333014

DeMarco, C., & Kyle, C. (2017). *Digital publishing: A home for faculty in the library—exercises in innovation from Harvard Law School. Working paper.* Retrieved from http://nrs.harvard.edu/urn-3:HUL.InstRepos:34864118

Dempsey, L. (2017). Library collections in the life of the user: Two directions. *Liber Quarterly, 26*(4), 338–359. doi:10.18352/lq.10170

Dotson, L., Bishop, C., & Beile, P. (2012). *The Research lifecycle at UCF: A library-led institutional collaboration to develop a mental model of research support and services.* Retrieved from https://stars.library.ucf.edu/cgi/viewcontent.cgi?article=1042&context=ucfscholar

Duke University, Graduate School. (2017). *Duke University graduate school strategic plan, 2016–2026.* Retrieved from https://gradschool.duke.edu/sites/default/files/documents/Duke%20Graduate%20School%20Strategic%20Plan_2016-2026.pdf

Duke University, Graduate School. (2019). Responsible conduct of research forums. *Professional development programs.* Retrieved from https://gradschool.duke.edu/professional-development/programs/responsible-conduct-research/rcr-forums

Duke University Libraries. (2016). *Engage, discover, transform: Duke University Libraries, 2016–2021.* Retrieved from https://library.duke.edu/sites/default/files/dul/users/Joyce%20Chapman/Duke%20University%20Libraries%20Strategic%20Plan%2016%20June%202016.pdf

Duke University, Office of the Provost. (2017). *Together Duke: Advancing excellence through community.* Retrieved from https://strategicplan.duke.edu/wp-content/uploads/sites/15/2017/09/TogetherDuke-Sept2017-text.pdf

Finley, P., & Skarl, S. (2018). Research lifecycles as the basis for library service plans: An annotated bibliography. *Codex, 4*(4), 62–76.

Fong, B. L., Wang, M., White, K., & Tipton, R. (2016). Assessing and serving the workshop needs of graduate students. *The Journal of Academic Librarianship, 42*(5), 569–580. doi:10.1016/j.acalib.2016.06.003

Fourie, I., & Bakker, S. (2013). Value of a manageable research life cycle for LIS. *The Electronic Library, 31*(5), 648–663. doi:10.1108/EL-04-2012-0034

Garwood, D. A., & Poole, A. H. (2018). Project management as information management in interdisciplinary research: "Lots of different pieces working together." *International Journal of Information Management, 41*, 14–22. doi:10.1016/j.ijinfomgt.2018.03.002

Hansen, D., Milewicz, L., Mangiafico, P., Shaw, W., Begali, M., & McGurrin, V. (2018). *A framework for library support of expansive digital publishing.* Retrieved from https://expansive.pubpub.org/pub/framework

Leiss, C., & Gregory, K. (2016). Visability and impact of research: Bibliometric services for university management and academic staff. *Proceedings of the IATUL Conferences.* Paper 3. Retrieved from http://docs.lib.purdue.edu /iatul/2016/plenary/3

Lucky, S., & Harkema, C. (2018). Back to basics: Supporting digital humanities and community collaboration using the core strength of the academic library. *Digital Library Perspectives, 34*(3), 188–199. doi:10.1108/DLP-03 -2018-0009

Mathews, B. (2012). *Too much assessment not enough innovation: R&D models and mindsets for academic libraries.* Retrieved from https://vtechworks.lib.vt.edu /bitstream/handle/10919/19047/Too_Much_Assessment_R&D_Paper _Mathews_Enhanced_Version.pdf

McClellan, S., Detmering, R., Martinez, G., & Johnson, A. M. (2017). Raising the library's impact factor: A case study in scholarly publishing literacy for graduate students. *portal: Libraries and the Academy, 17*(3), 543–568. doi:10.1353/pla.2017.0034

Oberlies, M. K., & Mattson, J. (2018). *Framing information literacy: Teaching grounded in theory, pedagogy, and practice.* Chicago, IL: Association of College & Research Libraries.

Peacemaker, B., & Roseberry, M. (2017). Creating a sustainable graduate student workshop series. *Reference Services Review, 45*(4), 562–574. doi:10.1108/ RSR-04-2017-0010

Reed, K., McFarland, D., & Croft, R. (2016). Laying the groundwork for a new library service: Scholar-practitioner & graduate student attitudes toward altmetrics and the curation of online profiles. *Evidence Based Library and Information Practice, 11*(2), 87–96. doi:10.18438/B8J047

Russell, J. E., & Hensley, M. K. (2017). Beyond buttonology: Digital humanities, digital pedagogy, and the ACRL framework. *College & Research Libraries News, 78*, 588–600.

Shirazi, R. (2018). The doctoral dissertation and scholarly communication: Adapting to changing publication practices among graduate students. *College & Research Libraries News, 79*, 34–37.

Speare, M. (2018). Graduate student use and non-use of reference and PDF management software: An exploratory study. *The Journal of Academic Librarianship, 44*(6), 762–774. doi:10.1016/j.acalib.2018.09.019

Stommel, J. (2014). Critical digital pedagogy: A definition. *Hybrid Pedagogy.* Retrieved from http://hybridpedagogy.org/critical-digital-pedagogy -definition

Tancheva, K., Gessner, G. C., Tang, N., Eldermire, E., Furnas, H., Branchini, D., . . . Foster, N. F. (2016). *A day in the life of a (serious) researcher: Envisioning the future of the research library.* New York, NY: Ithaka S+R. doi:10.18665 /sr.277259

Vaughan, K. T. L., Hayes, B. E., Lerner, R. C., McElfresh, K. R., Pavlech, L., Romito, D., . . . Morris, E. N. (2013). Development of the research lifecycle model for library services. *Journal of the Medical Library Association, 101*(4), 310–314. doi:10.3163/1536

Weiland, S. (2018). *The scholarly workflow in the digital age: What do we know? What should we do?* Paper presented at the Charleston Conference, Charleston, SC. Retrieved from https://pdfs.semanticscholar.org/0b40/7 0c6c7969d701ca66294066c77d9d739f40f.pdf

Whitmire, A. L. (2015). Implementing a graduate-level research data management course: Approach, outcomes, and lessons learned. *Journal of Librarianship and Scholarly Communication, 3*(2), 1–22. doi:10.7710/2162-3309.1246

Appendix 5.1: Common Research Tasks

- Searching existing literature for data needed for research (including a wide range of specialized kinds of information—from data sets to engineering standards to images and primary sources);

- Searching existing literature (i.e., literature review) for information needed in order to better understand and apply research methodology (e.g., experimental design; systematic reviews; using primary sources (contextual); theory; examples and demonstrations; tests and measurements; meta-analysis);

- Discovering new research (e.g., setting up alerts and RSS feeds; consuming social media and other online informal publications; evaluating new media formats);

- Understanding and tracking research impact and metrics (e.g., through social media, alt-metrics, web analytics, open access repositories, nontraditional CVs, LinkedIn);

- Managing and documenting research process (e.g., note-taking, citation management);

- Managing and analyzing research data (e.g., data analysis, visualization, text and data mining);

- Organizing research/data for future use (e.g., file naming; description, including use of metadata schemas; lossless formats; tools and principles for organizing research data for collaboration);

- Being conversant on scholarly communication issues (e.g., authors' rights; publishing options, including open access; assessing impact of scholarship, including using alternative metrics; embargos);

- Promoting scholarly work through different communication channels (e.g., social media, presentations at conferences, professional websites, open access repositories, nontraditional CVs, LinkedIn, as well as posters and other visualizations of research);

- Managing information workflows (e.g., how to organize information during the research-gathering phase, including selecting tools for interoperability and appropriateness for data; deciding what information to use for different purposes); and

- Using archival and special collections materials (how to identify, access, and use special collections and archival materials relevant to one's research; capturing and organizing research collected from archives).

CHAPTER SIX

The Research Commons: Transforming the Graduate Experience through Interdisciplinary Programming and Collaboration

Heather De Forest, Rebecca Dowson, Alison J. Moore, and Nicole White

Introduction

As an inherently interdisciplinary unit within a traditionally siloed institution, the academic library has the capacity to transform the graduate student experience. Increasingly, academic libraries are establishing units known as Scholars or Research Commons. These units provide space, infrastructure, and services that support the research endeavors of graduate students during all stages of the research life cycle. Research Commons are uniquely situated to support graduate students as future academics in a number of ways, including cultivating communal on-campus spaces, and encouraging participation in cross-disciplinary workshops on research methods, scholarly communications, and digital tools. In addition, these units frequently offer low-stakes leadership opportunities for graduate students, which further helps to support their professional development. This chapter demonstrates how Simon Fraser University (SFU) Library's Research Commons fosters interdisciplinary community among graduate students using the following three case studies: a graduate peer program; "Thesis Boot Camp"; and communities of practice. In addition to their benefits for community development, these initiatives also enable graduate students to build technical, leadership, and other professional development skills.

Background

Simon Fraser University (SFU) is a comprehensive, doctoral-granting university located in British Columbia, Canada, on the unceded and traditional territories of the xʷməθkʷəy̓əm (Musqueam), S̲kwx̲wú7mesh (Squamish), Səl̓ílwətaɬ (Tsleil-Waututh), q̓íc̓əy̓ (Katzie), qiqéyt (Qayqayt), Semiahmoo, sc̓əwaθən məsteyəxʷ (Tsawwassen), and kʷikʷəƛ̓əm (Kwikwetlem) peoples. In the 2017–2018 academic year, SFU had an annualized headcount of 4,444 graduate students, of whom 1,283 were doctoral students, 2,444 were master's students, and 716 were graduate students in other programs, such as certificate programs (SFU Institutional Research and Planning, 2018). Self-identified female students make up 57.6% of SFU's total graduate student population, and 31% of SFU's total graduate student population is international students (SFU Institutional Research and Planning, 2018, 2019). With three campuses, three campus libraries, and 34 full-time librarians in public service roles, the SFU Library serves a variety of patrons in a busy research environment. The SFU Library Research Commons, located in the W.A.C. Bennett Library at the SFU Burnaby campus, is an incredibly popular space for graduate students. Often at or over capacity by the third week of term, the Research Commons space is equipped with 22 dual-monitor desktop workstations, team rooms, sit-stand desks, a seminar room, and six staff offices.

However, the Research Commons is far more than a space. Since its inception in 2012, the Research Commons has transformed from a department of two librarians offering a virtual suite of programs and services to a dynamic team comprised of eight librarians and two library assistants in 2019. The speed at which the department has expanded over the past eight years is a testament to the growing need for graduate student support at SFU. The department is divided into teams serving three major areas: data services (such as research data management, programming, software support for quantitative and qualitative data analysis, and GIS), digital scholarship (including support for publishing, open access, research impact, online presence, data visualization, and the digital humanities), as well as outreach and engagement to graduate students and postdoctoral fellows. Additionally, support for graduate student writing, learning, and English as an Additional Language (EAL) is provided through the Research Commons and administratively managed by the Student Learning Commons, another department located in the library.

Literature Review

Why a "Research Commons"?

The Research Commons model is based on the concept of the "Learning Commons" or "Information Commons," however, with a distinctly graduate focus (Daniels, Darch, & de Jager, 2010; Roberts, 2007). Dowson (2016) notes, "as scholarship reaches further and further across methodological traditions, scholars require dedicated spaces and structures designed to build communities of practice around emerging methods and areas of study" (p. 2). Research Commons spaces are an interdisciplinary incubator for graduate research at the university. Students are free to engage with Research Commons events, services, and programming without the burden of evaluation because it operates as an entirely extracurricular support space. Thus, the Research Commons becomes a laboratory environment where early-career researchers can participate in low-stakes knowledge creation by asking questions, developing their skills, and connecting with peers in other disciplines.

One of the reasons that the SFU Library Research Commons has been successful is that it has demonstrated a commitment to developing services, events, and programs in partnership with, and/or in response to, student feedback. Workshops, for example, are one of the most significant ways that the Research Commons supports graduate students: there are more than 200 free workshops available to graduate students each year on topics such as research data management, scholarly publishing, quantitative and qualitative data analysis tools, and other skills or tools. Like other academic library units providing support for graduate students, the Research Commons has found that for these workshops to be effective, it is critical to ensure that the topics, timing, and mode of instruction meet student needs (Fong, Wang, White, & Tipton, 2016; Rempel, Hussong-Christian, & Mellinger, 2011).

Preparing Future Academics?

Although this chapter will focus on how SFU Library's Research Commons strives to support graduate students as future academics, it is important to recognize that all graduate students enter the academy as whole people with a variety of backgrounds, experiences, goals, and aspirations. Therefore, to support graduate students as future academics is also to support them in their simultaneous roles as students, employees, and caregivers, aiming to meet all students at their point(s) of need. It is no secret that the academy and, by extension, academic libraries, are changing. Canadian postsecondary institutions are receiving lower levels of federal and provincial funding (Statistics Canada, 2017; Usher, 2018), and as a vocation, higher education is shifting from a secure and practical-if-underpaid career option to one of intense pressure and precarity (Courtois & O'Keefe, 2015; Pasma & Shaker, 2018). Although many graduate students do transition into productive academic careers, many more do not. In fact, only approximately 13% of SFU's graduate students secure positions as researchers or instructors after graduation (SFU Graduate and Postdoctoral Studies, 2018). As such, the goal of the Research Commons is to ensure that graduate students are as well prepared as possible for wherever their futures may take them, including academia.

Transforming the Graduate Student Experience at SFU Library

The Research Commons supports graduate students in preparing for their careers through a wide variety of programming, services, technology, and spaces; however, there are several flagship programs that have a demonstrable impact on students' success, both while they are at SFU and in their future endeavors. This section will detail two such initiatives, the Research Commons' Peer Program and "Thesis Boot Camp," and will explore the emergence of informal programs to support specialized research communities of practice.

The Research Commons' Peer Program

The Research Commons makes use of a peer program to support graduate students as they engage with emerging research methods and tools. This peer program was inspired by the success of the Student Learning Commons' Writing, Learning, and EAL Peer programs. The Research Commons' Peer Program is designed to be flexible and responsive to students' needs. Because peers in the Research Commons can be hired for specific skill sets and are able to administer consultations and instruction related to new and emerging research tools and practices, this program allows the SFU Library to move with agility in these areas. Indeed, peer learning programs can be generally beneficial to the operational flexibility of the academic library (Ramaswamy, Garrett, & Currie, 2018). The peer model also allows the Research Commons to align its work with the SFU Library's current strategic plan, which emphasizes an enhanced graduate student experience. Through the peer program, the SFU Library has also been able to offer "employment, mentorship, and training opportunities to students to enhance student engagement and employability" (SFU Library, 2016).

Overview

The Research Commons' Peer Program currently employs 10 to 15 peers in the following four support areas: qualitative data analysis software (QDAS), research programming and data, digital humanities (DH), and geographic information systems (GIS). The peer team is composed of graduate students, at both the master's and doctoral levels, from a range of disciplines across the institution including Criminology, Education, English, Communications, Statistics and Actuarial Science, and Geography. The peers bring their knowledge of particular content areas and their facilitation skills to the positions, and they gain experience and professional development in both areas. Peers support researchers through consultations by e-mail, phone, video calls, and/or in person to individuals and small groups. The scope of their peer activities may also include leading workshops open to the campus community, providing discipline-specific workshops within graduate research methods courses, producing resource materials, hosting office hours online and/or virtually, and participating in other activities as they arise. The peers are paid for their time, and they work approximately 6 to 10 hours per week. In addition to these semester-long contracts, the Research Commons has also engaged students with unique expertise for one-off or short-lived events and workshops, for example, student-led *Wikipedia* editing workshops and edit-a-thons.

The Research Commons' Peer Program was built out from a pilot GIS program and followed by the hiring of two QDAS facilitators in 2015. The development of this program has been shaped by both environmental scans and assessments. As needs are identified, additional peers are hired to ensure effective support for graduate students, even in niche areas. The hiring of peers is not subject to collective agreements or to legacy processes and policies; as such, the Research Commons is able to continually reevaluate our peer recruitment practices to ensure that they align with the library's commitments to diversity and inclusion (SFU Library, 2016). Peers report to a librarian supervisor who oversees scheduling, shapes the direction of the program, and gives feedback. Recently, the Research Commons has formalized the ad hoc work of the peers into an organized Peer Program to achieve more consistency in procedures, as well as to ensure enhanced opportunities for training, networking, and referral across the program. These initiatives have included a focus on training on library procedures, informal opportunities for socializing, and greater integration within library structures.

The Peer Program offers students opportunities to increase their professional competencies in technical skills, communication and facilitation, pedagogy, and interdisciplinarity. Peers also benefit from integration into the library's organizational structure, equipping them with an extended network of professional colleagues and access to structural supports such as professional development opportunities. Students who have participated in the Peer Program enjoy a high degree of engagement with the institution and their work in the library, and are well positioned to build on the networks and skills they have established to further their academic and professional careers.

Benefits to Peers

Software Skills. Although graduate students and faculty benefit from the support offered through the peer program, the peers themselves also report significant benefits from their roles. Through their work, they gain skills that are useful in academic, alternative academics ("alt-ac"), and nonacademic contexts. Teaching and consulting on software as well as software practices creates opportunities for peers to deepen their knowledge. In their peer roles, these graduate students encounter issues and solutions beyond the scope of their own research projects. The Peer Program allows them to apply learning from one project or consultation to the next. In responding to queries, peers test practices for viability and are exposed to a multiplicity of data types and analysis needs. Peers also extend their range of troubleshooting supports for software, becoming members of online and in-person communities and discovering new sources of solutions. Beyond this wider exposure to the uses of software, stepping into an instructional role requires the peers to engage with different approaches to the material and supports them to develop enhanced cognitive processes (Bargh & Schul, 1980; Topping, 1996).

In many instances, peers are also able to deepen their knowledge by accessing additional training in specific software and applications; institutional licenses come with training credits, which the Research Commons makes available to the peers to support them in their learning. Additionally, working in the Research Commons may provide peers with practical experience, which software credentialing programs sometimes require. For example, QSR International, the makers of the QDAS software NVivo, offers a certification program that a peer facilitator recently completed. Her practical work made it possible for her to complete some of the requirements, and the Research Commons was able to defray the associated registration fees.

Further, many of the Research Programming peers have been able to advance through the credentialing process of The Carpentries, an organization that builds capacity in data and computational skills for research, and of which the SFU Library is a member organization. To gain these credentials, the peers have joined a network of Carpentries instructors and have fulfilled lesson delivery obligations through Software Carpentry and Data Carpentry workshops hosted by the Research Commons. In addition to offering valuable professional development for individual peers, partnership with The Carpentries supports the library's value of diversity, as articulated in our 2017–2021

Strategic Plan. Embedded in the ethos of The Carpentries and into its code of conduct is a desire to extend a welcome "to everyone regardless of their background, ethnicity, skill level, gender, career stage, or beliefs" (The Carpentries, 2018).

Facilitation Skills. A core component of the Peer Program is to give graduate students opportunities for skill development in teaching practices. Peers participate in the preparation and delivery of sessions ranging from hosted drop-in hours to scripted demonstrations to activity-driven, hands-on workshops. In course-integrated sessions, they liaise with the subject faculty to make the session meaningful in the context of the syllabus. Where appropriate, sessions are delivered in an online environment through the university's learning management system. Instruction is sometimes delivered by an individual facilitator and, at other times, involves cooperative teaching. Peers are careful to deliver instruction in the software itself rather than in research methodologies. Through these multiple contexts, peers gain experience with delivering presentations, engaging participants, providing salient examples, conducting assessment, and iterating their teaching approach.

For many of the peers, the program serves as a lab for their facilitation and instructional skills. The instructional opportunities inherent in these positions allow them to experiment and to test concepts learned through their coursework and/or co-curricular teaching workshops. For example, one of the peers created an instructional design framework to integrate various aspects (consultations, workshops, handouts/resources, online modules) of the software he supported. The peers continue to refine their approaches to workshop delivery in response to other professional development opportunities they take up across the university. An "Instructional Skills Workshop" (ISW) offered by the Teaching and Learning Centre is particularly beneficial in this regard, and the peer role supports graduate students to apply the concepts and ideas they encounter in this and other workshops.

Communication Skills. From time to time, we conduct informal surveys with Research Commons peers, for the purposes of reporting on the program and for ongoing program development. When asked, in the course of this survey, to comment on his experiences as a Research Commons peer, one graduate student told us that beyond software and facilitation experiences, "a key skill [he] developed during [his] time at the Research Commons was communication." The two different position streams among the DH peers exemplify the breadth of communication skills with which peers can be involved. Peers in the Technical Development stream are involved with documentation, testing, creation of test plans, and use cases for the digital research projects developed by the library's DH lab. They document decisions and design processes, they create best practices and how-to guides for end users, and they share skills through workshops and consultations. Peers in the Communications stream help with event planning and management, promotions and outreach, website design, blog content creation, social media, and grant writing. In both cases, DH peers gain experience with different forms of nonacademic communication, in areas such as technical writing, marketing, knowledge mobilization, and group collaboration processes. All peers, including those in QDAS, GIS, and programming, have opportunities for presentation and public speaking and may be called on to exercise these skills in different contexts. For example, several peers have prepared and delivered introductions of guest speakers.

Interdisciplinarity. Each of the peer portfolios supports graduate students and faculty from across the campus community. Scholars from a diversity of departments use services in the peer portfolios of GIS, QDAS, and the programming languages R and Python. Offering support to researchers from disparate disciplines affords the peers a unique opportunity to gain knowledge about varying epistemological and methodological traditions. In order to promote effective campus-wide use of software, peers must also become familiar with different research approaches and discipline-specific needs. To this end, peers can also serve as resources to one another. Because they come from different disciplines and work in close collaboration together, the peers are, within themselves, a network of researchers, and they often share ideas and questions with one another. In several instances, peers from across portfolios have collaborated to design interdisciplinary workshops. These collaborations have resulted in reaching new audiences; for example, peers working together have tailored GIS and QDAS resources to the digital humanities community. These opportunities for interdisciplinary collaboration position peers to transition to future work at a variety of scales, whether within or outside academia. They are situated to work anywhere along the spectrum of interdisciplinarity, "ranging from intrapersonal—where an individual tackles research from multiple perspectives; to the interpersonal—working with others; to the interfield and intercommunity—working with nonacademic stakeholders" (Pfirman & Martin, 2017, p. 588). In their workshops, the peers also contribute to the interdisciplinary education of the participants by presenting examples from multiple fields. Indeed, many aspects of the Research Commons' Peer Program support formal and informal interactions with scholars from multiple disciplines through a combination of "research symposia, methodological workshops, social events and dedicated physical space to foster brainstorming" (Pfirman & Martin, 2017, Table 40.1).

Other Professional Skills. Not only does the focus on providing broad service to a wide range of stakeholders give peers an advantage on interdisciplinarity—"a lauded goal for many educational institutions" (Dooling, Graybill, & Shandas, 2017)—it also engages them with a network of other users of their software. Often, these networks include faculty members and other researchers who may wish to employ the peers as research assistants or collaborate with them in other ways. For example, one of the peers, a communications student, was invited to offer a multiday workshop at another institution's nursing school via a recommendation from a faculty member he supported through the Research Commons. Through this process, he was given the chance to engage as a professional consultant, setting a fee for his expertise and travel expenses and preparing to teach in a context with different structures. Another peer reflected on her experiences in the Peer Program:

> I was super satisfied with the level of professionalism in the workplace and the amount of things that I have learned and experienced. It definitely made me ready to take on new responsibilities and look for new challenges in my professional life.

The Peer Program also creates an opportunity for peers to straddle the divide between novice and expert, student and professional. Importantly, leading course-integrated workshops in many disciplines and consulting for faculty projects gives graduate students in the program a chance to engage with more senior researchers in a peer-to-peer fashion, rather than as subordinates. They are brought in as experts in the software rather than as learners.

The Peer Program offers professional work experience that goes beyond the classic RA or TA positions that are available to many graduate students on campus. A former peer sums up their experience this way:

> Without question, it has been one of the most invaluable experiences that I have had in my academic journey. More so than the technical skills that I have been able to cultivate as part of my employment obligations, being a graduate peer facilitator has also served to enhance my other more universal aptitudes, such as public speaking, delivering presentations, leadership and management, networking, and creativity.

In addition to developing these "universal" or transferable skills through their teaching and consultation responsibilities, peers may also have the opportunity to participate in operational decisions, as well as event planning and management within the Research Commons. Through various software-related events that the Research Commons has hosted, peers have been able to meet and interact with high-profile, advanced researchers in their areas, from beyond the local community. They are sometimes involved in the interviewing of new peer candidates, sitting for the first time on the other side of the hiring process. Peers also gain experience with setting their own workloads and schedules, working within structures that require regular meetings, reporting and planning, and juggling responsibilities for various projects.

Engagement and Connection. A final way in which the Research Commons' Peer Program enhances the student experience is by fostering a deepened connection and engagement with the university. Research conducted with undergraduates has established that engagement in educationally purposeful activities is the strongest predictor of student learning and development (Kuh, 2001; Kuh, Schuh, & Whitt, 1991); graduate students also show higher rates of "persistence to degree" when they have more interactions with peers, staff, and faculty (Lovitts, 2001). In addition to the supervision they receive from their thesis or doctoral advisors, and from the researchers or teachers for whom they may be a TA or RA, peers receive supervision and mentorship from their librarian supervisor. They have a network of other peers outside of their disciplinary silos, and constant interaction with student participants—and may consequently feel less isolated than graduate students may typically feel. They may experience a greater bond with the institution because they have an academic home that is also their work home. The library, as a nondisciplinary body, can foster this sense of engagement for students from all departments, by providing a "meaningful orientation to the institution beyond academic units" (Pontius & Harper, 2006, p. 52).

Impact on the Graduate Student Community. In addition to the value the Peer Program offers to the students employed therein, there is a strong impact on attendees of peer-led workshops and consultations. In 2014 and 2018, the Research Commons undertook a survey of graduate students' needs and found a strong desire for both access to and assistance with a range of digital research tools and methods. This type of responsive programming is not possible with traditional library staffing models. The Peer Program gives the library the agility to hire those with the most sought-after skills in a timely way, for a limited set of tasks. The program also circumvents the expert-novice paradigm through its inherent peer-to-peer structure. In this structure, exploration is scaffolded through "social and cognitive interaction with a more experienced peer in relation to a task of a level of difficulty within the tutee's 'zone of proximal development'" (Topping, 1996, p. 324). In this way, our program provides a friendly and welcoming interface within a community of graduate students and supports these students in their learning, regardless of their home department or discipline. Graduate student participants in the Research Commons' peer-led workshops indicated accelerated completion rates—for example, one student commented "without the support I would most certainly have had to spend another year in the PhD program. So I thank you for making this process so much more manageable." The participants also report that they enjoy learning new digital research skills and feel excited about the academic and career impacts of these skills. Another student responding to the survey noted:

> The workshops helped me understand the capabilities of GIS which is very important before starting research [. . .] I was then able to help out with an SFU volunteer project where I provided the GIS support through aerial photography analysis [. . .] I was able to refer back to the handouts from the

workshops. I have enjoyed using GIS, and was even hired to a new job recently because I had a working knowledge of the program. Thanks to the GIS team!

Overall, the SFU campus community has felt a positive impact from the operation of the Peer Program, through its capacity-building outcomes.

Thesis Boot Camp

Universities are complex, hierarchical, and at times labyrinthine institutions. To flourish in the academy, graduate students and early career researchers need to develop strategies for understanding, navigating, and managing institutional structures, expectations, and priorities (Grallo, Chalmers, & Baker, 2012). The Research Commons helps graduate students build this capacity through "Thesis Boot Camp" (TBC), an interdisciplinary writing retreat that builds community, equips students with strategies to manage significant research- and writing-intensive projects, and highlights the supports available to them from across the university.

Overview

"Thesis Boot Camp" is one of the Research Commons' longest running and most consistently popular programs. First made available in the spring of 2014, the program is currently in its 26th iteration. TBC is an immersive, cohort-based, interdisciplinary, extracurricular writing and researching experience. It invites graduate students to dedicate three full days to writing and to the skills training most appropriate to their individual needs. Along with a comfortable, quiet working environment, writing and research support, snacks and lunches, TBC offers students community and motivation while they progress toward the completion of their dissertations or theses. In a mixed-methods survey, participants self-report that TBC enhanced their learning by broadening their skill sets, improved their experience by creating a sense of community, and increased their sense of agency. After participating in TBC, students' confidence, optimism, and attitudes toward their theses and completion all improved.

Participants

"Thesis Boot Camp" is available to graduate students in all disciplines. The only requirement for registration is that participants are at a stage in their programs where they are prepared to write. Although students were initially required to pay a $40 registration fee to attend TBC, the registration fee was replaced by a no-show fee in 2017, in recognition of the fact that the fee may

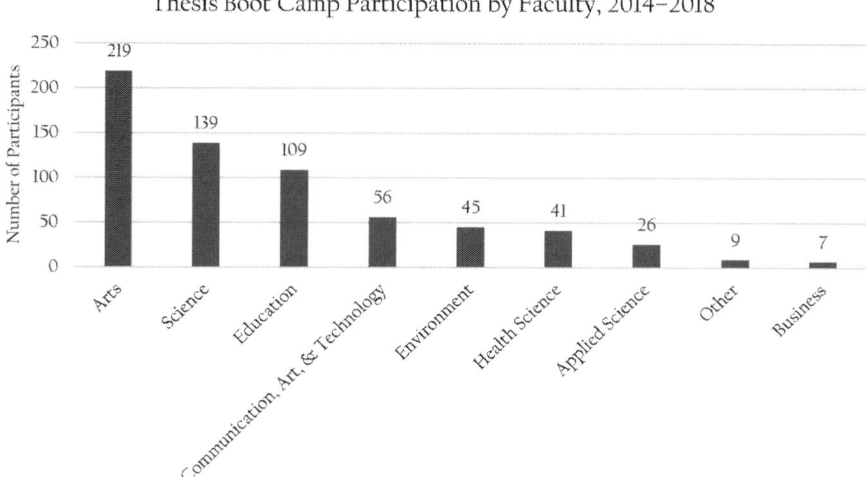

Figure 6.1   Research Commons' Thesis Boot Camp participation by faculty

create a barrier to attending for some students. Due to high demand for the program, first-time attendees are prioritized and returnees are only granted admission if unfilled spaces remain in the week leading up to the program. Since 2014, 56% of participants were master's students and 44% were doctoral students. In 2015, a questionnaire revealed that approximately 75% of TBC participants identify as female, 21% male, with the remaining identifying as nonbinary or preferring not to disclose. The largest percentage of students attending the program were between 26 to 45 years of age. Of the participants, 5% were 55 and over, and only 7% were between 18 and 25. Figure 6.1 shows participation, broken down by faculty. Roughly 31% of students are from the Faculty of Science while 34% are from the Faculty of Arts and Social Science. Students in the Faculty of Education made up 17% of attendees (see Figure 6.1).

Structure of Program

"Thesis Boot Camp" is offered between four and five times annually, across the university's three campus locations. TBC cohorts range in size from 25 to 30 participants. The program is structured to include dedicated writing time, workshops on a variety of topics, and individual consultations. In addition, there is a strong emphasis placed on building community among the participants. Students are encouraged to engage in open and honest discussions about the challenges and successes that arise when trying to make progress on a thesis. Facilitators also support the participants to establish an "accountability partner," with whom they develop SMART (specific, measurable, achievable/attainable, realistic, timely/time bound) goals that are revisited daily throughout the program.

Participation in TBC workshops was originally mandatory. However, this requirement changed in response to feedback received from participants. Now students' participation in workshops and consultations throughout the TBC program is optional, acknowledging that participants are at varying stages of degree completion and are in programs with vastly different requirements. Although students in the early stages of their programs tend to focus on writing and citation management data workshops, students in later stages of their degrees often attend fewer workshops and instead invest their time in one-to-one consultations with experts.

Campus Partners and Collaborators

Although overall coordination of "Thesis Boot Camp" is managed by the Research Commons librarian, there is a large team of individuals from both inside and beyond the library who collaborate to make the program a success. Graduate writing facilitators lead icebreakers, discussions on challenges in the graduate student experience, and address perennial issues of procrastination, perfectionism, time management, and motivation. The facilitators also guide daily goal-setting activities, which require students to reflect on and report their success at the end of each day.

Departmental librarians are invited to an informal meet and greet with participants on the first day of the program. This meeting is an opportunity for networking and connection, and it frequently results in consultation and reference support requests during and after the TBC. Other specialists integral to the program include members of the data services team, the copyright officer, professionals from Health & Counselling, and the library's thesis assistant for support with formatting and submission policies and procedures. Faculty guests also frequent the program, presenting on a range of topics. The ombudsperson, Graduate Student Society advocate, and Graduate Studies associate dean serve on a panel that focuses on how students can develop and sustain positive relationships with their supervisors, and presents avenues for support when supervisory issues develop. As one TBC participant reflected, these workshops can have a major impact:

> After two years of feeling stressed over the little progress made in my work, I sought out three services mentioned at the TBC. I am now in a better situation and will be defending within a semester. Thank you!

The cross institutional collaboration by so many campus partners ensures that students have wraparound support that contributes to the success of the program.

Assessment of the Program

The Research Commons has used a variety of mechanisms to assess the "Thesis Boot Camp" program in the approximately five years it has run. Enrollment by faculty, school, and/or department is tracked at the point of registration, as is stage of degree (early, middle, late), and anticipated areas of support needed. At the end of each camp, the Research Commons circulates feedback forms (satisfaction surveys) that ask students to comment on their productivity and accomplishments over the three-day period. These feedback forms also solicit suggestions to improve and/or change the program in the future. A more fulsome program evaluation of TBC was completed as a portion of a grant-funded research project in 2015, *Investigating the Impact of Professional Development Programming for Grad Students*. The mixed-methods investigation included a survey, focus groups, and in-depth interviews.

Benefits of the Program

The greatest benefit of "Thesis Boot Camp," as reported by its participants, is the space, support, and structure it provides to enable progress on research and writing. Students frequently comment that TBC allowed them to complete chapters, finish drafts, and perform substantive amounts of data analysis and interview transcription, to name a few accomplishments. Although this opportunity to make progress is, in itself, a significant benefit to both students and the university in terms of swifter degree completion, there are other benefits of the program that position graduate students to be successful both within and beyond the academy.

Results of the program survey suggest that participants leave "Thesis Boot Camp" with an increased sense of agency. Over 90% of students report feeling more confident and in control of their research and writing processes and feeling that they have the skills needed to complete their programs. Participants also indicate an increased familiarity with the wide range of services and supports available through the university that could assist them in overcoming future challenges. A total of 70% of participants also agreed that attending "Thesis Boot Camp" increased their self-esteem. Benefits to participants' sense of optimism and positive sentiment are also reflected in the 87% who indicated that they were looking forward to entering the next stage of their studies, research, or work. One participant wrote,

> Thesis boot camp refreshed and refocused me, pushing me over the seemingly insurmountable hurdle of starting the writing process after a lengthy life-work, coursework related gap. Thesis boot camp were the three most important days of my degree progress, focusing on myself, my needs, my direction, my plans, and my completion.

Another significant benefit of "Thesis Boot Camp" is the facilitators' success in cultivating a strong sense of academic community among the participants. This community development is accomplished through collaborative activities designed to surface common challenges that include writing, work-life balance, perfectionism, time management, and supervisory relationships. Participants articulate their struggles and, more importantly, identify strategies that have helped them overcome barriers to making progress on their research and writing. Through this work, they report an increased sense of belonging, with 62% of respondents noting that they feel more connected to their peers after attending TBC. Participating in an in-depth interview, one student commented,

> For me, the hardest part about writing my thesis was the psychological boundaries [. . .]. It helped me realize I am not alone in this struggle—and there are other people who are finding it difficult to complete their masters degree, too. So, it helped me mentally in the fact that I understand that it can be accomplished and there are resources I can use—so I am not completely alone in this.

Libraries can play a significant role in improving the graduate student experience through the provision of infrastructure, space, and services. Directing these resources toward a shared goal via dedicated programs such as "Thesis Boot Camp" empowers students to explore challenges and approaches to improving their research and writing processes. Furthermore, the cohort nature of "Thesis Boot Camp" provides a positive and safe environment in which participants examine and acculturate to the expectations of academia, and build a sense of agency as academics by developing their understanding of existing campus supports. The student experience is also enhanced through the facilitated interactions between participants, which serve to create a sense of community that extends across the institution and beyond the dedicated time at "Thesis Boot Camp."

Communities of Practice (CoP)

Success as academics and future professionals requires strong skills in self-directed learning, collaboration, and interdisciplinary research. The formation of Communities of Practice (CoP) around particular research interests supports graduate students in developing these skills while simultaneously building a strong personal network. Communities of Practice, defined by Wenger (2011) as "groups of people who share a concern or a passion for something they do and learn how to do it better as they interact regularly" (p. 1), may form organically, but more often are facilitated by the implementation of a collaborative structure to serve as the point of connection. These structures may be physical, such as access to dedicated space and specialized equipment necessary to the work of the community, or may be virtual, such as access to online educational resources that can be referenced at point of need. Through provision of dedicated spaces, access to research infrastructure and expertise, and diverse programming, the Research Commons facilitates the emergence of various CoP among graduate students and early career researchers.

Partnerships with Existing Communities of Practice

Many CoP form in response to a recognized interest in developing or refining a particular skill necessary for a research practice or project. These groups may develop within a department via personal connections or shared research interests and can be effective in building disciplinary capacity. However, the evolving scholarly ecosystem requires students to engage in diverse research practices that for many fall outside their disciplinary training. In these cases, partnerships between the library and a nascent CoP can expand the reach of the community, integrate additional specialized knowledge, and offer a stable home base from which to grow.

In 2015 the Research Commons partnered with the student-led SFU Scientific Programming Study Group (SciProg) as it was being established. SFU SciProg (2018) is dedicated to:

> building a community of SFU researchers who perform computational data analysis as part of their academic work. SciProg promotes skill sharing and collaboration by (1) organizing one-hour interactive workshops covering a wide range of software tools, (2) providing Q&A sessions for peer-to-peer assistance and collaboration, and (3) bringing researchers together at social events like Hacky Hours.

SciProg's student organizers work with the CoP members to define shared interests and respond with appropriate programming, while the Research Commons leverages its space, administrative structures, and expertise to amplify the impact of the CoP. SciProg events are featured on the Research Commons' website, advertised through newsletters, and promoted by the library's social media accounts. Research Commons' staff manage registration for SciProg workshops and ensure space is available for dedicated meetings held throughout the semester. The Research Commons also works closely with the organizers to respond to training requests, including funding specialized workshops and incorporating peers or librarians in the CoP where expertise aligns with identified SciProg needs.

With the support of the Research Commons, SciProg has increased their visibility, established a dedicated home for weekly meetings, and increased programming. These structures have enabled SciProg to fulfill its mission to grow the CoP in an inclusive manner, expanding from the original group of students and postdoctoral fellows from computational biology by inviting participants from areas as diverse as health sciences, psychology, geography, communication, computer science, and education. The partnership has benefited the wider student community by promoting the development of a cross-disciplinary research community accessible to any student interested in computational data analysis. These peer-to-peer research networks are particularly important for students who may feel a level of isolation if their research falls outside the core methods of their discipline.

Seeding Communities of Practice

Research Commons programming also serves as fertile ground for the development of additional CoP. As an example, there has been a strong demand for Qualitative Data Analysis Software (QDAS) and training since the founding of the Research Commons. Researchers attending open workshops have provided ample feedback on support required to further their competencies in this area, and in response, the Research Commons has developed specialized training opportunities and experimented with structures that enable cross-pollination between researchers using the same QDAS software. In April 2015, SFU Library partnered with the University of British Columbia (UBC) Library to host an NVivo Symposium. This event brought together researchers across the city who use NVivo, an industry standard QDAS tool, to learn more about its capabilities and its integration into a diverse range of research projects. The symposium featured a keynote and masterclass by expert researcher Pat Bazeley, as well as introductory NVivo workshops, and researcher lightning talk presentations. The event, facilitated by SFU and UBC Research Commons librarians, also included guided discussion among participants designed to spark new connections. Feedback on the event highlighted the benefits of bringing together practitioners to advance their skills and the opportunity to begin building a network of local expertise. We received the following comments from participants at the symposium:

Participant 1: I think it is great to have the opportunity to hear and see how others are making use of the software. It is otherwise easy to restrict yourself to keep doing what you have always done and feel comfortable with.

Participant 2: The two days were a very worthwhile investment of time. This event really deepened my sense of how to use NVivo and gave me some concrete ideas on how to improve my current project in it.

Participant 3: I feel much more connected to others who I could reach out to if I have questions in the future.

Participant 4: The opportunity to meet with other researchers at other institutions was great.

This feedback from participants illustrates the value in leveraging institutional resources and expertise to facilitate the development of new research communities of practice. Building on the Research Commons' experience providing QDAS support, the NVivo Symposium created an opportunity for like-minded scholars to learn from one another and begin building an interdisciplinary and cross-institutional network. Once connected through this large community-focused event, researchers self-initiated discussions about establishing a regional community of practice to support cross-disciplinary explorations into qualitative research. Participants suggested strategies to support this CoP, such as hosting ongoing workshop series, exploring online platforms and tools to enable asynchronous discussion, holding space for meet-ups or other informal information sharing opportunities, and continuing to offer formal large-scale events like the NVivo Symposium. Work toward implementing this community of practice at SFU has thus far included the following: surveying active NVivo users; hosting several in-person meetings to discuss shared goals and strategies; and establishing a group in SFU's learning management system to share resources and host discussions. The decentralized nature of this CoP, coupled with the usual challenges of limited time and capacity for researchers, has ultimately resulted in participation slowing over time. Although this particular community of practice was short-lived, its members benefited from strengthening their interdisciplinary networks, gaining exposure to research-in-practice via the NVivo Symposium and local meetings, and further developing their technical skills in qualitative data analysis. Peers and librarians also benefited as members of the CoP, gaining insight into the implementation of the research tools the library supports, hearing directly from the community about issues of importance to applying qualitative methods, and identifying potential intersections with other areas of the library, such as research data management for qualitative data.

Collaborating with campus and external stakeholders to form and sustain local CoP allows graduate students to grow interdisciplinary networks, advance their approaches to research and technical skills, and to take on leadership opportunities as co-organizers of CoP events. As future academics, students and early career researchers will be expected to successfully build these types of interpersonal connections and professional competencies. Leveraging the Research Commons' infrastructure and expertise in these ways allows students to advance their skills and contribute to their own professional growth, while simultaneously extending Research Commons' programming and services into unique areas of inquiry.

Conclusion

The Research Commons model has proven to be an effective way to provide SFU graduate students with the tools, skills, and support they need to succeed as future academics. As a result of attending "Thesis Boot Camp," serving as a graduate peer, or facilitating a community of practice, graduate students who previously may not have had clear career aspirations gain confidence to take on new academic, professional, and personal challenges, such as applying for further graduate education, postdoctoral work, or assistant professor positions. In sum, therefore, the Research Commons staff, services, and infrastructure all reinforce the academic library's capacity to transform the graduate student experience in positive ways.

References

Bargh, J. A., & Schul, Y. (1980). On the cognitive benefits of teaching. *Journal of Educational Psychology, 72*(5), 593–604. https://doi.org/10.1037/0022-0663.72.5.593

The Carpentries. (2018). *Updates to the Carpentries' code of conduct: Background to the recent revision of the code.* Retrieved from https://carpentries.org/blog/2018/09/coc-revision-release

Courtois, A. D. M., & O'Keefe, T. (2015). Precarity in the ivory cage: Neoliberalism and casualisation of work in the Irish higher education sector. *Journal for Critical Education Policy Studies, 13*(1), 43–66. *Retrieved from* http://www.jceps.com/archives/2458

Daniels, W., Darch, C., & de Jager, K. (2010). The Research Commons: A new creature in the library? *Performance Measurement and Metrics, 11*(2), 116–130. https://doi.org/10.1108/14678041011064043

Dooling, S., Graybill, J. K., & Shandas, V. (2017). Doctoral student and early career academic perspectives on interdisciplinarity. In R. Frodeman (Ed.), *The Oxford handbook of interdisciplinarity* (2nd ed.). New York, NY: Oxford University Press. https://dx.doi.org/10.1093/oxfordhb/9780198733522.013.46

Dowson, R. (2016). Research Commons: Site of innovation, experimentation, and collaboration in academic libraries. *Scholarly and Research Communication, 7*(2), 1–9. https://doi.org/10.22230/src.2016v7n2/3a259

Fong, B. L., Wang, M., White, K., & Tipton, R. (2016). Assessing and serving the workshop needs of graduate students. *The Journal of Academic Librarianship, 42*(5), 569–580. https://doi.org/10.1016/j.acalib.2016.06.003

Grallo, J. D., Chalmers, M., & Baker, P. (2012). How do I get a campus ID? The other role of the academic library in student retention and success. *The Reference Librarian, 53*(2), 182–193. https://doi.org/10.1080/02763877.2011.618787

Kuh, G. D. (2001). *The national survey of student engagement: Conceptual framework and overview of psychometric properties.* Bloomington: Indiana University Center for Postsecondary Research & Planning.

Kuh, G. D., Schuh, J. S., & Whitt, E. J. (1991). *Involving colleges: Successful approaches to fostering student learning and personal development outside the classroom.* San Francisco, CA: Jossey-Bass.

Lovitts, B. E. (2001). *Leaving the ivory tower: The causes and consequences of departure from doctoral study.* Lanford, MD: Rowan & Littlefield.

Pasma, C., & Shaker, E. (2018). *Contract U: Contract faculty appointments at Canadian universities.* Canadian Centre for Policy Alternatives. Retrieved from https://www.policyalternatives.ca/sites/default/files/uploads/publications /National%20Office/2018/11/Contract%20U.pdf

Pfirman, S., & Martin, P. J. S. (2017). Facilitating interdisciplinary scholars. In R. Frodeman (Ed.), *The Oxford handbook of interdisciplinarity* (2nd ed.). New York, NY: Oxford University Press. https://doi.org/10.1093/oxfordhb /9780198733522.013.47

Pontius, J. L., & Harper, S. R. (2006). Principles for good practice in graduate and professional student engagement. *New Directions for Student Services, 2006*(115), 47–58. https://doi.org/10.1002/ss.215

Ramaswamy, M., Garrett, J., & Currie, D. (2018). *Crowd sourcing expertise: Learnings from a peer to peer teaching experiment.* Poster presented at the 16th Biennial Conference of the United States Agricultural Information Network, Pullman, WA. Retrieved from https://hdl.handle.net/1813/58741

Rempel, H. G., Hussong-Christian, U., & Mellinger, M. (2011). Graduate student space and service needs: A recommendation for a cross-campus solution. *The Journal of Academic Librarianship, 37*(6), 480–487. https://doi.org/10 .1016/j.acalib.2011.07.004

Roberts, R. L. (2007). The evolving landscape of the learning commons. *Library Review, 56*(9), 803–810. https://doi.org/10.1108/00242530710831257

Simon Fraser University (SFU), Graduate and Postdoctoral Studies. (2018). *Graduate student exit survey 2017.* Retrieved from http://www.sfu.ca/content/sfu /dean-gradstudies/blog/year/2018/12/student-survey-2017/_jcr_content /main_content/download/file.res/2017%20Graduate%20Student%20 Exit%20Survey%20Report.pdf

Simon Fraser University (SFU), Institutional Research and Planning. (2018). *Annualized 2017/18 graduate enrolment report.* Retrieved from http://www .sfu.ca/content/dam/sfu/irp/enrollment/EnrollmentDashboard/documents /gr.enrol.report.2017.2018.pdf

Simon Fraser University (SFU), Institutional Research and Planning. (2019). *International students and SFU international experience: By country, graduate.* Retrieved from https://www.sfu.ca/content/dam/sfu/irp/students/documents /ST23.pdf

Simon Fraser University (SFU) Library. (2016). *SFU Library strategic plan 2017– 2021.* Retrieved from https://www.lib.sfu.ca/system/files/26348/strategic -plan-2017-2021-compressed.pdf

Simon Fraser University (SFU), Scientific Programming Study Group (SciProg). (2018). *What we do.* Retrieved from http://sciprog.ca

Statistics Canada. (2017, July 13). *Financial information of universities and degree-granting colleges, 2015/2016.* Retrieved from https://www150.statcan.gc.ca /n1/daily-quotidien/170713/dq170713c-eng.htm

Topping, K. J. (1996). The effectiveness of peer tutoring in further and higher education: A typology and review of the literature. *Higher Education, 32*(3), 321–345. https://doi.org/10.1007/BF00138870

Usher, A. (2018). *The state of post-secondary education in Canada, 2018.* Toronto, ON: Higher Education Strategy Associates. Retrieved from http://higheredstrategy.com/wp-content/uploads/2018/08/HESA_SPEC_2018_final.pdf

Wenger, E. (2011). *Communities of practice: A brief introduction.* Retrieved from https://scholarsbank.uoregon.edu/xmlui/handle/1794/11736

The Nuts and Bolts of Scholarly Publishing: Guiding Graduate Student Authors through the Journal Publication Process

Julia Hon and Rochelle Lundy

Introduction

For many graduate students, publication in scholarly journals is a crucial step toward establishing their careers (Flaherty, 2017; Stoilescu & McDougall, 2010). However, formal instruction on scholarly communication topics is rarely offered within degree programs (Jalongo, Boyer, & Ebbeck, 2013). Although students often receive ad hoc guidance from advisors, these senior researchers may be unfamiliar with or even dismissive of emerging digital publication models (Coonin, 2011; Coonin & Younce, 2009; Nicholas et al., 2015), and ill equipped to field questions around publishing contracts and author rights (Sims, 2011). Graduate students, who face high stakes as they begin their careers, are therefore in pressing need of guidance as they consider options for disseminating their research.

Academic libraries are well positioned to provide the foundational "scholarly publishing literacy" (Zhao, 2014) that will assist graduate students in navigating a rapidly changing scholarly communication ecosystem. However, although many libraries offer consultations, guides, and workshops on scholarly communication issues (Radom, Feltner-Reichert, & Stringer-Stanback, 2012), these are often limited to specific topics, such as citation metrics, open access, or contract addenda, which might be unfamiliar to novice authors or seem disconnected from their immediate publishing concerns.

This chapter discusses an introductory publishing workshop series developed at the University of Washington Libraries to address this training gap and to promote confidence in scholarly publishing among emerging researchers. To meet graduate students at their points of need, the workshops focused primarily on offering practical advice and demonstrating useful tools, weaving open access and author rights concepts throughout rather than making them an explicit focus. The two complementary sessions walked attendees through the process of publishing a journal article from start to finish. The first session covered the preacceptance period, introducing a framework to help participants select publication venues, while the second addressed the steps from acceptance to publication, explaining the implications of a journal publication contract. This approach to scholarly communication instruction can be adapted to a variety of populations and institutional contexts, offering tractable guidance that graduate students can carry forward into the next phase of their careers.

Literature Review: Scholarly Publishing Perceptions and Practices

Selecting Publication Venues

The growth of digital distribution and the emergence of open access publications have caused a "paradigmatic shift" in the scholarly communication environment (Rowley, Johnson, Sbaffi, Frass, & Devine, 2017, p. 1201). For researchers, these developments have created new possibilities, but have also fostered discomfort with a rapidly changing publishing ecosystem (Lewis, 2012; Rowley et al., 2017) and uncertainty as to current publication options (Kocken & Wical, 2013; Morris & Thorn, 2009; Odell, Palmer, & Dill, 2017; Otto, 2016). Accordingly, the criteria by which academics choose publication venues have remained consistent in spite of this expansion of opportunities (Blankstein & Wolff-Eisenberg, 2019). When deciding where to submit their work, scholars continue to rely on characteristics long valued in traditional publishing environments: presence of peer review, journal prestige, impact metrics, level of fit between the submission and the journal's typical publications, and speed of review and publication (Bird, 2010; Blankstein &

Wolff-Eisenberg, 2019; Coonin, 2011; Nariani & Fernandez, 2012; Russell & Kent, 2010).

Open access journals have risen significantly in scholars' esteem in recent years (Coonin & Younce, 2010; Rowley et al., 2017), but are nevertheless perceived as falling short of traditional counterparts with regard to these selection criteria. For instance, many researchers believe that open access journals operate without peer review or employ less-than-rigorous peer review (Bird, 2010; Coonin, 2011; Coonin & Younce, 2009; Mulligan & Mabe, 2011; Nicholas et al., 2015). Open access publications are also frequently viewed as less prestigious than traditional publications (Cullen & Chawner, 2011; Dallmeier-Tiessen et al., 2011; Rowley et al., 2017; Xia, 2010). Although some authors now embrace the view that open access publishing will not restrict career advancement (Nariani & Fernandez, 2012, pp. 187–88), many continue to shy away out of concern that it will negatively affect promotion and tenure decisions (Peekhaus & Proferes, 2016).

Even features touted as particular benefits of open access publishing are often perceived by scholars as "oversold" or not unique to open access. For instance, scholars acknowledge that open access journals publish rapidly, but feel that traditional journals have quickened their publication timelines such that speed is no longer exclusive to the open access model (Nariani & Fernandez, 2012, p. 187; Rowley et al., 2017). Similarly, authors agree that open access journals circulate widely, but most are more concerned about reaching other scholars in their field than a large audience (Warlick & Vaughan, 2017). Unless researchers are collaborating with international or community-based colleagues who may not have access to subscription publications (Nariani & Fernandez, 2012, pp. 186–87), they do not necessarily view the broader readership of an open access publication as valuable, and report ambivalence regarding the idea that publishing open access leads to an increased citation rate (Rowley et al., 2017).

Researchers also view open access publishing as having drawbacks not present with traditional publishing models. Lack of funding for processing charges is frequently cited as a barrier to open access publishing (Dallmeier-Tiessen et al., 2011; Nariani & Fernandez, 2012), but many scholars also object to publishing charges on principle (Nariani & Fernandez, 2012; Schultz & Medaille, 2019). Others dislike charges because they associate payment with "vanity" or "predatory" publishing, believing fees suggest that a journal's peer review process is lax and its content of low quality (Coonin, 2011; Nariani & Fernandez, 2012; Nicholas et al., 2015). These attitudes vary across academic disciplines, with those in the life sciences and medicine—where many subscription journals levy publishing fees—objecting less strenuously to open access processing charges (Coonin, 2011; Nariani & Fernandez, 2012).

Copyright and Contractual Considerations

Academic researchers have traditionally demonstrated poor knowledge of copyright law as it relates to scholarship (Gadd, 2017; Gadd, Loddington, & Oppenheim, 2007). Recent studies suggest increasing variation in scholars' copyright proficiency (Gadd, 2017; Rapple, 2017), but continue to indicate that the level of understanding held by most researchers remains relatively low (Charbonneau & McGlone, 2013; Di Valentino, 2015; Kim, 2010; Lovett, Rathemacher, Boukari, & Lang, 2017; Sims, 2011).

Scholars often evince a particularly poor grasp of what rights they retain after signing a publication agreement, with many incorrectly interpreting contracts to permit unrestricted use and distribution of published articles. Sims (2011), for instance, found that 25% of surveyed faculty erroneously believe they automatically maintain significant rights to make use of their work when transferring copyright ownership to a publisher. Lovett et al. (2017) and Schultz and Medaille (2019) similarly observed minimal understanding of the self-archiving options spelled out in publication agreements. Rapple (2017) discovered that 21% of surveyed faculty did not even realize that publication contracts might affect their ability to share work with other scholars postpublication.

There has, perhaps accordingly, been minimal investigation into scholars' willingness to negotiate the contracts offered by publishers. However, when surveyed, scholars report little interest in better understanding author rights (Russell & Kent, 2010). This appears true even among researchers who receive funding that imposes open access or other publishing-related requirements: Charbonneau and McGlone (2013) found that 35% of researchers funded by the National Institutes of Health failed to even examine the copyright terms of their contracts prior to signing and only 2% sought contract modifications. Attempts to engage with these issues may be more prevalent among scholars already interested in nontraditional scholarly communication models. A survey conducted at the University of Pennsylvania found that among faculty respondents, many of whom had deposited items in an institutional repository, a significant minority had sought to negotiate a publication agreement (24%) or to publish work under a Creative Commons license (29%) (Wipperman, 2018).

Scholars' lack of interest in author rights is often attributed to the complex nature of copyright law, but the efforts of academic publishers to reassure authors about the consequences of signing agreements may also be to blame (Gadd, 2017). Although exclusive licenses of all rights under copyright have virtually the same effect as transfers of ownership, publishers often emphasize that authors remain copyright owners in name under such agreements, creating understandable confusion regarding postpublication rights (Gadd, 2017).

Graduate Student Experience and Attitudes

Scholarly publishing issues are increasingly relevant to graduate students, as many now face pressure to publish prior to completing their degrees. As one professor recently wrote, "the convention . . . of waiting to publish until after the Ph.D. has broken down" (Flaherty, 2017, para. 3). Graduate students may need publications under their belt to compete for research-oriented positions or even jobs at teaching institutions (Stoilescu & McDougall, 2010, p. 80).

However, graduate students receive little, if any, formal guidance on the scholarly publishing process. According to Jalongo et al. (2013), graduate students must acquire the "tacit knowledge" of scholarly publishing "through a combination of informal mentoring experiences and the individual doctoral candidate's initiative, diligence, and persistence at publication" (p. 242). This concept echoes testimonies from graduate students about their relative ignorance of the ins-and-outs of publishing and reliance on advisors for publishing decisions (Mertkan, 2016, p. 136). One survey reported that 80% of graduate student respondents agreed that "I publish where my supervisors recommend I publish" (Stanton & Liew, 2011, Influences on Publishing Behavior section, para. 2). Although there is little research on graduate student understanding of copyright and author rights, anecdotal evidence suggests that, like their faculty counterparts, students' knowledge is limited. For example, McClellan, Detmering, Martinez, and Johnson (2017) report that, after a session on contract negotiation, one student remarked that they "didn't even have an idea that that was something authors were allowed to do" (p. 560).

Underrepresented and marginalized graduate students, including international students, may face additional barriers to gaining confidence with the publishing process. International students may bring different understandings of research processes (Click, 2018) and scholarly writing and publishing norms; as Morrissey and Given (2006) note, citation strategies, plagiarism, and copyright are areas of concern for international students (p. 236). Studies have also shown that first-generation graduate students and students of color consistently receive less mentoring and training in professional development skills, including publishing (MacLachlan, 2006). A recent study of Latinx doctoral students revealed that because of "inadequate faculty mentorship," students relied on the advice of peers to "demystify scholarly processes, such as . . . publishing and presenting at conferences" (Ramirez, 2017, p. 35).

Despite career-related anxieties and lack of formal mentoring, recent studies suggest that, compared to established scholars, graduate students may be more inclined toward new publishing models. Unlike faculty, graduate students have not yet established a "publishing routine" (Dawson, 2018), making them more receptive to experimenting with nontraditional and open access publications. Rodriguez (2014) concluded that open access publishing caused "less concern about tenure implications" among younger scholars than has been previously reported (p. 609). There is a cautious optimism that graduate students coming of age alongside new models of scholarly publishing are developing a different mind-set about the dissemination of research than established scholars (Tenopir et al., 2017). In fact, at least some early-career researchers report frustration with the traditional system and a desire for openness and transparency in publications and the publication process (Nicholas et al., 2015, p. 18). As the scholarly ecosystem shifts and graduate students reevaluate their publishing options, there is an opportunity for librarians who understand the scholarly communication landscape to step in.

Library Approaches to Scholarly Publishing Instruction

Academic libraries are well positioned to act as resources for graduate students in the publishing process, and many institutions have already taken on this role. Zhao (2014) contends that promoting "scholarly publishing literacy" (p. 12) is well within libraries' wheelhouse thanks to traditions of research support and information literacy instruction. Most academic libraries provide some scholarly communication support—89% of respondents in a survey of ARL libraries offered one or more services in this area (Radom et al., 2012, p. 13). However, recognition that libraries are suited to this role is far from universal, as a significant subset of both librarians and researchers believe there is little need or capacity for library involvement in scholarly communication (Klain-Gabbay & Shoham, 2016).

The degree and type of scholarly publishing support differs significantly between institutions. Support is often provided through ad hoc consultations with researchers who approach the library for advice on particular topics, such as contract negotiation or publisher reputation (Zhao, 2014). A significant number of academic libraries also offer online reference guides to "scholarly publishing," but the breadth, depth, and focus of these resources varies widely. Most guides serve as a basic resource on issues like copyright or open access, often prioritizing links to external resources or focusing heavily on their parent institutions' policies, with little contextual information on the publishing process. A smaller number of guides serve as comprehensive orientations to the modern scholarly publishing landscape, such as the University of California at Berkeley's "Publishing Lifecycle" guide or Arizona State University's guide, which pairs an overview of publishing models with in-depth advice on topics such as author rights (Perry, 2017; University of California, Berkeley Library, n.d.). Although online guides are advantageous in their ease of access, they may not provide sufficient guidance for graduate students new to the publishing process.

Workshops and other library programming can more effectively fill gaps in scholarly publishing knowledge but are less widespread and more labor-intensive than consultations or guides. Scholarly publishing instruction often focuses on specific topics in libraries' traditional domain, such as impact metrics or open access, or is integrated with other research or professional development content, such as writing a literature review or obtaining grant funding (McClellan et al., 2017). Some universities have recently ventured into broader workshops that bring together multiple strands of the scholarly publishing landscape. For instance, in 2016, Ohio State University hosted a workshop that sought to introduce participants to scholarly publishing, including answering questions about publishing agreements and new publication models (The Ohio State University, University Libraries, 2016).

These workshops are typically open to all researchers, rather than targeted specifically at a graduate student audience. According to Baruzzi and Calcagno (2015), only 18% of libraries offered workshops on the publishing process aimed at graduate students (p. 399). Of eight examples of "graduate student professional skills" events presented in one article, only two limited participation to graduate students (McClellan et al., 2017, pp. 549–551). The literature does contain a few notable examples of graduate student-specific workshops. The University of Colorado Libraries' "Publish Not Perish" online tutorial was an ahead-of-its-time virtual course that bundled discussion of open access into a tutorial on the basics of publishing (Knievel, 2008). Although open to all users, the tutorial's target audience was early career faculty and graduate students, who comprised about 65% of the user group (Knievel, 2008, p. 184). Texas A&M University developed trainings focused on copyright for graduate students, including a mandatory introductory module and a workshop series featuring fair use, publishing contracts, and author rights (Secker, 2017, para. 18). The University of Louisville's ambitious five-part "Publishing Academy" was also open only to graduate students, and covered a range of publishing topics, including publication value, metrics, copyright, contracts, and open access, as well as advice from faculty panels on writing for publication (McClellan et al., 2017).

Piloting Scholarly Publishing Instruction at the University of Washington

Background

The University of Washington is a large public research university spread across three campus locations. In 2017, the university's largest campus in Seattle had a graduate and professional student enrollment of approximately 15,000 students, of whom 18% were international students and 11% were underrepresented minority students (University of Washington Board of

Regents, 2018). The University of Washington Libraries ("the Libraries") support graduate students by operating 16 libraries, serving more than 5 million users each year, and offering specialized librarian assistance in 70 subject areas (University of Washington Libraries, n.d.-a).

The Libraries' Scholarly Communication and Publishing department provides outreach and services related to copyright, electronic theses and dissertations, open access, digital scholarship, and research data management. The department, on its own and in conjunction with other units within the Libraries, has offered workshops on specific scholarly communication topics, such as digital identifiers, citation metrics, and dissertation writing.

While completing Master of Library and Information Science degrees at the University of Washington, we collaborated with the Scholarly Communication and Publishing department to identify new opportunities for programming that would meet the scholarly communication-related needs of the University of Washington community. Surveys and assessments conducted by the department in 2017–2018 revealed a growing interest in new and more open forms of publishing. However, as is the case at many institutions, there were few formal avenues for researchers to expand their understanding of scholarly communication (McClellan et al., 2017).

Anecdotal evidence gathered by librarians suggested that graduate students were particularly eager for opportunities to learn about the scholarly publishing process. University of Washington graduate students, like those studied in the literature (Jalongo et al., 2013; Stanton & Liew, 2011), look primarily to their advisors for publishing guidance. Advice is provided on an ad hoc basis, and its amount and quality are inconsistent. Students indicated that an advisor who takes on a mentoring role around publishing can be enormously helpful, but that students who lack such support may struggle to navigate the publication process.

Program Design

Aiming to provide the support necessary for University of Washington graduate students to operate within an evolving scholarly communication environment, we developed a workshop series open to emerging researchers in any discipline. Rather than structure the workshops around specific scholarly communication topics, we elected to organize content chronologically, walking through the process of publishing a journal article from start to finish. This was motivated by a desire for the programming to be accessible without regard to existing levels of scholarly publishing knowledge. Focusing the workshops on specific topics, such as citation metrics or contract addenda, may have proven intimidating to novice authors, who might not yet have even heard of these concepts.

Programming taking a comprehensive approach to multimodal topics had also recently proven successful at the University of Washington Libraries. During the spring of 2017, the Libraries, in partnership with University of Washington Learning Technologies and the Simpson Center for the Humanities, offered a "Digital Scholarship: Planning for Success" workshop that introduced conceptual and practical foundations for scholarly digital projects. The workshop filled quickly, even garnering a waiting list due to space constraints. Another recent offering, an online non-credit-bearing course introducing graduate students to digital storytelling, attracted over 130 applicants. The positive reception to these integrated workshop series suggested that a similar approach might be successful in addressing the need for scholarly publishing instruction.

The workshops were envisioned as user-centered, designed to respond to student needs rather than to put forth a particular point of view or to educate participants about the broader costs and benefits of specific publishing models. Open access, in particular, is often viewed by librarians as "such an obvious public good" that the desire to advocate for it may occasionally overshadow researchers' points of need (Dawson, 2018, p. 6). Although many scholars are eager to learn more about open access, some dislike attempts to shepherd them toward a particular mode of publication (Cirasella, 2017; Corbett, 2009; Dawson, 2018). Younger researchers, although often interested in open access models, may find engaging with broader scholarly communication controversies incompatible with their already crowded schedules.

Many librarians have creatively incorporated advocacy into services that directly address scholar concerns, modifying the open access message for specific audiences and explaining the benefits of alternative publishing models on an individual rather than systemic level (Cirasella, 2017; Dawson, 2018). Following this lead, we elected to weave open access and author rights concepts throughout the workshops, but focused primarily on offering practical advice, demonstrating useful tools, and addressing common concerns rather than advocating for specific publishing outcomes. The result was "The Nuts and Bolts of Scholarly Publishing," a workshop series styled as an introduction to publishing in scholarly journals, with content divided across two complementary sessions.

Program Implementation and Delivery

Logistics and Outreach

We endeavored to make workshop attendance as frictionless, welcoming, and low-stakes as possible for graduate students, who often have competing responsibilities and variable schedules (Lambert, 2014). We selected a classroom in the Research Commons, a collaborative space in the Libraries on the Seattle campus, as the workshop venue. Located near the building's main entrance, the glass-walled classroom is both accessible and flexible. Participants were urged to bring computers or tablets, but those without devices could complete activities in groups, a tech-flexible arrangement aimed at encouraging engagement and discussion. The two sessions were held approximately one week apart, and, to align with the "nuts-and-bolts" theme, we decided on a relatively short, low-commitment, 60-minute timeframe, over the lunch period, during which fewer classes are scheduled.

Outreach materials framed workshop content as a guide to the process of submitting a scholarly article. Content was targeted toward graduate students, but we chose not to limit attendance in order to encourage those with a variety of perspectives and needs to share their experiences. Announcements were disseminated through library and graduate school electronic newsletters, which reach wide audiences. However, the most effective form of outreach occurred through liaison librarians, who generated the majority of interest in the workshops.

Registration for the sessions was encouraged but optional so as to not dissuade those with unpredictable schedules. A Google form was used for registration and to gather preliminary information on attendees, including their department, status, and interest in the workshop, to better target content. The majority of responses indicated a general interest in the basics of publishing and little or no experience with the workshop content.

Session 1: Evaluating Academic Journals

The first session was intended to introduce emerging researchers to the scholarly publishing landscape and to strategies for evaluating publishing venues. The workshop began by asking attendees to complete a Poll Everywhere questionnaire—a real-time, anonymous survey tool—which provided a sense of participants' prior knowledge and concerns.

The presentation portion of the session framed the process of venue selection as considering the *fit, impact, and quality* of a prospective submission outlet. To discuss *fit*—how research aligns with a journal and its audience—we demonstrated how to research a journal's submission requirements, aims, and scope. The *impact* frame considered how a journal reaches the scholarly community, including a critical discussion of impact factors and altmetrics. Here we also discussed open access publications through the lens of making an impact beyond the scholarly community and provided contextual information on the basics of open access publishing models. Journal *quality* was the final consideration discussed. Here, we provided an overview of traditional and emerging peer review models, and addressed concerns about journals with deceptive practices. As scholars often conflate open access issues with predatory publishing concerns, we intentionally structured the workshop to frame these as separate (although linked) issues.

The remainder of the workshop was devoted to hands-on, interactive components. In a small-group activity, we provided a list of three open access journals within a single discipline and asked participants to help a hypothetical researcher from that field decide where to submit their work. Each small group explored the websites of two of the three journals in order to make a preliminary evaluation of journal impact and quality and subsequently discussed their assessments in the larger group. We then presented a series of tools for evaluating journals, including journal recommenders, citation reports, quality guides, and whitelists, and attendees were given time to apply them to journals in their own fields.

Session 2: Contracts and Copyright

The second workshop aimed to help participants understand why copyright is relevant to journal publishing, to recognize the major parts of a publishing contract, and to be aware of negotiation strategies. The first part of the session provided an overview of copyright, and discussed who owns the copyright to scholarly work and how rights can change hands via publishing contracts. We then demystified the most important terms authors encounter in publishing contracts and discussed the specific rights authors can license or retain.

A hands-on exercise followed, framed by a discussion of how to decide whether to sign a contract. Authors may wish to share an article on a personal website or institutional repository, but publishing contracts often prohibit or restrict such activities. Participants reviewed a sample publishing agreement to determine whether it permitted the sharing and reuse actions described in several hypothetical scenarios. Open access issues were folded into this discussion, as the "green" open access model relies on the ability of authors to openly distribute some version of their published work.

Finally, we guided participants through negotiation of a contract when a proposed agreement does not align with the rights the author needs or wants to retain. We discussed specific strategies and tools, including prefabricated addenda, and described different outcomes that could result from a negotiation, emphasizing that authors have the agency to suggest contract changes to retain more of their rights.

Program Assessment and Sustainability

The level of interest in these pilot workshops and attendee feedback confirmed a need for instruction in scholarly publishing for graduate students and other emerging researchers at the University of Washington, and that the format of these sessions provided an effective way of reaching this audience. Overall, 25 people registered for the first workshop, and 30 registered for the second, with 65% of registrants signing up for both sessions. According to librarians in the Scholarly Communication and Publishing department, these numbers were on the high end for workshops from their department. The workshops also attracted participants from diverse disciplinary backgrounds: registrants were fairly evenly divided between the humanities and social sciences; health sciences and nursing; and engineering and environmental sciences.

We received limited feedback through our follow-up survey, but those who responded stated that workshop content was novel and helpful. Qualitative feedback such as "[the workshops were] an excellent use of two hours" confirmed that the sessions effectively filled knowledge gaps. Respondents also indicated an interest in going beyond the "nuts and bolts"; attendees selected research data management, navigating peer review, and developing an online scholarly presence as potential topics for future workshops.

To promote the sustainability of these workshops, we took steps to encourage sharing of workshop content. We created a "Nuts and Bolts of Scholarly Publishing" online reference guide that acts as a repository of workshop content for attendees (University of Washington Libraries, n.d.-b). The guide also expands on the topics covered, allowing participants to delve deeper into areas of interest. Finally, the guide functions as a workshop substitute for those who could not attend, and we encouraged attendees to share the guide broadly.

To promote adaptation and reuse of the workshop content, we made slides and handouts publicly available under a "Creative Commons Attribution–NonCommercial" license. We also shared detailed presenter notes internally within the Libraries. The "Contracts and Copyright" workshop was already presented by another librarian during Open Access Week in the fall of 2018, and University of Washington health sciences librarians have expressed interest in developing a version to suit the specific needs of their community. We envision these sessions becoming part of a larger ecosystem of scholarly publication instruction for emerging researchers, potentially occurring as one-off sessions, during onboarding for new students, or as part of a series of related sessions on publishing or open access.

Discussion and Conclusions

Developing and delivering this workshop series raised issues that we will carefully consider as we look toward future programming on scholarly publishing. We targeted workshop content toward graduate student researchers, recognizing that while the needs "of graduate students and faculty are closely aligned, the lack of programming tailored to graduate students as a unique group with particular needs may suggest a potential growth area for libraries" (McClellan et al., 2017, p. 548). However, participation in the pilot sessions was not restricted to graduate students, and attendees included faculty members at later stages of their careers. The combination of junior and senior researchers yielded unanticipated benefits: faculty members shared their personal publishing experiences, enriching the workshop for all participants, and graduate students were able to build relationships with future colleagues. However, faculty members' greater experience occasionally resulted in questions outside the scope of the sessions' back-to-basics approach that may have confused student participants. Graduate program orientations and training sessions for graduate research assistants may be suitable venues for experimenting with student-only sessions that can provide useful points of comparison.

Delivery of the workshops also raised the question of whether it would be beneficial to target sessions toward specific disciplines. Participation in our pilot workshops was not restricted by discipline, and the sessions attracted a diverse pool of researchers divided between the humanities and social sciences (37%); health sciences and nursing (30%); and engineering and environmental sciences (33%). Workshop discussion reflected that scholarly publishing conventions vary across academic fields, such that researchers in different disciplines may encounter substantially different publishing practices. Focusing instruction in a particular subject area would allow the workshops to introduce discipline-specific practices to graduate students. However, it would also preclude the interdisciplinary exchange of experiences that took place during pilot workshops and could create a more intimidating environment by placing students alongside those with whom they may compete for advisor attention or departmental resources. Offering workshops that group related departments together, such as health sciences or humanities, may be a way to achieve some of the benefits of a more targeted session without these potential drawbacks.

Finally, we emerged from the pilot workshops believing that scholarly publishing instruction presents opportunities for fruitful library collaboration with campus partners. A writing center could contribute to a workshop on drafting and preparing a manuscript for submission, a session that could precede the existing journal selection and contract workshops. Faculty mentors or a campus professional development center could expand content regarding the peer review process, providing guidance around responding to reviewers and revising submissions. Although libraries are well positioned to support graduate students as they enter the world of scholarly publishing, integrating library services with other campus offerings can only enhance the contribution librarians make toward graduate student professional development.

Acknowledgments

The authors thank the University of Washington Libraries for supporting the development and delivery of these workshops, particularly Verletta Kern, the Scholarly Communication and Publishing department, the Research Commons, and Gabriella Dahlin, who designed the logo and marketing materials. The authors also thank Dr. Ricardo Gomez, who supported this research in its very early stages.

References

Baruzzi, A., & Calcagno, T. (2015). Academic librarians and graduate students: An exploratory study. *portal: Libraries and the Academy, 15*(3), 393–407. https://doi.org/10.1353/pla.2015.0034

Bird, C. (2010). Continued adventures in open access: 2009 perspective. *Learned Publishing, 23*(2), 107–166. doi:10.1087/20100205

Blankstein, M., & Wolff-Eisenberg, C. (2019, April 12). *Ithaka S+R US faculty survey 2018.* https://doi.org/10.18665/sr.311199

Charbonneau, D. H., & McGlone, J. (2013). Faculty experiences with the National Institutes of Health (NIH) public access policy, compliance issues, and copyright practices. *Journal of the Medical Library Association, 101*(1), 21–25. https://doi.org/10.3163/1536-5050.101.1.004

Cirasella, J. (2017). Open access outreach: SMASH vs. suasion. *College & Research Libraries News, 78*(6), 323–326. https://doi.org/10.5860/crln.78.6.323

Click, A. B. (2018). International graduate students in the United States: Research processes and challenges. *Library & Information Science Research, 40*(2), 153–162. https://doi.org/10.1016/j.lisr.2018.05.004

Coonin, B. (2011). Open access publishing in business research: The authors' perspective. *Journal of Business & Finance Librarianship, 16*(3), 193–212. doi:10.1080/08963568.2011.581606

Coonin, B., & Younce, L. (2009). *Publishing in open access journals in the social sciences and humanities: Who's doing it and why?* Paper presented at ACRL Fourteenth National Conference, Seattle, WA. Retrieved from http://www.ala.org/acrl/sites/ala.org.acrl/files/content/conferences/confsandpreconfs/national/seattle/papers/85.pdf

Coonin, B., & Younce, L. (2010). Publishing in open access education journals: The authors' perspectives. *Behavioral and Social Sciences Librarian, 29*(2), 118–32. https://doi.org/10.1080/01639261003742181

Corbett, H. (2009). The crisis in scholarly communication, part I: Understanding the issues and engaging your faculty. *Technical Services Quarterly, 26*(2), 125–134. https://doi.org/10.1080/07317130802268522

Cullen, R., & Chawner, B. (2011). Institutional repositories, open access, and scholarly communication: A study of conflicting paradigms. *The Journal of Academic Librarianship, 37*(6), 460–470. doi:10.1016/j.acalib.2011.07.002

Dallmeier-Tiessen, S., Darby, R., Goerner, B., Hyppoelae, J., Igo-Kemenes, P., Kahn, D., . . . van der Stelt, W. (2011) *Highlights from the SOAP project survey: What scientists think about open access publishing.* Retrieved from https://arxiv.org/abs/1101.5260

Dawson, D. (2018). Effective practices and strategies for open access outreach: A qualitative study. *Journal of Librarianship and Scholarly Communication*, 6(1), eP2216. http://doi.org/10.7710/2162-3309.2216

Di Valentino, L. (2015). *Awareness and perception of copyright among teaching faculty at Canadian universities.* Paper presented at ABC Copyright Conference, Winnipeg, Manitoba. http://dx.doi.org/10.21083/partnership.v10i2.3556

Flaherty, C. (2017). Renewed debate over whether graduate students should publish. *Inside Higher Ed.* Retrieved from https://www.insidehighered.com /news/2017/08/23/renewed-debate-over-whether-graduate-students -should-publish

Gadd, E. (2017). Guest post—Academics and copyright ownership: Ignorant, confused, or misled? [blog post] *The Scholarly Kitchen.* Retrieved from https:// scholarlykitchen.sspnet.org/2017/10/31/guest-post-academics-copyright -ownership-ignorant-confused-misled

Gadd, E., Loddington, S., & Oppenheim, C. (2007). A comparison of academics' attitudes towards the rights protection of their research and teaching materials. *Journal of Information Science*, 33(6), 686–701. https://doi.org/10.1177 /0165551506076396

Jalongo, M. R., Boyer, W., & Ebbeck, M. (2013). Writing for scholarly publication as "tacit knowledge": A qualitative focus group study of doctoral students in education. *Early Childhood Education Journal*, 42(4), 241–250. https://doi .org/10.1007/s10643-013-0624-3

Kim, J. (2010). Faculty self-archiving: Motivations and barriers. *Journal of the American Society for Information Science and Technology*, 61(9), 1909–1922. https://doi.org/10.1002/asi.21336

Klain-Gabbay, L., & Shoham, S. (2016). Scholarly communication and academic librarians. *Library & Information Science Research*, 38(2), 170–179. https:// doi.org/10.1016/j.lisr.2016.04.004

Knievel, J. E. (2008). Instruction to faculty and graduate students: A tutorial to teach publication strategies. *portal: Libraries and the Academy*, 8(2), 175– 186. https://doi.org/10.1353/pla.2008.0020

Kocken, G. J., & Wical, S. H. (2013). "I've never heard of it before": Awareness of open access at a small liberal arts university. *Behavioral & Social Sciences Librarian*, 32(3), 140–154. https://doi.org/10.1080/01 639269.2013.817876

Lambert, N. M. (2014). *Publish and prosper: A strategy guide for students and researchers.* New York, NY: Routledge.

Lewis, D. (2012). The inevitability of open access. *College & Research Libraries*, 73(5), 493–506. Retrieved from https://crl.acrl.org/index.php/crl/article /view/16255/17701

Lovett, J. A., Rathemacher, A. J., Boukari, D., & Lang, C. (2017). Institutional repositories and academic social networks: Competition or complement? A study of open access policy compliance vs. ResearchGate participation. *Journal of Librarianship and Scholarly Communication*, 5(General Issue), eP2183. https://doi.org/10.7710/2162-3309.2183

MacLachlan, A. J. (2006). Developing graduate students of color for the professoriate in science, technology, engineering, and mathematics (STEM). *Center for Studies in Higher Education: Research & Occasional Paper Series, CSHE.6.06.* Retrieved from http://escholarship.org/uc/item/3892k4rm

McClellan, S., Detmering, R., Martinez, G., & Johnson, A. (2017). Raising the library's impact factor: A case study in scholarly publishing literacy for graduate students. *portal: Libraries and the Academy, 17*(3), 543–568. doi:10.1353/pla.2017.0034

Mertkan, S. (2016). From a doctoral dissertation to journal articles. In C. Sugrue & S. Mertkan (Eds.), *Publishing and the academic world: Passion, purpose and possible futures* (pp. 136–149). Abingdon, Oxon: Routledge.

Morris, S., & Thorn, S. (2009). Learned society members and open access. *Learned Publishing, 22*(3), 221–239. https://doi.org/10.1087/2009308

Morrissey, R., & Given, L. M. (2006). International students and the academic library: A case study. *Canadian Journal of Information & Library Sciences, 30*(3/4), 221–239. Retrieved from http://muse.jhu.edu/journal/497

Mulligan, A., & Mabe, M. (2011). What journal authors want: Ten years of results from Elsevier's author feedback programme. *New Review of Information Networking, 16*(1), 71–89. https://doi.org/10.1080/13614576.2011.574495

Nariani, R., & Fernandez, L. (2012). Open access publishing: What authors want. *College & Research Libraries, 73*(2), 182–195. https://doi.org/10.5860/crl-203

Nicholas, D., Watkinson, A., Jamali, H. R., Herman, E., Tenopir, C., Volentine, R., . . . Levine, K. (2015). Peer review: Still king in the digital age. *Learned Publishing, 28*(1), 15–21. doi:10.1087/20150104

Odell, J., Palmer, K., & Dill, E. (2017). Faculty attitudes toward open access and scholarly communications: Disciplinary differences on an urban and health science campus. *Journal of Librarianship and Scholarly Communication, 5*(General Issue), eP2169. http://dx.doi.org/10.7710/2162-3309.2169

The Ohio State University, University Libraries. (2016). *Event listing—"The write stuff": Navigating the changing landscape of scholarly publishing.* Retrieved from https://library.osu.edu/researchcommons/event/sp16-write-stuff-workshop

Otto, J. J. (2016). A resonant message: Aligning scholar values and open access objectives in OA policy outreach to faculty and graduate students. *Journal of Librarianship and Scholarly Communication, 4,* eP2152. http://doi.org/10.7710/2162-3309.2152

Peekhaus, W., & Proferes, N. (2016). An examination of North American library and information studies faculty perceptions of and experience with open-access scholarly publishing. *Library & Information Science Research, 38,* 18–29. https://doi.org/10.1016/j.lisr.2016.01.003

Perry, A. (2017, December 13). *Arizona State University library guide: Scholarly communication: Scholarly publishing.* Retrieved from https://libguides.asu.edu/scholcomm/home

Radom, R., Feltner-Reichert, M., & Stringer-Stanback, K. (2012). *Organization of scholarly communication services. SPEC kit 332 (November 2012).* Washington,

DC: Association of Research Libraries. Retrieved from https://publications .arl.org/Organization-of-Scholarly-Communication-Services-SPEC-Kit -332

Ramirez, E. (2017). Unequal socialization: Interrogating the Chicano/Latino(a) doctoral education experience. *Journal of Diversity in Higher Education,* *10*(1), 25–38. https://doi.org/10.1037/dhe0000028

Rapple, C. (2017). Survey shows author sharing via scholarly collaboration net-works is widespread, despite strong support for copyright [blog post]. *Kudos.* Retrieved from https://blog.growkudos.com/2017/04/04/author -sharing-survey

Rodriguez, J. E. (2014). Awareness and attitudes about open access publishing: A glance at generational differences. *The Journal of Academic Librarianship,* *40*(6), 604–610. https://doi.org/10.1016/j.acalib.2014.07.013

Rowley, J., Johnson, F., Sbaffi, L., Frass, W., & Devine, E. (2017). Academics' behaviors and attitudes towards open access publishing in scholarly jour-nals. *Journal of the Association for Information Science & Technology, 68*(5), 1201–1211. http://doi.org/10.1002/asi.23710

Russell, J., & Kent, T. (2010). Paved with gold: An institutional case study on sup-porting open access publishing. *Serials: The Journal for the Serials Commu-nity, 23*(2), 97–102. doi:10.1629/2397

Schultz, T. A., & Medaille, A. (2019). *Spinning a scholarly story: Using faculty interviews to develop a scholarly communications agenda for liaison librarians.* Paper presented at ACRL 2019 Conference, Cleveland, OH. Retrieved from http://www.ala.org/acrl/sites/ala.org.acrl/files/content/conferences /confsandpreconfs/2019/SpinningaScholarlyStory.pdf

Secker, J. (2017). Just call me a copyright/fair use librarian [blog post]. *UK copy-right literacy.* Retrieved from https://copyrightliteracy.org/2017/09/20/just -call-me-a-copyrightfair-use-librarian

Sims, N. (2011). *Lies, damned lies, and copyright (mis)information: Empowering fac-ulty by addressing key points of confusion.* Paper presented at ACRL 2011 Conference, Philadelphia, PA. Retrieved from http://www.ala.org/acrl/sites /ala.org.acrl/files/content/conferences/confsandpreconfs/national/2011 /papers/lies_damned_lies.pdf

Stanton, K. V., & Liew, C. L. (2011). Open access theses in institutional reposito-ries: An exploratory study of the perceptions of doctoral students. *Infor-mation Research, 16*(4). Retrieved from http://www.informationr.net/ir/17 -1/paper507.html

Stoilescu, D., & McDougall, D. (2010). Starting to publish academic research as a doctoral student. *International Journal of Doctoral Studies, 5,* 79–92. https://doi.org/10.28945/1333

Tenopir, C., Dalton, E. D., Christian, L., Jones, M. K., McCabe, M., Smith, M., & Fish, A. (2017). Imagining a gold open access future: Attitudes, behaviors, and funding scenarios among authors of academic scholarship. *College & Research Libraries, 78*(6), 824–843. https://doi.org/10.5860/crl.78.6.824

University of California, Berkeley Library. (n.d.). *Scholarly communication: Publishing lifecycle.* Retrieved from http://www.lib.berkeley.edu/scholarly-communication/publishing/publishing-lifecycle

University of Washington Board of Regents. (2018). *2018 diversity metrics data book.* Retrieved from https://depts.washington.edu/dvrsty/BOR/DEI-Data-Book-2018.pdf

University of Washington Libraries. (n.d.-a). *About the libraries.* Retrieved from http://www.lib.washington.edu/about

University of Washington Libraries. (n.d.-b). *Nuts and bolts of scholarly publishing.* Retrieved from https://guides.lib.uw.edu/research/publishing

Warlick, S., & Vaughan, K. (2007). Factors influencing publication choice: Why faculty choose open access. *Biomedical Digital Libraries, 4*(1). https://doi.org/10.1186/1742-5581-4-1

Wipperman, S. (2018). Survey results on open access themes. *Operation Beprexit: Documenting Penn Libraries' journey toward open source repository solutions.* Retrieved from https://beprexit.wordpress.com/2018/07/25/survey-open-access

Xia, J. (2010). A longitudinal study of scholars' attitudes and behaviors toward open-access journal publishing. *Journal of the American Society for Information Science and Technology, 61*(3), 615–624. doi:10.1002/asi.21283

Zhao, L. (2014). Riding the wave of open access: Providing library research support for scholarly publishing literacy. *Australian Academic & Research Libraries, 45*(1), 3–18. https://doi.org/10.1080/00048623.2014.882873

Librarians in Dissertation Deposit: Infusing an Institutional Ritual with Scholarly Communication Instruction

Roxanne Shirazi and Jill Cirasella

Introduction

Most doctoral students are required to produce a dissertation that makes an original contribution to their field of study in order to fulfill their degree requirements. The scholarly nature of this requirement informs how students and faculty approach doctoral research, but universities often treat the dissertations themselves merely as student records, not scholarly contributions. Librarians, however, are uniquely situated to work with graduate students as emerging participants in the scholarly communication ecosystem and help them prepare their dissertations for an outside audience. Librarians have the expertise to advise students with questions regarding copyright, licensing, fair use, and authors' rights, as well as the awareness to spot such issues even when students are not aware of them.

The importance of treating graduate students as scholarly contributors was made evident when our institution, the Graduate Center of the City University of New York, moved responsibility for dissertation deposit from an administrative role to a librarian position. In this chapter, we offer as a case study our experience transforming the deposit process into a scholarly communication consultation with a copyright-literate librarian. We also provide prompts for considering ways to insert librarian-led scholarly communication consultations into the graduation checklist, regardless of which office manages dissertation deposit.

Literature Review

Scholarly communication librarians have paid considerable attention to developing effective strategies for outreach to various campus stakeholders pertaining to issues around open access publishing, authors' rights, fair use, and other scholarly communication topics (Dawson, 2018; Duncan, Clement, & Rozum, 2013). Davis-Kahl and Hensley's (2013) book-length examination of information literacy and scholarly communication was followed by an Association of College and Research Libraries (ACRL) white paper (2013), which identified three "intersections" in which current trends in scholarly communication and information literacy share common purpose: (1) economics of the distribution of scholarship, (2) digital literacies, and (3) new roles for librarians. An emphasis on the changing nature of scholarly publishing was thus deemed an essential part of teaching information literacy in academic libraries.

Practitioners involved in dissertation deposit generally come from two worlds on campus: the library and administrative offices, such as the Office of the Registrar and Student Services. The Council of Graduate Schools sponsors best practices initiatives that broadly concern dissertations in the context of doctoral education, such as the Future of the Dissertation Workshop (2016), while cross-professional organizations like the United States Electronic Thesis and Dissertation Association (USETDA) and the Networked Digital Library of Theses and Dissertations (NDLTD) sponsor annual conferences with published proceedings.

Typically, libraries have approached dissertations from a collections standpoint, focusing on issues of preservation, description, and access to the finished product. With the advent of electronic theses and dissertations (ETDs) in the late 1990s, the library world has focused on what we might call "the afterlife" of the dissertation—their use value as a research output. Suber (2006) famously characterized dissertations as "the most invisible form of useful literature and the most useful form of invisible literature" (para. 9), and the practitioner literature has since been overwhelmed with debates over access embargoes and book-publishing prospects (Cirasella & Thistlethwaite, 2017; Courtney & Kilcer, 2017). Some libraries offer scholarly communication instruction to depositing students outside of the required procedures for submitting their final work (Clement & Bianchi, 2013).

The literature around the *deposit* of the dissertation tends to focus on establishing workflows for electronic deposit (Cox, 2015), including metadata schema and repository-specific optimizations (Veve, 2016). An additional focus within the ETD community concerns the question of whether or not dissertations that are made available online are considered published, both for the sake of establishing the copyright status for digitization of legacy works (Clement & Levine, 2011) and for assessing an openly available dissertation's impact on the author's future publication prospects (Gurman & Brunner, 2015; Hawkins, Kimball, & Ives, 2013).

Although all these topics were of concern to our institution as we endeavored to rethink the library's approach to dissertation deposit, it was not until we began meeting with students under a new paradigm that we really understood the possibilities for attuning graduate students to the cadences of scholarly publishing as part of the deposit procedure itself. Policies and standards beget institutional culture and norms; by attending to our own role in the formation of these procedures and critically examining what we had previously taken for granted in deposit, we were able to structure the culminating experience of doctoral study into an outgoing scholarly communication literacy consultation.

Background

Institutional Context

In order to understand what is and is not generalizable about our experience, it is necessary to understand the structure of the City University of New York (CUNY), and the Graduate Center within it. CUNY is the largest urban university in the United States and is legislatively recognized as being "of vital importance as a vehicle for the upward mobility of the disadvantaged in the city of New York" (City University of New York, n.d.-a; NY Education Law § 6201). It consists of 25 campuses across the five boroughs of New York City: 11 senior colleges, seven community colleges, one honors college, and six graduate and professional schools, including the Graduate Center (City University of New York, n.d.-b).

Our campus, the Graduate Center, is a stand-alone entity that confers only graduate degrees; it is not a graduate school within a larger college or a graduate-only satellite of another campus. It is worth noting, though, that the Graduate Center's "campus" consists of only one building, albeit a large one: the former flagship B. Altman & Co. department store in Manhattan. It is diagonally across the street from the Empire State Building and a block away from Herald Square, justifying its tagline as "the life of the mind in the heart of the city" (Robinson, 2017).

As of this writing, the Graduate Center has 4,071 students in 15 master's programs and 31 doctoral programs. Many other CUNY schools also offer master's degrees, but only a small handful also grant doctoral degrees. Indeed, the Graduate Center is CUNY's primary doctorate-granting school, conferring more than 400 doctorates per year (CUNY, Office of Institutional Research, 2017, Degrees Granted section). The Graduate Center is notable among U.S. doctorate-granting institutions for the diversity of its doctorate recipients: it ranks sixth nationally in number of doctorates awarded to Hispanic or Latinx students between 2013 and 2017, and twentieth in number of doctorates awarded to black or African American students in the same time period (National Science Foundation, 2017, Table 9). In 2018, the Graduate Center's combined doctoral and master's student population was 6.2% Asian, 5.7% Black or African American, 10.5% Hispanic or Latinx, 42.2% white, 2.3% multiracial, 9.4% unknown, and 23.4% international; there were only three American Indian or Alaskan Native students, and only three Native Hawaiian or other Pacific Islander students. The student body was 56.6% female and 43.4% male (CUNY, Graduate Center, Office of Institutional Research and Effectiveness, 2019).

In some ways, the Graduate Center is the keystone of CUNY: it is supported by the other campuses and supports them in turn. In particular, it both draws on and augments the faculty of the other campuses. The Graduate Center has approximately 140 professors appointed solely to the Graduate Center and over 1,600 consortial faculty members—professors based at other CUNY schools who dedicate some of their workloads to teaching or advising at the Graduate Center (CUNY, Graduate Center, n.d.). At the same time, most of the Graduate Center's doctoral students have fellowship packages that require teaching at one or more of CUNY's undergraduate colleges. The campuses are spread out across the city, some an hour or more away by public transportation, so these teaching assignments limit the amount of time doctoral students can physically spend at the Graduate Center, in our library, and in consultation with our librarians.

However, almost all students are required to produce a dissertation, thesis, or capstone project that must be deposited with the library for archiving and distribution. Therefore, almost all students must interact at least once with the Dissertation Office, which is part of the library. Central to our transformation of the deposit process is a desire to infuse those interactions with scholarly significance, to provide graduating students with information literacy instruction that will be relevant to their postgraduation lives.

Mina Rees Library

Historically, the Graduate Center's Mina Rees Library was divided into two main departments: Collections and Public Services, which added a Scholarly Communication unit in 2013. The Dissertation Office arguably could have been in either of these departments but was in neither. Rather, in a decades-old arrangement, it was a separate nub on the organizational tree, staffed by the dissertation assistant, a nonlibrarian who reported directly to the chief librarian.

The dissertation assistant's primary duties consisted of the following: meeting individually with all depositing students; helping them understand deposit requirements and navigate deposit procedures; reviewing the formatting and front matter of all submissions; delivering all electronic submissions to ProQuest via their ETD Administrator site; overseeing binding of all print submissions; and maintaining records for all submissions. These were all vitally important tasks—crucial to the library's archiving of culminating student works and to the institution's conferral of degrees. However, under the dissertation assistant, dissertations were treated primarily as degree requirements and student records. Because the dissertation assistant was not a librarian, she could not engage with the works as a librarian would: as contributions to and continuations of the scholarly conversation, as works that will be sought, read, and cited by other researchers.

From Assistant to Librarian

In 2015, after 28 years in the position, the dissertation assistant announced her retirement, prompting library leadership to rethink everything about the position: title, rank, qualifications, duties, etc. From the outset, we agreed that students, the library, and the institution as a whole would benefit if we could transform the role into a faculty librarian position and hire a librarian with a deep understanding of systems of scholarly communication; such a librarian would be able to interrogate and refine our deposit requirements and communicate their scholarly significance to the Graduate Center community. However, we were aware that what seemed obvious to us was actually based on years of library experience and may not be self-evident to administrators. We needed to make the case to key decision makers: we had to get from idea to reality, from library request to administrative "yes."

One of our earliest decisions was to pitch the position as *dissertation research librarian*, for two reasons. First, we wanted to avoid the appearance of merely swapping out "assistant" for "librarian," without reinventing the position. Second, we thought this title would communicate that a faculty librarian could make deposit a meaningful extension of the research process and address the ways in which dissertations and theses are part of the scholarly conversation.

Of course, a strategic job title only goes so far. We also built a case around the needs expressed by earlier graduates: assistance with research management tools and techniques; expertise in copyright and licensing; and support for digital scholarship (i.e., scholarly works that include or consist entirely of digital projects). We also explained the scholarly importance of cataloging, storing, and disseminating culminating works according to best practices, such as the importance of applying metadata that adheres to appropriate standards.

Happily, we were able able to get to "yes" on transforming the position. As much as we might like to claim full credit for that victory, to congratulate ourselves on having an airtight argument, the approval probably had just as much to do with winds blowing around the Graduate Center—for example, encouragement for students to publish before graduating and a growing focus on the digital humanities—as with our powers of persuasion. The chief librarian's strong relationships with department heads and prominent faculty helped too: she sought buy-in from these faculty, who then voiced their support to administrators. Further, she made the case for transforming the position at the same time she put forward discontinuing print submissions, strategically tying these two proposals together to help show how different the new job would be from the old one. As a result of the chief librarian's conversations around campus, a call for updated and expanded dissertation services became part of the Graduate Center's swirling winds.

We also needed an immediate approval to fill the vacancy created by the dissertation assistant's retirement. Luckily, students, faculty, and administrators all understood the necessity of avoiding a halt in the processing of dissertations, theses, and capstone projects. Library vacancies are generally not seen as emergencies, but a vacancy in the Dissertation Office would have led to an inability to accept deposits, which would have led to an inability to grant degrees. With three graduation dates per year, even a short vacancy would have been catastrophic. The urgency was real and universally acknowledged.

We were able to avoid a vacancy, but, because of bureaucratic and budgetary constraints, it required some stop-gap measures. We had a short-term interim dissertation assistant in place a couple of days before the dissertation assistant retired and shortly thereafter appointed a dissertation research librarian for a temporary one-year term. During that year, the library conducted a national search and hired the tenure-track dissertation research librarian (coauthor Shirazi).

When we wrote the job description for the dissertation research librarian, we mirrored the arguments we made during our campaign to transform the position. We summarized the position thus: "The Dissertation Research Librarian will provide responsive, effective, and innovative coordination of the Library's collection, archiving, and distribution of dissertations, theses, and capstone projects (ETDs). The Dissertation Research Librarian also assists students and faculty in adapting to the evolving digital scholarly communication landscape." And we added several items to the list of responsibilities that we could not have expected of a dissertation assistant, including:

- Determines best practices for ETD submission and approval;
- Provides one-on-one guidance and workshop-based instruction on copyright (fair use, licensing, etc.) and tools for research management (citation management tools, file management tools, etc.);
- Formulates workflows to allow alumni to make their dissertations open access;
- Consults with creators of digital/nontextual works to anticipate successful archiving of those works; and
- Maintains professional currency in ETD archiving, distribution, and repository management.

We also changed the reinvented position's place in the organizational chart, moving it from reporting directly to the chief librarian to being part of the Scholarly Communication unit. There, we hoped, the dissertation research librarian would be in ongoing conversation with other librarians engaged in scholarly communication projects and issues—bouncing ideas off each other, illuminating nuances for each other, deepening each other's expertise, etc.

Moving Forward

From Product to Process

We were then poised to shift gears in the library's approach to dissertations, moving focus from *product* toward *process*. When deposit was handled by the dissertation assistant, finished products came to the library, and the library's role was to steward that product: we focused on preservation, description, and access. Now, with a librarian at the helm, the library has become fundamentally involved in the process of the underlying scholarship as well: manuscript preparation, rights clearance, and approval and submission systems. It's that expansion of responsibilities and oversight of the production of scholarship that has opened up new opportunities for engagement with our graduate students and, to an extent, with their faculty advisors. This is not to diminish the importance of product-minded activities such as cataloging and preservation—those are still core concerns for libraries, and we dedicated significant staffing and expertise to addressing issues related to ETD discovery and digital preservation as we moved to a fully electronic workflow. Yet, the idea that the library could tackle concerns related to the preparation of the dissertation, and not solely be there as a repository or container for the finished work, was new for administrators on our campus.

Students nearing completion of a doctoral dissertation often have scholarly publishing concerns that warrant librarian involvement. For example, as more universities make dissertations available online, uncertainty abounds about the appropriate use of images, responsible citation of social media, and fears over accidental plagiarism. There are also discipline-specific pain points: students in the humanities may agonize over access embargoes; art historians may remove crucial images entirely from their scholarship due to copyright concerns; and students in fields such as economics or biology may not realize they signed away their copyright to those previously published articles they now want to include in their dissertations (Shirazi, 2018).

Whom do these students turn to for answers? This was the core question for us as we began to insert a scholarly communication consultation into the deposit procedure. We discovered that, prior to our intervention, these questions were routinely referred to ProQuest's customer service department despite the library's active scholarly communication initiatives. Our librarians were separated from depositors' point of need, resulting in a disconnect between services that the library offered and the help the students received.

We are now taking a more holistic approach to ETD submission, with a Dissertation Office that is administratively and *conceptually* located in the library and led by a librarian. We discovered that when we advise students on manuscript preparation in the Dissertation Office, this is really an opportunity to discuss scholarly communication topics like copyright, fair use, and authors' rights at a student's point of need. Indeed, our doctoral students actively seek out this information, and now the dissertation research librarian is positioned to provide scholarly communication instruction that will better prepare our graduates for their roles as future academics.

Professionalizing as Academics through a Proto-Publication Experience

Hswe (2014) encourages us to consider the implications of ETD management using a student-centered approach: "First-hand exposure to copyright and fair use issues, including the deposit agreement(s) students are obliged to understand, can amount to a formative authorship experience" (p. 3.10). When librarians debate whether or not dissertations are published, we're usually concerned with figuring out the kind of access we can provide to the finished product. But as Hswe points out, the submission process is imbued with potential pitfalls for graduate students who may very well be experiencing publishing—in whatever form it may be—in the library, through the university, for the first time. As we restructured the library's procedures, we foregrounded thinking about dissertation and thesis deposit from this perspective: what are we teaching students about publishing?

We began by asking ourselves, "How can we structure the dissertation deposit procedure to provide opportunities for a deeper engagement with the changing nature of scholarly publishing? How can we bring librarian expertise into these conversations?" As with most processes in libraries, everyone seems to do dissertation deposit differently. So while it's difficult to generalize our experience in a way that could be readily applied elsewhere, we'll share some of the details of what we learned as we reimagined the dissertation deposit experience at our institution.

Our first step was to cease archiving print dissertations and move to an online submission procedure. Previously, students had been required to schedule an in-person appointment with the dissertation assistant to deposit their finished manuscript after successfully completing their defense. Students were responsible for printing out their manuscript on premium paper and bringing it to that appointment, where they would physically submit the pages to be bound by the library. If format corrections were required, students would complete them and return with a *new* printout, to be checked again. If the manuscript passed muster, students would then take a deposit clearance form to a series of administrative offices (Bursar, Financial Aid, Registrar, Library Circulation) to obtain signatures stating that they owed no fees and were cleared to graduate. Students then uploaded a PDF version of their manuscript to ProQuest using the ETD Administrator submission system, with which they could optionally register their copyright in the work with the U.S. Copyright Office. At no point in this procedure was there a consultation with a librarian. As stated earlier, questions surrounding copyright permissions and fair use were routinely referred to ProQuest's customer service department.

Now, students submit directly to the Graduate Center's ETD series of CUNY's bepress Digital Commons repository, CUNY Academic Works. Students also submit to ProQuest using the ETD Administrator system, both to aid in discovery and to enable purchase of personal bound copies. Crucially, there is no appointment required because the deposit occurs asynchronously as students self-submit online and receive feedback via e-mail. The deposit clearance form has been replaced by an online application for graduation, which is administered by Student Services. For the time being, an approval page still must be submitted, in hard copy and with original signatures, to the library for verification of the deposit.

Our online submission workflow is now similar to what academics encounter when submitting an article to a journal for publication. We believe that there is value in learning how to adapt one's manuscript to a set of formatting rules, submitting the work electronically for review, and responding to requested revisions. As graduate students are increasingly advised to publish earlier in their careers (Alvarez, Bonnet, & Kahn, 2014; Flaherty, 2017), some undoubtedly have this experience already. But there are many for whom this is the first time, including those whose mentors handled such formalities in coauthored publications.

Further, the library has expanded review of dissertation formatting to address concerns related to scholarly publishing. We now pay close attention to whether prior publications and funding information have been properly identified in the Acknowledgments section; we inspect image credit lines to ensure proper citation and discuss the principles of fair use in relation to third-party materials; and we consult with students about the implications of open access to their final work. Throughout, the dissertation research librarian is able to situate these requirements in the broader context of modern scholarly publishing conventions and approach them *in conversation* with students, just as we would with faculty. This is a far cry from our institution's previous conception of the Dissertation Office as taskmaster, enforcing arcane formatting rules that were designed to suit the requirements of the library's bindery or ProQuest's microfilm format.

Meeting Students Where They Were

Eliminating the requirement for an in-person meeting was a priority for our campus community, but it meant that the library could no longer rely on a guaranteed personal interaction with every graduating student. Dissertation deposit had been a rite of passage that was fraught with anxiety and tension as students competed for limited appointment times, and freeing them from this scheduling requirement was essential to transforming the procedure into a more dignifying experience for our future academics. Instead, we began to hold regular and dedicated "office hours" in the library's Dissertation Office, which were publicized as time for one-on-one consultations to learn about depositing the dissertation and discuss questions or concerns with the new dissertation research librarian.

We also scheduled group information sessions, mostly in the evening, so that working (and teaching) students could hear the procedure explained in person and ask questions at the end of the presentation. These group sessions quickly became the most attended classes offered by the library, bringing students from different fields to connect with and learn from their peers—in contrast with the typically isolating atmosphere of graduate school. From the library's perspective, the interdisciplinary and group dynamic of the Q&A helps to surface broader issues that might go unseen in individual appointments. The music student's question about listing a proper credit line for a musical excerpt, for example, might spark a conversation about identifying federally funded research in a biology dissertation. Each one of these real-life examples demonstrates the intricacies of academic publishing for students and thus prepares them to consider a variety of aspects of their published works that they'd never before considered.

For students who are unable or unwilling to come to the library, we have borrowed techniques from asynchronous reference to use e-mail constructively—keeping a conversation flowing, using open-ended questions, and so forth. E-mail conversations might escalate into telephone calls or in-person appointments, depending on the student's situation and preference. Finally, finding allies in the departments, whether the department secretary or the chair, was key to our success in reaching students who were no longer required to meet with the library. We also found that our subject librarians' liaison practices adapted well to these purposes. Through all of these methods of outreach, we encounter about a third of graduating students for each degree period who still want a one-on-one, in-person meeting outside of general office hours or group instruction.

Despite our efforts to draw out more substantive conversations, the more routine inquiries persist. Lack of a writing center at our institution means that our students still need help wrangling Microsoft Word, and there are legitimate questions that might not be in the scope of a scholarly communication consultation that must still be addressed, such as more general citation questions. For these questions, we try to refer out to the Reference Desk, but it can be difficult to take this kind of tiered reference approach in part because students don't always trust other sources of information; they want to hear it directly from the Dissertation Office. We learned, then, to set reasonable boundaries, particularly with more demanding students—an approach to service that is more common in campus administrative offices, but was somewhat unfamiliar for librarians who might engage in more hand-holding than other service providers on campus.

Taking Stock

We have now gone through several degree cycles under the new system and have begun to take stock of the outcomes of our efforts. For faculty and departmental staff, there is greater awareness of authors' rights and copyright issues, and that the library can advise on these matters. As an example, many did not know about copyright concerns related to students' previously published materials until we told them that this is an issue. The library is now engaged in larger conversations with department chairs as they consider guidelines for composite theses (i.e., dissertations that consist of articles or manuscripts that have been accepted for publication). We also know that students are benefiting from our dedicated office hours and group information sessions. A significant part of our students' anxiety was caused by all the hurdles they had to jump just to get an answer to a policy or formatting question; librarians already have the infrastructure to service questions in this way. We're able to direct them to our in-house expertise instead of sending them to an outside vendor, and we're able to provide more up-to-date information by using our LibGuides instead of the college website.

A librarian consultation and involvement in the ETD submission process can also benefit a library's existing activities of preservation and access, for the simple reason that we are involved in setting up the submission guidelines. We are able to determine what kinds of information about the deposit we want to capture and thus better align the submission form with our cataloging needs. Looking ahead, we are exploring ways to integrate more robust digital preservation tools with our ETD management workflow, implement PDF standards into our submission guidelines, and expand our capacity to accept a variety of digital research outputs as dissertations.

As part of our reflective assessment of our own work, we developed a worksheet for librarians looking to get more involved in the dissertation deposit process (Shirazi & Cirasella, 2018). Over the course of our professional conversations about our efforts to reimagine dissertation deposit, we were struck by how often our interlocutors were unfamiliar with the procedures at their own institutions. The prompts on the worksheet are designed to guide practitioners through an environmental scan of current practices and to identify specific individuals or offices on campus who bring expertise in areas such as open access, publisher policies, licensing, citation styles, digital file formats, and data sharing. We ask users to consider: Whose buy-in would be necessary to bring a scholarly communication consultation into the deposit process? Are there faculty committees or working groups that their library could reach out to, or other entities on campus such as a writing center? What collaborations already exist that could be put to use in these efforts?

Conclusion

Buckland (2015) has encouraged librarians to approach students as content creators, arguing that "discussions about scholarly publishing [should] become a standard part of all library outreach" (p. 202). With doctoral students, libraries have a built-in mechanism for addressing scholarly communication issues at a student's point of need: the deposit of their dissertation. A critical understanding of the system of scholarly publishing will be especially useful for those students who are going on to work as academics, and examining that system through the lens of their own contribution can demonstrate the delicate balance between authors' rights, publishers' rights, and the public's right to publicly funded research.

With deliberate planning and organizational restructuring, the Mina Rees Library was able to infuse an institutional ritual with scholarly communication instruction. Instead of having a strictly administrative meeting with the dissertation assistant, graduating students now receive help on a range of deposit-related topics—in person, on the phone, and by e-mail—from a dissertation research librarian who is informed about scholarly communication issues, particularly as they pertain to culminating student works. Taken together, these interactions constitute a final, outgoing information literacy experience that addresses graduate students as content creators rather than information consumers. These librarian-led sessions cover various aspects of scholarly communication—information they'll need and considerations they'll need to weigh in their upcoming professional scholarly lives.

References

Alvarez, B., Bonnet, J., & Kahn, M. (2014). Publish, not perish: Supporting graduate students as aspiring authors. *Journal of Librarianship and Scholarly Communication*, 2(3). https://doi.org/10.7710/2162-3309.1141

Association of College and Research Libraries. Working Group on Intersections of Scholarly Communication and Information Literacy. (2013). *Intersections of scholarly communication and information literacy: Creating strategic collaborations for a changing academic environment*. Chicago, IL: Association of College and Research Libraries. Retrieved from http://acrl.ala.org/intersections

Buckland, A. (2015). More than consumers: Students as content creators. In M. Bonn & M. Furlough (Eds.), *Getting the word out: Academic libraries as scholarly publishers* (pp. 193–202). Chicago, IL: Association of College and Research Libraries. Retrieved from http://hdl.handle.net/10214/12087

Cirasella, J., & Thistlethwaite, P. (2017). Open access and the graduate author: A dissertation anxiety manual. In K. L. Smith & K. A. Dickson (Eds.), *Open access and the future of scholarly communication: Implementation* (pp. 203–224). Lanham, MD: Rowman & Littlefield. Retrieved from https://academicworks.cuny.edu/gc_pubs/286

City University of New York (CUNY). (n.d.-a). *About*. Retrieved February 15, 2019, from http://web.archive.org/web/20190207210859/http://www2.cuny.edu/about/university-resources/yes-we-can/about

City University of New York (CUNY). (n.d.-b). *Colleges & schools*. Retrieved February 15, 2019, from http://www2.cuny.edu/about/colleges-schools

City University of New York (CUNY), Graduate Center. (n.d.). *Faculty*. Retrieved February 15, 2019, from https://www.gc.cuny.edu/faculty

City University of New York (CUNY), Graduate Center, Office of Institutional Research and Effectiveness. (2019, March 11). *Student diversity* [Tableau visualization]. Retrieved from https://public.tableau.com/profile/cuny.gc.edu.oire.2018#!/vizhome/GraduateCenterStudentDiversity_0/Diversity

City University of New York (CUNY), Office of Institutional Research. (2017). *Student data book*. Retrieved from http://www2.cuny.edu/about/administration/offices/oira/institutional/data/student-data-book-archive/fall-2017

Clement, G., & Bianchi, J. A. (2013). *Copyright and publishing literacy for ETD authors: Applying the theft of the mind model*. Poster session presented at the meeting of Texas ETD Association. Retrieved from http://oaktrust.library.tamu.edu/handle/1969.1/147616

Clement, G., & Levine, M. (2011). Copyright and publication status of pre-1978 dissertations: A content analysis approach. *portal: Libraries and the Academy*, *11*(3), 813–829. Retrieved from http://oaktrust.library.tamu.edu/handle/1969.1/149190

Council of Graduate Schools. (2016). *Proceedings of the CGS Future of the Dissertation Workshop (January 2016)*. Retrieved from http://cgsnet.org/future-dissertation-workshop

Courtney, K. K., & Kilcer, E. (2017). From apprehension to comprehension: Addressing anxieties about open access to electronic theses and dissertations. In K. L. Smith & K. A. Dickson (Eds.), *Open access and the future of scholarly communication: Implementation*. Lanham, MD: Rowman & Littlefield. Retrieved from http://nrs.harvard.edu/urn-3:HUL.InstRepos :38475918

Cox, N. S. (2015). How did we get here: Binding of print theses and dissertations to processing electronic theses and dissertations? *North Carolina Libraries*, 73(1), 20–24. Retrieved from http://www.ncl.ecu.edu/index.php/NCL /article/view/415

Davis-Kahl, S., & Hensley, M. K. (Eds.). (2013). *Common ground at the nexus of information literacy and scholarly communication*. Chicago, IL: Association of College and Research Libraries. Retrieved from https://digitalcommons .iwu.edu/bookshelf/36

Dawson, D. (DeDe). (2018). Effective practices and strategies for open access outreach: A qualitative study. *Journal of Librarianship and Scholarly Communication*, 6(1), eP2216. https://doi.org/10.7710/2162-3309.2216

Duncan, J., Clement, S., & Rozum, B. (2013). Teaching our faculty: Developing copyright and scholarly communication outreach programs. In S. Davis-Kahl & M. K. Hensley (Eds.), *Common ground at the nexus of information literacy and scholarly communication* (pp. 269–285). Chicago, IL: Association of College and Research Libraries. Retrieved from https://digitalcommons .usu.edu/lib_pubs/117

Flaherty, C. (2017, August 23). Renewed debate over whether graduate students should publish. *Inside Higher Ed*. Retrieved from https://www.inside highered.com/news/2017/08/23/renewed-debate-over-whether-graduate -students-should-publish

Gurman, D., & Brunner, M. (2015). Dissertation to book: Successful open access outreach to graduate students. *Journal of Library Innovation*, 6(1), 40–59. Retrieved from https://sites.google.com/site/journaloflibraryinnovation/vol -6-no-1-2015

Hawkins, A. R., Kimball, M. A., & Ives, M. (2013). Mandatory open access publishing for electronic theses and dissertations: Ethics and enthusiasm. *The Journal of Academic Librarianship*, 39(1), 32–60. https://doi.org/10.1016/j .acalib.2012.12.003

Hswe, P. (2014). Briefing on copyright and fair use issues in ETDs. In M. Schultz, N. Krabbenhoeft, & K. Skinner (Eds.), *Guidance documents for lifecycle management of ETDs* (pp. 3.1–3.20). Atlanta, GA: Educopia Institute. Retrieved from https://educopia.org/guidance-documents-for-lifecycle -management-of-etds

National Science Foundation. (2017). *Survey of earned doctorates* [data set]. Retrieved from https://ncses.nsf.gov/pubs/nsf19301/data

New York State Legislature. NY EDN § 6201. *Legislative findings and intent*. Retrieved from https://www.nysenate.gov/legislation/laws/EDN/6201

Robinson, C. (2017, August 22). *Convocation 2017 address by President Robinson.* Retrieved from https://www.gc.cuny.edu/Page-Elements/News/2017/August/Convocation-2017-Address-by-President-Robinson

Shirazi, R. (2018). The doctoral dissertation and scholarly communication: Adapting to changing publication practices among graduate students. *College and Research Libraries News, 79*(1), 34–37. https://doi.org/10.5860/crln.79.1.34

Shirazi, R., & Cirasella, J. (2018). *Not just degree-seekers: Graduate students as scholarly contributors* [worksheet]. Retrieved from https://digitalcommons.kennesaw.edu/cgi/viewcontent.cgi?filename=0&article=1035&context=gradlibconf&type=additional

Suber, P. (2006). Open access to electronic theses and dissertations (ETDs). *SPARC Open Access Newsletter.* Retrieved from http://nrs.harvard.edu/urn-3:HUL.InstRepos:4727443

Veve, M. (2016). Harvesting ETD metadata from institutional repositories to OCLC: Approaches and barriers to implementation. *Journal of Library Metadata, 16*(2), 69–79. https://doi.org/10.1080/1051712X.2016.1215730

PART 3

Focusing on Future Professionals: Professional Expectations of the "Real World"

CHAPTER NINE

Finding and Evaluating the Evidence: Collaborating with Future Social Work Practitioners and Scholars on Systematic Reviews

Jennifer Bowers

Introduction

The job market demand for social workers is strong and is projected to grow by 16% over the next 10 years (Bureau of Labor Statistics, 2019). Central to professional expectations will be the need for graduate social work students to excel in evidence-based practice (EBP), in order to evaluate the effectiveness of interventions, programs, and services to be used with their future clients, organizations, and communities. Through an EBP approach, students are taught how to construct effective research questions and translate them into search strategies, survey the published (and sometimes unpublished) research literature, evaluate applied methodologies, and assess the quality of the findings. EBP techniques are often integrated into research methods courses where students are introduced to the hierarchy of research evidence and learn the strengths of these different types of research studies and syntheses. Positioned at the top of the evidence pyramid, systematic reviews, which may involve a meta-analysis of quantitative research data or a meta-synthesis of qualitative studies, play a key role in applying research to practice. In contrast to a review of the literature that is selective by nature, a systematic review "provides a comprehensive synthesis of the available evidence to allow the researcher to draw broad and robust conclusions" (Siddaway, Wood, & Hedges, 2019, p. 751) and is characterized by being "methodical, comprehensive, transparent, and replicable" (Siddaway et al., 2019, p. 751) in order to minimize bias (Kugley et al., 2016). Systematic reviews are highly valued for their synthesis of research findings and are used to inform social work practice and policy decisions (Crisp, 2015; Maynard & Dell, 2018). Moreover, systematic reviews guide decisions for busy practitioners, who may not have the time or resources to survey and synthesize the comprehensive field of research.

Librarians are natural partners to collaborate with social work faculty to prepare graduate students with a strong foundation in EBP. Even though master's level students may not go on to conduct systematic reviews, it is important that they gain a solid understanding of the process of systematic and thorough reviews of the research evidence so that they are prepared to critically evaluate published reviews in their field and have the knowledge to be informed consumers of research literature. Social work faculty and doctoral student teams, on the other hand, are increasingly conducting systematic reviews as part of their research activity. Long established in the medical and health sciences fields, the prevalence of systematic reviews in other disciplines, especially those in the social sciences with an applied research orientation such as social work, is on the rise (Gore & Jones, 2015). These reviews are published in the leading journals and can also be integral to research grant proposals. Some social work doctoral candidates are writing systematic reviews that comprise their entire dissertation. Liaison librarians can support the EBP research needs of social work students by collaborating on developing EBP curricular assignments and supporting materials, and by acting as consultants or coauthors on systematic reviews. In particular, librarians can share their expertise with complex search strategies, database recommendations, and bibliographic management tools, among other contributions, to strengthen systematic review projects.

This case study presents how I, as the social sciences librarian liaison to the Graduate School of Social Work (GSSW) at the University of Denver, have provided systematic review support for master's and doctoral students. The chapter will also discuss challenges and opportunities related to these liaison partnerships and will suggest recommended practices for supporting and promoting systematic review services, as well as list resources that other social sciences librarians may find useful. As expectations for EBP proficiency expand, librarians have an exciting opportunity, through systematic review assignments and collaborations with students, to prepare future practitioners and scholars to find and incorporate the best evidence to serve their clients and communities.

Background

Founded in 1864, the University of Denver (DU) is a private university of approximately 12,000 students, on a quarter-based system, with an almost even distribution of undergraduates and graduates. Graduate enrollment in the fall of 2017 was 5,669 students, of whom 3,416 were women and 1,288 were people of color (University of Denver, 2017). The Graduate School of Social Work (2019), ranked among the top 20 social work graduate programs nationally, offers both master's and doctoral degrees. In addition to the on-campus master's and PhD programs, which enroll approximately 450 students, GSSW also has satellite campuses in Durango, Colorado (Four Corners MSW program), Glenwood Springs, Colorado (Western Colorado MSW program), and a fully online MSW@DU degree. Students can pursue a range of clinical, policy, and community social work degree concentrations, including aging services and policy, child welfare, family systems practice, mental health, and organizational leadership and policy practice, among others, in addition to certificates in animal-assisted and Latinx social work. The PhD program typically enrolls six students in each cohort. Across its master's and doctoral programs, the school emphasizes a commitment to social justice and preparing its graduates to be agents for social change. As the social sciences librarian, I am the liaison to the GSSW, among other social sciences graduate and undergraduate degree programs at DU, and provide the primary library support for the on-campus, distance, and online GSSW programs through in-person and online instruction and research consultations. The University Libraries Research Center features a tiered approach to reference services, with a research desk staffed by graduate students for answering quick questions (15 minutes or less) and a consultation room where we offer scheduled and walk-in 60-minute research consultations with subject specialist and general librarians (Meyer, Forbes, & Bowers, 2010). This configuration greatly facilitates more in-depth research support that is well suited to systematic review consultations.

Literature Review

Evidence-Based Practice and Social Work Education

The National Association of Social Workers (NASW, 2019) defines EBP as:

a process involving creating an answerable question based on a client or organizational need, locating the best available evidence to answer the question, evaluating the quality of the evidence as well as its applicability, applying the evidence, and evaluating the effectiveness and efficiency of the solution. EBP is a process in which the practitioner combines well-researched interventions with clinical experience, ethics, client preferences, and culture to guide and inform the delivery of treatments and services. (paras. 4–5)

The NASW emphasis on EBP as a process is important, since definitions of evidence can sometimes be misunderstood and the phrase "evidence-*based* has taken on the connotation, by some, to imply that nonresearch factors are not important in the EBP process" (Parrish, 2018, p. 408). Indeed, recognizing the integration of research with client preferences and practitioner experience is consistent with social work values, whereby the client is empowered through collaborative decision making about their treatment (Bender, Altschul, Yoder, Parrish, & Nickels, 2014; Gambrill, 2007). EBP has additional social justice implications since social workers have an ethical obligation to find and apply the best available evidence for their clients, tailored specifically to their cultural and community contexts (Bender et al., 2014; Parrish, 2018; Shlonsky, Baker, & Fuller-Thomson, 2011).

The EBP paradigm has been central to social work since the mid-1990s, and represents a continued trajectory "to forge a service profession grounded in empirical research" (Okpych & Yu, 2014, p. 3). It wasn't until the first part of the 21st century, however, that social work educators began to call for integrating EBP training into graduate curricula (Gambrill, 2007; Howard, Allen-Meares, & Ruffolo, 2007; Howard, Himle, Jenson, & Vaughn, 2009; Howard, McMillen, & Pollio, 2003; Jenson, 2007). Early proponents, such as Howard et al. (2003) from the George Warren Brown School of Social Work at Washington University, called for a new pedagogy for practice education that "fully anticipates and capitalizes on the dramatic accumulation of practice-relevant research findings" (p. 235). To prepare their master's students for EBP, they implemented several changes to the curriculum so that students would value an evidence-based perspective; learn how to select empirically tested interventions or practice methods; understand how social work theories and policies are research-based; deliver empirically supported practice interventions; adapt recommendations from practice guidelines, treatment manuals, and systematic reviews for use with specific clients and agency settings; evaluate the effectiveness of their own practice; and identify their information needs, from developing research questions to finding, appraising, and applying interventions (Howard et al., 2003). Gambrill (2007) offered recommendations for curricular change, in concert with Council on Social Work Education (CSWE) guidelines, that would be grounded in problem-based learning in order to emphasize client-focused, empirically supported decision making.

Since those early articles, EBP has been widely adopted by social work schools and is taught, most commonly, in research methods courses (Bender et al., 2014; Traube, Pohle, & Barley, 2012). The CSWE (2019), the accrediting organization for baccalaureate and master's social work education in the United States, states that "teaching social work students how to access, analyze, interpret, and appropriately employ evidence is critical to effective social work practice" (para. 1), and their standards outline and reinforce these goals (Teater & Chonody, 2018). Recent concerns highlight the need to integrate EBP more broadly into clinical practice courses and field placements, and to form partnerships with service agencies so that "social work students can help bridge the gap between science and service in the community" (Rollo & Kleiner, 2018, p. 1). EBP is seen by many as a way to narrow the divide between research and practice and researchers and practitioners, especially when integrated into both practice and research courses (Drisko, 2014). Doctoral students face different challenges for addressing the research practitioner divide. As Goodman (2015) notes, while

> advancing the principles and methods of science *in* the profession, social work doctoral education must maintain professional values and the transmission of practice knowledge as it develops *for and from* practitioners working in the field. Consequently, integration of both research and practice at the micro- and macrolevels is essential for realizing stewardship in social work. (p. 31)

Guerrero, Moore, and Pitt-Catsouphes (2018) identified EBP as the most prevalent model currently employed in doctoral social work education, with its emphasis on applied research and practice and policy efficacy.

To what extent do social work practitioners believe their education prepared them to implement the EBP model in their professional practice? Several studies have been conducted to assess the perceived impact and applicability of evidence-based methods in real-world settings. Most recently, Teater and Chonody (2018) surveyed social workers in the United States through an online questionnaire to measure their attitudes toward, access to, and confidence in EBP, as well as their educational preparation and identification with the EBP movement. They found that more than 90% of respondents had positive attitudes toward EBP, recognizing its value in practice and its role in the social work curriculum; nevertheless, more than one-third (33.7%) indicated that it was challenging to implement evidence-based social work. Scurlock-Evans and Upton (2015) systematically reviewed research from the United States, Canada, and other Western cultural regions about social workers' EBP attitudes and implementation. Their findings revealed generally positive attitudes about EBP despite some confusion about what is meant exactly by the term *evidence*. They also noted significant facilitators of and barriers to implementing EBP, including positive influences from professional networks and colleagues and individual impediments such as lack of time, training, expertise, and mentoring. Organizational barriers, like an absence of support or funding, limited access to research evidence, and organizational cultures that don't prioritize EBP, as well as systemic factors such as a paucity of research findings for specific practice contexts, likewise impeded implementation.

Whereas many social work practitioners may be supportive of but struggle to integrate EBP fully in their professional work, social work students also appear to be strongly receptive to engaging in EBP, despite some concerns about feasibility (Bender et al., 2014; Knight, 2015; van der Zwet, Weling, Beneken genaamd Kolmer, & Schalk, 2017). Knight (2015) discovered that, while the majority of students at her institution felt prepared to engage in EBP, they also reported limited use of databases or online resources for their practice, not modifying their practice in response to research findings or using interventions and techniques found to be effective, and not consulting the research literature when they had questions about their practice, leading her to conclude that challenges still exist "to help students transfer their understanding of EBP into action" (p. 265). Surveys of social work students in the Netherlands and Israel had similar findings (Shapira, Enosh, & Havron, 2017; van der Zwet et al., 2017). Moreover, Shapira et al. (2017), describing social work students with some work experience, stressed the role of self-efficacy in implementation, stating that "workers who feel relatively confident in their research skills and understanding would make use of EBP-enabling conditions when such are available, whereas those lacking confidence and research knowledge would not" (pp. 195–196). Such observations underscore the continued importance for collaboration between educators and service agencies or organizations to facilitate the transition from EBP taught in the classroom to actualization in professional practice.

Systematic Reviews and the Social Sciences

Systematic reviews and meta-analyses in the social sciences present unique opportunities and specific challenges. Although Lundahl and Yaffe (2007) found that social work was significantly behind psychology and psychiatry in published meta-analyses in 2007, since that time systematic reviews within the field have increased, due in part to their importance for synthesizing research to inform social work practice (Crisp, 2015; McGinn, Taylor, McColgan, & McQuilkan, 2016) even though these review methods are still underutilized (Maynard, Littell, & Shlonsky, 2018). The Campbell Collaboration is the major publisher of systematic reviews in the social sciences and consists of nine coordinating groups: social welfare, crime and justice, education, international development, disability, business and management, knowledge translation and implementation, methods, and food security. Like the Cochrane Collaboration, which sets the gold standard for systematic reviews in medicine and health sciences, Campbell reviews are highly regarded and are essential for enabling "clinicians to accurately inform clients and significant others about the evidentiary status of recommended methods" (Gambrill, 2015, p. 159). Maynard and Dell (2018) determined that Campbell systematic reviews are downloaded and cited frequently, although it was difficult to assess their direct impact on social policy in Europe and the United States.

Searching for Studies: A Guide to Information Retrieval for Campbell Systematic Reviews provides a very useful model for conducting a social sciences review, from suggesting subject databases and other sources to developing search strategies, managing references, and reporting and documenting the search (Kugley et al., 2016). Other case studies offer advice and outline procedures for conducting systematic reviews for the social sciences in general (Papaioannou, Sutton, Carroll, Booth, & Wong, 2010; Siddaway et al., 2019), and in specific social science fields, including social work (Crisp, 2015; McFadden, Taylor, Campbell, & McQuilkin, 2012; McGinn et al., 2016; Shlonsky et al., 2011), crime prevention (Tompson & Belur, 2016), and education (Campbell, Taylor, Bates, & O'Connor-Bones, 2018). These studies also highlight particular challenges for social science systematic reviews, such as finding the right balance between sensitivity and precision, the need for initial test searches in databases, developing a robust list of synonyms to account for diversity of terminology, searching the grey literature, employing alternative search strategies (e.g., citation searching, reference lists, consulting experts), and searching across a wide range of disciplinary and multidisciplinary databases. Crisp (2015) cautions that research relevant for social work topics can be found in many disciplines and that cross-disciplinary coverage can also result in use of variable terminologies for similar topics. Searching specifically for qualitative evidence about intimate partner violence, McGinn et al. (2016) tested the effectiveness of 14 databases and web search engines and concluded, in this case, that *Social Services Abstracts* performed the best for the selected topic, but also recommended *PsycInfo*, *CINAHL*, and *Social Sciences Citation Index* for intervention process questions. Booth (2016) provides further recommendations for identifying research for qualitative systematic reviews, also referred to as qualitative evidence syntheses (QES). Since some social work questions are more appropriately addressed by qualitative studies, or mixed-methods research, practitioners, researchers, and librarian partners will need to be familiar with strategies for conducting systematic reviews that draw on both kinds of evidence. Shlonsky et al. (2011) detail how the use of database methodological search filters aid in making particular methodological studies more easily discoverable and, therefore, recommend that publishers increase their use of methodological descriptors assigned to journal articles. Finally, several authors acknowledge that time and other constraints often make it impractical for social sciences students, practitioners, and others to conduct systematic reviews to the exact standards expected of Campbell and Cochrane reviews, and offer suggestions for controlling the numbers of studies to be screened, minimizing publication bias, and navigating other concerns (Campbell et al., 2018; Siddaway et al., 2019; Tompson & Belur, 2016).

Librarians' Roles in Systematic Reviews

Most of the literature about the librarian's role in supporting systematic reviews is found in health and medical librarianship, despite the fact that systematic reviews in the social sciences have been published for several decades and that guides to conducting these reviews frequently recommend consulting librarians and other information specialists (Kugley et al., 2016; Petticrew & Roberts, 2006). In their scoping review, Spencer and Eldredge (2018) noted that health sciences librarians have been involved with systematic reviews since the 1990s, and they identified 18 roles that these librarians serve in connection with systematic reviews, from developing and evaluating search strategies and identifying databases to assisting with question formulation, protocol development, and teaching others how to perform systematic reviews. Speaking to the advantages of librarian collaboration, Koffel (2015) found that librarian involvement with systematic reviews was associated with higher quality reviews and use of recommended search methods. Some barriers to librarians participating in systematic reviews include time constraints, insufficient training, and lack of subject expertise in the review subject (Murphy & Boden, 2015; Spencer & Eldredge, 2018). Although health sciences and medical librarians most often collaborate with faculty and practitioners to produce systematic reviews, they also support student systematic review assignments and independent systematic reviews (Campbell & Dorgan, 2015; Hanneke, 2018; Wissinger, 2018).

Beyond the health sciences literature, librarian involvement with systematic reviews in the social sciences is being recognized, although articles about these new services are still limited (Foutch, 2016; Gore & Jones, 2015; Johnson, 2018; Kocher & Riegelman, 2018). Writing to help library managers plan for systematic review services, Gore and Jones (2015) noted that these services can generate income for libraries by charging fees for searches, can expand librarians' research output (as coauthors), and can increase the visibility of librarians as expert searchers and research collaborators. They also recommended that managers prepare to address issues about training and mentoring, as well as demands on librarians' time, and that managers decide to what extent librarians should provide assistance to students. Riegelman and Kocher (2018) described their recently launched systematic review service at the University of Minnesota, designed to meet the needs of social sciences faculty and students, which comprises formal systematic review training, expert search training in social sciences and medical databases, and grey literature discovery techniques for team members, in addition to strategies for service promotion and assessment. As the demand for systematic review support in the social sciences becomes more prevalent, the literature will likely reflect how academic libraries and librarians are responding to the needs of their communities.

To date, few articles have specifically addressed librarian support for systematic reviews for social work faculty or graduate students. In Bausman and Laleman Ward's (2016) national survey of social work librarians and information literacy instruction in the United States, 15% of survey respondents indicated that they collaborated with faculty on a research project, systematic review, or professional presentation; however, no further details about systematic review support in particular were provided. Bausman, Pell, and Mulliken (2018) briefly discuss how systematic review techniques can be applied to enhance social work graduate students' literature reviews in general, but conclude that "completing an actual systematic review that adheres to preferred reporting guidelines will be impractical in most programs" (p. 89). Although this is probably true for most master's students, in my experience, doctoral students may conduct full systematic reviews for their dissertations or with faculty teams. I believe that the number of online social work research guides related to EBP and which feature systematic review resources suggest that these services are becoming part of social work librarians' instruction and outreach efforts.

Systematic Review Support at DU

As the social sciences librarian, I have a strong relationship with the Graduate School of Social Work. Library instruction currently consists of orientation sessions focused on introducing students to social work resources and strategies for EBP literature reviews and policy research that are taught each summer to Advanced Standing students (an accelerated master's degree track for social work bachelor's students) and in the fall to incoming master's and doctoral students. I also provide tailored library instruction for specific courses when requested by instructors, for both online and in-person classes, in addition to individual research consultations for students. Although the University of Denver Libraries has no formal systematic review service, social work faculty and doctoral students have acted on their existing relationships with me to reach out for systematic review support.

Systematic review consultations reveal, to an even greater degree, the necessity for collaboration. To be successful, they need to draw on the strengths, experience, and knowledge of both graduate students and the librarian. Librarians can contribute their expertise with developing effective and complex search strategies and their knowledge of database subject coverage, controlled vocabulary, and special features, among other skills, while doctoral students (or faculty) can bring their extensive disciplinary knowledge, research skills, and their practical experience working with and passion for finding the best ways to serve their clients and communities. This collaborative approach is necessary not only for practical reasons, but also amplifies the strengths-sharing and collaborative-based priorities of the University Libraries Research Center and librarian faculty.

I was first contacted for systematic review assistance in the fall of 2015 by a doctoral student and faculty team, who were investigating the effectiveness of youth empowerment programs. That academic year, I worked with two other social work systematic review teams and one team conducting a scoping review. Since that time, I have provided support for three social work doctoral students doing solo systematic reviews, either for an independent study or dissertation; a faculty-student team from the GSSW Institute for Human Animal Connection; and doctoral students from the Psychology and Counseling Psychology departments and the Graduate School of Professional Psychology. In each case, it was the first time for the students to undertake a systematic review, and I approached these consultations as a learning opportunity for both of us. With each consultation, I've gained experience with the systematic review process and have learned important lessons that have been useful for subsequent research consultations.

As noted above, a systematic review contains the following basic elements: defining the research question; determining the search methods; setting inclusion and exclusion criteria; and reporting the results (Crisp, 2015). Within that process, reviewers also need to formulate a search query, which may be tested against and revised after initial scoping searches, and further tailored to specific databases; develop a protocol that describes the rationale, hypothesis, and methods to be employed; identify relevant databases; search the grey literature and employ alternative search methods (e.g., hand-searching journals, contacting experts); export results to a citation manager; document the searches so they can be reported and replicated; and determine the process for how the retrieved studies will be evaluated (against the inclusion and exclusion criteria) and selected for inclusion in the final review (Kugley et al., 2016; Siddaway et al., 2019). Librarians, whether they participate as full systematic review team members (as coauthors) or serve as advisors, typically focus their contribution to the search and retrieval parts of the review process. Foutch (2016), however, described also being involved in the initial review of articles for eligibility, which required training by a team member, so that she could interpret the research results. My efforts so far have been concerned primarily with the search phase of the process.

Formulating a Search Query

Doctoral students usually come to our first meeting with their research question already formulated, either with their team members or on their own, and an initial list of keywords for searching. They may also have a good sense of the extent of literature they expect to find on the topic during their review due to previous research, or it may be a new topic of investigation. Our meeting typically begins then with a discussion about what the individual or team has done so far and then identifies the next steps that we want to accomplish together. First, we look at the research question and break it down into the major concepts and work together to develop relevant search terms, adding to those already identified. At this point we might also search together for an existing, published systematic review or meta-analysis on a similar topic or on one aspect of the research question. Since each systematic review must record the search query, this has proven to be a productive strategy for identifying additional relevant search terms. Next, we review the list of search terms to eliminate redundancy, truncate terms to account for plural and relevant endings, employ quotations or proximity operators for phrase searching (depending on the database search features), use wildcards or include different English spellings of terms (e.g., marginalize or marginalise) and, following some exploratory searching, add relevant database subject headings. Since most systematic reviews aim to be as comprehensive as possible, referred to as *sensitivity*, compiling an extensive list of search terms is crucial. *Specificity*, or relevancy, however, needs to be a balanced part of the equation.

Database Selection

As noted above, social work topics can be very interdisciplinary, so selected search terms need to account for variable disciplinary terminology, which may not be apparent until after conducting initial searches and scanning titles, abstracts, and subject headings from the retrieved results. The cross-disciplinary nature of social work research also factors into database selection. I've worked with students on systematic and scoping reviews that have investigated, for example: toxic stress and the adverse effects of poverty; trauma-informed interventions for adolescents in the juvenile justice system; animal-assisted interventions that affect engagement in mental health services; restorative practice interventions with K–12 youth; and outcomes linked to intergenerational programming. Depending on the specific research topic, the student and I will discuss relevant disciplines and then proceed to identify potential social science, medical, and other databases for searching. At this stage, we also outline strategies for searching beyond subscription databases and note resources for finding grey literature.

Setting Inclusion and Exclusion Criteria

In addition to generating search terms and identifying databases, we also discuss inclusion and exclusion criteria, which are central to keeping the searching as relevant as possible and maintaining a sensitivity and specificity balance. The student often has an initial list of potential criteria that will define the review scope, which may include language, publication date range, research design, measures or key variables, and data (such as effect size), among other considerations (Siddaway et al., 2019). Siddaway et al. (2019) caution that inclusion and exclusion criteria should be established only on the research question at hand and not revised after searching; however, they also acknowledge that, depending on the reviewers' level of experience, it may be necessary to make postsearch adjustments. Furthermore, they note that inclusion and exclusion criteria will need to be justified based on theoretically and empirically defensible grounds and that appropriate steps are taken to avoid potential bias. In my experience, students often need to revise the initial criteria after trying the search and applying the criteria in different databases in order to create a more relevant search (increase specificity) or to work within practical constraints. For example, after retrieving thousands of possible hits from just one database with the selected search query, the student and I revised the search to make it more precise while still keeping it reflective of the research question and criteria decisions.

Developing a Protocol

The search terms and query, databases, and inclusion and exclusion criteria comprise my collaborative contribution to the student's or team's systematic review search protocol. Protocols are written and often registered before searching begins; some are officially registered with an organization such as PROSPERO, an international register of systematic reviews in health and social care, welfare, education, crime, and international development with a health outcome. Registering the protocol is recommended to avoid duplication and to reduce reporting bias (PROSPERO, n.d.). The PRISMA (Preferred Reporting Items for Systematic Reviews and Meta-Analyses) website (2015) provides a 27-item checklist that outlines elements to consider when planning the protocol, although its main purpose is to guide writing the final report, and the PRISMA flow diagram is a template for documenting the systematic review search, retrieval, and eligibility screening process. Most of the students I've worked with are aware of the PRISMA guidelines and, to my knowledge, they all prepare a protocol; however, I'm not certain if these are formally registered or not. At our first meeting, I might also suggest to students general resources for conducting a systematic review.

Exporting Sources to a Citation Manager

Students often return for a follow-up consultation or continue to ask for advice by e-mail. Managing numerous citations is of paramount concern, and we discuss strategies and citation management tools at the first meeting, but this becomes more of an issue after searches are conducted and citations retrieved. In particular, students frequently have questions about how to export hundreds of citations at one time from databases and how to organize the results.

EBP and the Systematic Review Assignment

In addition to supporting doctoral students conducting systematic reviews, I have also partnered with the lead instructor of the foundation year social work class, "Evidence for Practice," to enhance an existing abbreviated systematic review assignment and to develop online supportive materials. The course fosters master's students' skills in identifying, analyzing, and applying empirical evidence, and encourages them to critically examine evidence for biases and relevancy to the specific clients, populations, and contexts they encounter in their practice. "Evidence for Practice" is a multisection course and is offered throughout the academic year for both in-person and online students. With these goals in mind, the students work during the quarter on a mock systematic review that scaffolds them through the key steps of the review process.

The first step is for the students to write a strong, well-formulated, research question using the PICO(S) model, which organizes the clinical question into its four, and occasionally five, main elements: **P**atient/**P**opulation (client type and/or problem); **I**ntervention (what you might do); **C**omparison (alternative course of action); **O**utcome (what you want to accomplish); and **S**tudy type. COPES (client-oriented, practical, evidence search) is another question formulation model that is used in social work and which is comprised of the same elements. The next stages guide the students through brainstorming synonyms, constructing a search query with Boolean operators, and identifying relevant subscription and publicly available databases for their research questions, and following up with additional sources or search methods, such as checking a clearinghouse or registry, reviewing journal tables of contents, or consulting a librarian or subject expert. Students keep track of their searches and results with a search history table in order to document their process, revisions, and evaluation decisions. Students are reminded to construct searches to find studies that are specific to their question and that are also highest on the evidence research hierarchy, which places systematic reviews, meta-analyses, and practice guidelines at the top, followed by experimental studies (randomized controlled trials and quasi-experimental studies), then observational studies (case control and cohort), with the last rungs comprising preexperimental group studies, surveys, and qualitative studies. After the searches, students summarize what they found and answer questions about the research designs most commonly used for the topic and the research placement on the effectiveness hierarchy; which populations were addressed or left out; and how the databases or other sources performed in terms of providing useful evidence. Finally, the students select four articles or sources that represent the best evidence relevant to their question and evaluate those sources for the quality of study execution and fit for population and context, including describing the sample size and characteristics, methodological design, threats to internal validity, and key findings as they pertain to the question.

From my experience, I've found that the biggest challenge some students face is finding systematic reviews, meta-analyses, practice guidelines, and randomized controlled trials (sources considered the best evidence), which may not exist for certain types of social work questions or topics. This is a recognized problem within evidence-based social work, where randomized controlled trials may not be possible due to ethical concerns, or where the majority of studies are qualitative in nature (Crisp, 2015; Drisko, 2014; Howard et al., 2009; Traube et al., 2012). Although qualitative systematic reviews are becoming more common, they still aren't as prevalent in the published literature as those comparing quantitative studies. Students researching topics such as high school college preparation programs for first-generation college students, or intergenerational programming, might have more difficulty finding evidence than those investigating the effectiveness of substance abuse, bullying, or suicide prevention interventions, which are more frequently assessed by quantitative studies. Likewise, students interested in investigating newer interventions or programs that haven't been assessed extensively might not find enough published studies yet, and will have to bring in related research.

In addition to addressing practical issues and challenges, research consultations with students in the "Evidence for Practice" class and, to some extent, doctoral students conducting systematic reviews, can provide emotional support. Students may need an empathetic listener to let them express their frustration with the assignment, or to express their disappointment that a topic about which they are very passionate has yet to be studied extensively by the field. Some students may feel anxious about their research skills, and the consultations can be an opportunity either to strengthen or affirm their abilities and thereby boost their confidence, setting them up for future research-intensive assignments. Doctoral students conducting their own systematic reviews may also need advice about what is possible to accomplish; if they are faced with time or other constraints (such as those for an independent study or for an upcoming grant deadline) that might prohibit pursuing a full systematic review, proposing alternatives, such as a scoping or rapid review, might be a better option (Crisp, 2015; Grant & Booth, 2009).

Recommendations for Supporting Student Systematic Reviews

Subject librarians are generally very knowledgeable about the best ways to support their student communities through instruction, reference consultations, online research guides, video tutorials, and other methods. Providing systematic review support can be incorporated into these traditional efforts but may also benefit from the following suggestions.

Training

Unless educated to be a medical librarian, it is likely that librarians will need additional training on how to conduct a systematic review in order to understand the elements, process, and specific requirements. The Campbell Collaboration offers a series of Introductory Methods training videos that cover the basic elements of a systematic review, including problem formulation, literature searching, coding, effect size calculation and basic meta-analysis, and an introduction to meta-analysis, all of which were recorded during the 2011 and 2013 Campbell Colloquia. The Campbell Collaboration website presents additional training materials and also advertises upcoming online training opportunities. In their article about developing a systematic review service at their library, Riegelman and Kocher (2018) opted to bring in an outside expert for a two-day, in-person training for their systematic review team and other interested library staff members. The team supplemented that training with sessions led by subject librarians, or other expert searchers, on advanced search techniques for education, psychology, medical, and agriculture databases, in addition to grey literature discovery. Learning advanced search techniques from colleagues about social sciences databases outside one's area of expertise is highly recommended. Moreover, librarians should be sure to learn the differences in and strategies for conducting quantitative and qualitative systematic reviews. Although intended for medical reviews, Sampson et al. (2009) have published guidelines for peer reviewing search strategies, which could be used either as a tool for evaluating librarian-generated search strategies, or integrated into library systematic review services generally. Finally, librarians should also become familiar with reporting requirements, protocol registries, systematic review tools, and the principal disciplinary databases (Kocher & Riegelman, 2018). See the recommended resources section in Appendix 9.1 of this chapter.

Workshops

Offering systematic review workshops for the university community has several benefits. A well-designed workshop can introduce attendees (whether students or faculty) to the process and resources for conducting a systematic review, so that they are either better prepared to proceed on their own, or have a solid foundation when they meet with a librarian for a consultation. Campbell, Kung, and Dennett (2016) established the following outcomes for their student workshop on systematic reviews: identify systematic reviews and distinguish them from other reviews; understand the range of resources required for a systematic search; develop a well-formulated PICO(S) question; know how to apply appropriate limits; document the search; understand the importance of peer reviewing the search; and recognize the level of expert searching required for a systematic review. Workshops can focus on the searching phases of a systematic review, with recommended strategies and resources, or can present an overview of the entire process, depending on the knowledge and skills of the librarian. It might also be effective to coteach the workshop with a faculty member who has systematic review experience and who can provide insights and practical recommendations. Additional advantages to workshops comprise educating the university community about librarian support for systematic reviews in the social sciences. A workshop is also an excellent way to bring together doctoral students from different social sciences departments on campus who may be writing systematic review dissertations. These students are often isolated and can benefit from the opportunity to share experiences, frustrations, and recommendations with other graduate students. Parker and Neilson (2015) described creating several tools to support asynchronous learning, including a quick reference chart, or cheat-sheet, for database descriptions and features, a comprehensive guide for less experienced learners that includes screen shots, and a video tutorial, the most comprehensive of the three tools. These types of materials could be developed to enhance workshop content and offer additional support to researchers.

Determining Levels of Support

Medical and health sciences librarians often work on systematic review teams where they are entirely responsible for the literature searching, and may also be involved in exporting and screening records (Gore & Jones, 2015). This type of support can be extremely time consuming, is often conducted for a fee, and may not be feasible for social sciences subject librarians who often liaison to several departments for which they provide instruction, reference, and collection development support (Gore & Jones, 2015). Depending on the size of the institution and the number of subject librarians, existing commitments, and other factors, librarians will need to consider what level of systematic review support is practical and feasible. This may entail establishing a systematic review service carried out by a team of librarians, such as that described by Riegelman and Kocher (2018), or librarians may incorporate systematic review consultations into their current liaison reference support. In either case, it is important to set the expectations and boundaries for what role the librarian will serve on the review and the extent of the service (Gore & Jones, 2015). At the University of Denver Libraries, we have a teaching mission, and so it is more in line with our goals to guide students with how and where to search, rather than doing the searches for them.

Promotion of Services

Once the level of service to be provided is established, promoting systematic review services can be addressed. Riegelman and Kocher (2018) set both internal (library) and external (university) communication plans to inform people about the role of the service and to promote it to faculty and researchers. They developed a library webpage, advertised in the campus newsletter, and contacted individual researchers who had published systematic reviews at their institution. Although they mentioned students as the recipients of the newsletter, their promotion efforts were targeted primarily to faculty and researchers. Additional suggestions for reaching students would be to contact the dean or lead instructor for doctoral education and promoting the service on graduate student and departmental listservs. Riegelman and Kocher (2018) advised taking a gradual approach to institution promotion so as not to be overwhelmed with consultation requests, since they anticipated supporting reviews that could range from a single consultation to those lasting up to several months or years long.

Conclusion

Preparing graduate social work students for EBP is an integral goal of social work education and should be supported by the subject librarian. In this role, the librarian can partner with social work faculty to introduce students to strategies for identifying, evaluating, and applying research studies and syntheses to better serve their clients and communities, not only during their educational program but especially once they are established practitioners or faculty members themselves. Future employers are likely to value social workers who are confident and accomplished searchers, who know how to use and to think critically about the evidence, and who also understand the challenges and complexities that encompass evidence-based practice, or evidence-informed practice in real-world settings.

Although most graduates of social work programs will not be required to conduct systematic reviews themselves, having the experience of performing an abbreviated systematic review strengthens their search skills and introduces them to techniques for finding relevant evidential resources, whether those are published systematic reviews or research studies that they can use to inform their work. Social work doctoral students are conducting full systematic reviews more frequently, either for their dissertation, or with faculty in their department as part of a systematic review team. Knowing how to produce a systematic review will provide them with valuable experience that will serve them well in multiple ways as future faculty members, whether for research projects, community partnerships, or grant applications. As systematic reviews become increasingly common in the social sciences, librarians can embrace this opportunity to collaborate with our students and faculty in new ways that not only make use of our expertise with search query construction, database searching, and bibliographic citation managers but also expand our roles to become advisors and active partners in research endeavors.

References

Bausman, M., & Laleman Ward, S. (2016). The social work librarian and information literacy instruction: A report on a national survey in the United States. *Behavioral & Social Sciences Librarian, 35*(3), 109–122. doi:10.1080/01639269.2016.1243439

Bausman, M., Pell, J., & Mulliken, A. (2018). Library services and resources in graduate-level social work education. In C. Renfro & C. Stiles (Eds.), *Transforming libraries to serve graduate students* (pp. 85–101). Chicago, IL: Association of College and Research Libraries.

Bender, K., Altschul, I., Yoder, J., Parrish, D., & Nickels, S. J. (2014). Training social work graduate students in the evidence-based practice process. *Research on Social Work Practice, 24*(3), 339–348. doi:10.1177/1049731513506614

Booth, A. (2016). Searching for qualitative research for inclusion in systematic reviews: A structured methodological review. *Systematic Reviews, 5*(1), 74–97. doi:10.1186/s13643-016-0249-x

Bureau of Labor Statistics, U.S. Department of Labor. (2019, April). Social workers. *Occupational Outlook Handbook.* Retrieved from https://www.bls.gov/ooh/community-and-social-service/social-workers.htm

Campbell, A., Taylor, B., Bates, J., & O'Connor-Bones, U. (2018). Developing and applying a protocol for a systematic review in the social sciences. *New Review of Academic Librarianship, 24*(1), 1–22. doi:10.1080/13614533.2017.1281827

Campbell, S., & Dorgan, M. (2015). What to do when everyone wants you to collaborate: Managing the demand for library support in systematic review searching. *Journal of the Canadian Health Libraries Association/Journal de l'Association des bibliothèques de la santé du Canada, 36*(1), 11–19. doi:10.29173/jchla/jabsc.v36i1.24353

Campbell, S. M., Kung, J. Y. C., & Dennett, L. (2016). A curriculum for introductory systematic review searching for researchers. *Journal of the Canadian Health Libraries Association/Journal de l'Association des bibliothèques de la santé du Canada, 37*(1), 2–5. doi:10.5596/c16-003

Council on Social Work Education. (2019). *Teaching evidence-based practice (EBP)*. Retrieved from https://www.cswe.org/Centers-Initiatives/Initiatives/Teaching-Evidence-Based-Practice

Crisp, B. R. (2015). Systematic reviews: A social work perspective. *Australian Social Work, 68*(3), 1–12. doi:10.1080/0312407X.2015.1024266

Drisko, J. (2014). Split or synthesis: The odd relationship between clinical practice and research in social work and in social work education. *Clinical Social Work Journal, 42*(2), 182–192. doi:10.1007/s10615-014-0493-2

Foutch, L. J. (2016). A new partner in the process: The role of a librarian on a faculty research team. *Collaborative Librarianship, 8*(2), 80–83.

Gambrill, E. (2007). Transparency as the route to evidence-informed professional education. *Research on Social Work Practice, 17*(5), 553–560. doi:10.1177/1049731507300149

Gambrill, E. (2015). Avoidable ignorance and the role of Cochrane and Campbell reviews. *Research on Social Work Practice, 25*(1), 147–163. doi:10.1177/1049731514533731

Goodman, H. (2015). Current issues in social work doctoral education. *Journal of Teaching in Social Work, 35*(1–2), 29–45. doi:10.1080/08841233.2015.1007802

Gore, G. C., & Jones, J. (2015). Systematic reviews and librarians: A primer for managers. *Partnership: The Canadian Journal of Library and Information Practice and Research, 10*(1), 1–16. doi:10.21083/partnership.v10i1.3343

Graduate School of Social Work, University of Denver. (2019). *A social work degree with a social justice focus*. Retrieved from https://socialwork.du.edu/academics/master-social-work-programs

Grant, M. J., & Booth, A. (2009). A typology of reviews: An analysis of 14 review types and associated methodologies. *Health Information & Libraries Journal, 26*(2), 91–108. doi:10.1111/j.1471-1842.2009.00848.x

Guerrero, E. G., Moore, H., & Pitt-Catsouphes, M. (2018). A scientific framework for social work doctoral education in the 21st century. *Research on Social Work Practice, 28*(3), 243–253. doi:10.1177/1049731517709077

Hanneke, R. (2018). The hidden benefits of helping students with systematic reviews. *Journal of the Medical Library Association, 106*(2), 244–247. doi:10.5195/jmla.2018.420

Howard, M. O., Allen-Meares, P., & Ruffolo, M. C. (2007). Teaching evidence-based practice: Strategic and pedagogical recommendations for schools of social work. *Research on Social Work Practice, 17*(5), 561–568. doi:10.1177/1049731507300191

Howard, M. O., Himle, J., Jenson, J. M., & Vaughn, M. G. (2009). Revisioning social work clinical education: Recent developments in relation to evidence-based practice. *Journal of Evidence-Based Social Work, 6*(3), 256–273. doi:10.1080/15433710802686963

Howard, M. O., McMillen, C. J., & Pollio, D. E. (2003). Teaching evidence-based practice: Toward a new paradigm for social work education. *Research on Social Work Practice, 13*(2), 234–259. doi:10.1177/1049731502250404

Jenson, J. M. (2007). Evidence-based practice and the reform of social work education: A response to Gambrill and Howard and Allen-Meares. *Research on Social Work Practice, 17*(5), 569–573. doi:10.1177/1049731507300236

Johnson, A. (2018). Connections, conversations, and visibility: How the work of academic reference and liaison librarians is evolving. *Reference & User Services Quarterly, 58*(2), 91–102. doi:10.5860/rusq,58.2.6929

Knight, C. (2015). Social work students' use of the peer-reviewed literature and engagement in evidence-based practice. *Journal of Social Work Education, 51*(2), 250–269. doi:10.1080/10437797.2015.1012924

Kocher, M., & Riegelman, A. (2018). Systematic reviews and evidence synthesis: Resources beyond the health sciences. *College & Research Libraries News, 79*(5), 248–252. doi:10.5860/crln.79.5.248

Koffel, J. B. (2015). Use of recommended search strategies in systematic reviews and the impact of librarian involvement: A cross-sectional survey of recent authors. *PloS One, 10*(5), e0125931. doi:10.1371/journal.pone.0125931

Kugley, S., Wade, A., Thomas, J., Mahood, Q., Jørgensen, A. K., Hammerstrøm, K., & Sathe, N. (2016). *Searching for studies: A guide to information retrieval for Campbell systematic reviews.* Campbell Methods Guides. doi:10.4073/cmg.2016.1

Lundahl, B., & Yaffe, J. (2007). Use of meta-analysis in social work and allied disciplines. *Journal of Social Service Research, 33*(3), 1–11. doi:10.1300/J079v33n03_01

Maynard, B. R., & Dell, N. A. (2018). Use and impacts of Campbell systematic reviews on policy, practice, and research. *Research on Social Work Practice, 28*(1), 13–18. doi:10.1177/1049731517722637

Maynard, B. R., Littell, J. H., & Shlonsky, A. (2018). Introduction to the special issue on Campbell Collaboration systematic reviews. *Research on Social Work Practice, 28*(1), 3–5. doi:10.1177/1049731517722638

McFadden, P., Taylor, B. J., Campbell, A., & McQuilkin, J. (2012). Systematically identifying relevant research: Case study on child protection social workers' resilience. *Research on Social Work Practice, 22*(6), 626–636. doi:10.1177/1049731512453209

McGinn, T., Taylor, B., McColgan, M., & McQuilkan, J. (2016). Social work literature searching: Current issues with databases and online search engines. *Research on Social Work Practice, 26*(3), 266–277. doi:10.1177/1049731514549423

Meyer, E., Forbes, C., & Bowers, J. (2010). The research center: Creating an environment for interactive research consultations. *Reference Services Review, 38*(1), 57–70. doi:10.1108/00907321011020725

Murphy, S. A., & Boden, C. (2015). Benchmarking participation of Canadian university health sciences librarians in systematic reviews. *Journal of the Medical Library Association, 103*(2), 73–78. doi:10.3163/1536-5050.103.2.003

National Association of Social Workers. (2019). *Evidence-based practice.* Retrieved from https://www.socialworkers.org/News/Research-Data/Social-Work-Policy-Research/Evidence-Based-Practice

Okpych, N. J., & Yu, J. L. (2014). A historical analysis of evidence-based practice in social work: The unfinished journey toward an empirically grounded profession. *Social Service Review, 88*(1), 3–58. doi:10.1086/674969

Papaioannou, D., Sutton, A., Carroll, C., Booth, A., & Wong, R. (2010). Literature searching for social science systematic reviews: Consideration of a range of search techniques. *Health Information & Libraries Journal, 27*(2), 114–122. doi:10.1111/j.1471-1842.2009.00863.x

Parker, R. M., & Neilson, M. J. (2015). Lost in translation: Supporting learners to search comprehensively across databases. *Journal of the Canadian Health Libraries Association/Journal de l'Association des bibliothèques de la santé du Canada, 36*(2), 54–58. doi:10.5596/c15-014

Parrish, D. E. (2018). Evidence-based practice: A common definition matters. *Journal of Social Work Education, 54*(3), 407–411. doi:10.1080/10437797.2018.1498691

Petticrew, M., & Roberts, H. (2006). *Systematic reviews in the social sciences: A practical guide.* Malden, MA: Blackwell.

PRISMA. (2015). Retrieved from http://www.prisma-statement.org

PROSPERO. (n.d.). Retrieved from https://www.crd.york.ac.uk/prospero

Riegelman, A., & Kocher, M. (2018). For your enrichment: A model for developing and implementing a systematic review service for disciplines outside of the health sciences. *Reference & User Services Quarterly, 58*(1), 22–27. doi:10.5860/rusq.58.1.6837

Rollo, C. M., & Kleiner, D. A. (2018). From clinic to classroom: Creating evidence-based practice champions in a graduate social work program. *Journal of Social Work Education, 54*(Suppl. 1), 76–89. doi:10.1080/10437797.2018.1434435

Sampson, M., McGowan, J., Cogo, E., Grimshaw, J., Moher, D., & Lefebvre, C. (2009). An evidence-based practice guideline for the peer review of electronic search strategies. *Journal of Clinical Epidemiology, 62*(9), 944–952. doi:10.1016/j.jclinepi.2008.10.012

Scurlock-Evans, L., & Upton, D. (2015). The role and nature of evidence: A systematic review of social workers' evidence-based practice orientation, attitudes, and implementation. *Journal of Evidence-Informed Social Work, 12*(4), 1–31. doi:10.1080/15433714.2013.853014

Shapira, Y., Enosh, G., & Havron, N. (2017). What makes social work students implement evidence-based practice behaviors? *Journal of Social Work Education, 53*(2), 187–200. doi:10.1080/10437797.2016.1260507

Shlonsky, A., Baker, T., & Fuller-Thomson, E. (2011). Using methodological search filters to facilitate evidence-based social work practice. *Clinical Social Work Journal, 39*(4), 390–399. doi:10.1007/s10615-010-0312-3

Siddaway, A. P., Wood, A. M., & Hedges, L. V. (2019). How to do a systematic review: A best practice guide for conducting and reporting narrative reviews, meta-analyses, and meta-syntheses. *Annual Review of Psychology, 70,* 747–770. doi:10.1146/annurev-psych-010418-102803

Spencer, A. J., & Eldredge, J. D. (2018). Roles for librarians in systematic reviews: A scoping review. *Journal of the Medical Library Association, 106*(1), 46–56. doi:10.5195/jmla.2018.82

Teater, B., & Chonody, J. M. (2018). Identifying as an evidence-based social worker: The influence of attitudes, access, confidence, and education. *Social Work Education, 37*(4), 442–457. doi:10.1080/02615479.2017.1421161

Tompson, L., & Belur, J. (2016). Information retrieval in systematic reviews: A case study of the crime prevention literature. *Journal of Experimental Criminology, 12*(2), 187–207. doi:10.1007/s11292-015-9243-x

Traube, D. E., Pohle, C. E., & Barley, M. (2012). Teaching evidence-based social work in foundation practice courses: Learning from pedagogical choices of allied fields. *Journal of Evidence-Based Social Work, 9*(3), 241–259. doi:10.1080/15433714.2010.525417

University of Denver. (2017, Fall). *Factbook: Institutional quick facts.* Retrieved from https://www.du.edu/ir/factbook/index.html

van der Zwet, R. J., Weling, J., Beneken genaamd Kolmer, D. M., & Schalk, R. (2017). Exploring MSW students' and social workers' orientation toward the evidence-based practice process. *Social Work Education, 36*(1), 75–87. doi:10.1080/02615479.2016.1266321

Wissinger, C. (2018). Is there a place for undergraduate and graduate students in the systematic review process? *Journal of the Medical Library Association, 106*(2), 248–250. doi:10.5195/jmla.2018.387

Appendix 9.1: Selected Resources

Books

Boland, A., Cherry, M., & Dickson, R. (Eds.). (2017). *Doing a systematic review: A student's guide* (2nd ed.). Los Angeles, CA: Sage Publications.

Cooper, H. (2017). *Research synthesis and meta-analysis: A step-by-step approach* (5th ed.). Los Angeles, CA: Sage Publications.

Gough, D., Oliver, S., & Thomas, J. (Eds.). (2017). *An introduction to systematic reviews* (2nd ed.). Los Angeles, CA: Sage Publications.

Petticrew, M., & Roberts, H. (2006). *Systematic reviews in the social sciences: A practical guide*. Malden, MA: Blackwell Publishing.

Websites (and Databases)

Campbell Collaboration: https://www.campbellcollaboration.org

Searching for Studies: A Guide to Information Retrieval for Campbell Systematic Reviews

https://www.campbellcollaboration.org/information-retrieval-guides

Campbell Collaboration: The Introductory Methods

https://campbellcollaboration.org/the-introductory-methods.html

Cochrane Library of Systematic Reviews

https://www.cochranelibrary.com

EPPI (Evidence for Policy and Practice Information) Centre Knowledge Library

http://eppi.ioe.ac.uk/cms/Publications/Indexofsystematicreviewtopics/tabid/60/Default.aspx

PRISMA

http://www.prisma-statement.org

PROSPERO

https://www.crd.york.ac.uk/prospero

Sage Research Methods

http://methods.sagepub.com

Trip Database

https://www.tripdatabase.com

Empowering Graduate Students as Distance Learners: Access, Relevance, and Success

Yi Ding and Melissa A. Rassibi

Introduction

Graduate students and distance learners are two groups of underrepresented students for information literacy education. Although it might be commonly recognized among librarians that graduate students who are emerging professionals need a set of information literacy skills to succeed in their academic work, providing information literacy education that is easily accessible, highly relevant, and as a result beneficial for their career development is also considered challenging for many librarians. The challenges are even more evident when these graduate students are distant learners, which poses additional hurdles for high-quality information literacy education due to, not only constraints in time, space, and technology, but also the multiple roles these distance learners play that may limit their ability to access and utilize the information literacy and library services available for traditional graduate students.

Bearing in mind this unique student population, our Learning Management System (LMS) team at the California State University Northridge (CSUN) library spearheaded a collaboration with instructional designers from our distance learning college to create an information literacy module for graduate students who are distance learners. During the process, we considered different learning styles and needs, guided by theories of distance learners and universal design that inform the whole design process, as well as our selection of content and technology. Our goal was to design the kind of online information literacy education that is accessible, relevant, and conducive to the success of distance graduate students in professional life. The multiple roles these students play also made the design project a perfect opportunity for our LMS team to reflect on and thus create more inclusive library services that benefit the overall success of graduate students on our campus.

Background

CSUN is located within the Los Angeles environs. It is the second largest public master's level institution in the country. With more than 38,000 students from 93 countries, it is a designated Hispanic Serving Institution (HSI) and Asian American Native American Pacific Islander Serving Institution (AANAPISI), enrolls the largest number of deaf and hard-of-hearing students of any U.S. state university, and has been ranked by the *Wall Street Journal* as the second most diverse university in the nation. CSUN is a social elevator serving more students on Pell Grants than any other institution in California. It is a majority minority university with 52.6% of undergraduates reporting as Latinx. The top three reported categories of race and ethnicity among graduate students are white (34.9%), Latinx (33.8%), and Asian (10.3%) with 64.9% of graduate students reporting as female. The Tseng College for Graduate, International and Professional Education specializes in developing graduate-degree and certificate programs that prepare mid-career adults for advancement in rapidly growing fields. Tseng College offers 12 master's degrees, primarily online. The Oviatt Library is the heart of the CSUN campus, serving all 38,000 plus students through one central location and online.

Literature Review

Practitioners and researchers in higher education have been exploring ways to better educate distance, adult, and nontraditional learners for decades. Specifically, when describing the graduate student population at Tseng College, instructional designers indicated they are usually nontraditional students, who enter the program with life experiences and work responsibilities while in the program. Therefore, in the design of the information literacy modules, our LMS team has applied learning theories of not only distance learners, but also adult learners and nontraditional students. In particular, we take into consideration what has been the focus of literature around adult learning, andragogy, a theoretical framework developed by Knowles (1984).

In recent literature about library instruction for adult learners, andragogical learning was recognized by many librarians when developing instruction programs. The unique characteristics of adult learners were taken into consideration. Caravello (2001) described some effective activity learning exercises in an information literacy course. Simmonds (2001) summarized the feedback from adult students, faculty, and administrators on the needs for library instruction. Fox (2001) talked about providing remote access to both library collections and services. Turcotte (2015) examined the common struggle of adult learners with technology. While in an extensive literature review, Gold (2005) discovered "a lack of administrative guidance or support beyond the library" (p. 470); it is noticeable that all articles emphasized the room for improvement on the libraries' side to provide resources and guidance both about technology and research.

In terms of distance learning, although there are abundant articles investigating strategies to design online learning experiences (Shea, Fredericksen, Pickett, & Pelz, 2003), there are few about library modules. Even among those that address library instruction, they were usually supporting for-credit library courses (Finch & Jefferson, 2013), instead of courses with only one-shot library sessions or even those without a librarian presence at all. There are also articles about general suggestions on improving the library's role in online learning (Fletcher & Stewart, 2001; Lippincott, 2005). Lastly, most of the above mentioned literature on adult learning discussed regular students instead of distance learners.

Therefore, this chapter aims to look into the development of an online information literacy module in a course from the perspectives of both distance learners and adult learners.

Universal Design for Learning

Most education is developed for the average learner. Identical instructional methods and content are seen as equal, and modifications are sometimes considered an advantage for those students for whom they are made. Educators who make these modifications are accused of not treating their students equally. But as we are constantly discovering, there is high variability in learning. Treating all students the same is unfair as all students are not the same—neither do they learn the same way. Furthermore, often the obstacles and hindrances to learning are not the material itself, but the tools and methods used to present the subject matter. In the past, a heavy reliance on textbooks and other print materials stood as a barrier to students with any print disability. Rapid advances in technology have helped to eliminate some of these barriers by rendering print materials accessible and allowing for the easier creation of multimedia learning objects.

We have seen that teaching to students' strengths and intelligences is more effective than supplementing for their weaknesses. Gay (2018) illustrates this with students from typically marginalized racial and ethnic backgrounds, while Meyer, Rose, and Gordon (2014) do so for students with identified learning disabilities. Although it is important to treat students as individuals, it is neither practical nor even possible to teach to the learning strengths of each individual learner.

Fortunately, learning variability is highly predictable and can be addressed systematically along three networks of neural systems: the affective, the recognition, and the strategic (Meyer et al., 2014, p. 42). The affective encompasses the emotional part of learning, or the learner's motivation: the learner needs to want to learn the material. Recognition addresses how the learner internalizes the content, drawing from patterns that help them make sense of the new input. Differences in experience, age, racial, ethnic, and socioeconomic background can all influence the learners' ability to recall (or not recall) background content that helps contextualize the information. And strategy refers to the learners' ability to self-regulate, to make and adjust goals toward the comprehension of new content.

Universal Design for Learning (UDL) draws from a multiyear review of thousands of research articles on how the brain learns, as well as effective teaching practices to provide a framework to address learner variability systematically using knowledge about these three neural networks. It is furthermore based on the advantages brought about by the rapid developments in technology and the field of Universal Design for products and architecture. It holds the tenet that what is "essential for some" is almost always "good for all" (Meyer et al., 2014, p. 51). An example of this can be seen in captioned videos. Learners with different hearing abilities cannot fully access the content of a video that is not captioned. For them captioning is essential. But other learners, including non-native speakers, learners with poor verbal reasoning, learners in noisy environments, and learners who need to access the content without sound, can access the content to a fuller extent with the addition of captions.

The ultimate goal of UDL is to produce expert learners, who know their own strengths and intelligences and are able to regulate their own learning in order to become highly motivated, resourceful, and strategic. Although previous instructional methods have been curriculum centered, UDL attempts to remove all hindrances and obstacles presented by teaching methods and tools to put the focus on the learner. In other words, instead of making modification for learners who are unable to access content to the fullest extent, it mandates the creation of curriculum that accounts for the needs of all users, with no subsequent needs for adjustments or modifications.

To enable educators to do this, UDL presents a framework that is not prescriptive but instructional, one that helps educators keep in mind the highly predictable and systematic variability in learning to ensure they are not introducing hindrances in learning through the material, tools, and methods they use. Each guideline—multiple means of representation, multiple means of action and expression, and multiple means of engagement—addresses one of the three neural systems and provides effective practices for each of these guidelines based on existing research. Enacting these guidelines accounts for most learner variability, thereby providing a possible solution for getting every learner to their destination.

Supporting Distance Learners at CSUN

Unlike all other departments at CSUN, there is no assigned liaison librarian supporting the academic needs of Tseng graduate students. Few librarians have provided any type of information literacy support to the college either virtually or physically. Although currently the instructional designers at Tseng College have designed and incorporated into the Learning Management System (LMS), Canvas, a page on library resources, it is a single page on general library services.

Understanding the Need

In the spring of 2018, we contacted the director of distance learning of Tseng College to inquire about a partnership between our two departments. We were referred to one of Tseng College's instructional designers, and subsequently met with the e-learning technology manager to discuss the possibility of creating a series of information literacy modules to be used by students during their orientation, as well as a resource for students to reference while conducting research assignments for their classes. Both of Tseng College's instructional designers, as instructors in multiple cohorts, had previously created modules on information literacy because research was a crucial component of most programs offered through Tseng. As was previously mentioned, there was no liaison librarian working with the Tseng College instructional designers on creating these modules, and, therefore, the modules were not frequently updated. The content was based on the previous ACRL Standards (2000), and, although accessible, was targeted toward the average learner.

The library's LMS team distributed an e-mail survey to all Tseng College faculty. Responses from a variety of departments indicated a need for various information literacy support for Tseng students, such as developing research strategies, effectively using databases, evaluating information, and creating citations. From this enthusiastic response, we began our partnership with Tseng College, developing a series of information literacy modules targeted at distance learning graduate students.

Developing Learning Goals

Creating inclusive content that promotes success among users with varied learning abilities and preferences begins with developing inclusive learning goals. Meyer et al. (2014) state that ineffective learning goals confound actual goals with the methods and tools used to impart them. To avoid this, they encourage being "tight on goals but loose on means" (Meyer et al., 2014, p. 98). It is imperative then that goals refer only to the content to be mastered without specifying how.

In developing learning goals for the information literacy modules for Tseng College, we referred to the needs of the specific students as expressed by the college's lead instructional designers, feedback from the teaching faculty as collected by the survey, and pertinent domain knowledge as informed by the standards of the Association of College and Research Libraries (ACRL). In 2016, the previous ACRL *Information Literacy Competency Standards for Higher Education* were replaced by the ACRL *Framework for Information Literacy for Higher Education*. Although the previous standards could sometimes be characterized as limiting, due to their prescriptive manner, the *Framework*, in the same spirit as UDL, provides a loose structure that can be used to inform the instructional goals of various institutions, without delineating specific tasks that fulfill those standards or specific tools or methods to impart them. Thus, learning goals were structured by the *Framework* in conjunction with the specific needs of the Tseng graduate students without mention of tools or methods. The following learning goals were developed for the Tseng College information literacy modules: "Using the Library;" "Improving your Search Results;" "Evaluating Information Sources;" "Finding Better Information with Google;" and "Crediting your Sources." Each learning goal was associated with an individual module that could stand alone by itself or be used in conjunction with the other modules. Each individual module utilized student learning outcomes that did not stipulate methods or tools.

Designing an Inclusive Learning Environment

Multiple Means of Engagement

The affective network deals with the emotional part of the brain. Addressing variability in learning means providing multiple methods of motivation or engagement, thereby causing the learner to want to learn. Often, previous experiences must be overcome. Gay (2018) mentions "stereotype threat"—a belief that failure will reinforce a negative stereotype held about a certain group—as a possible source of anxiety experienced by learners from different racial, ethnic, cultural, or sociocultural backgrounds. Meyer et al. (2014) mention that most students with print disabilities have experienced failures or difficulties that disrupt their desire to learn, or that modifications made to supplement weaknesses reinforce their concept of inferiority. As every learner has different interests and strengths, it is important to provide multiple means of engagement to account for a variety of learners. The ultimate goal of UDL is to produce purposeful learners with intrinsic motivation. Introducing learners to various learning techniques, often for the first time, can impart them with the tools needed for self-direction.

It was important to both the LMS team and the Tseng instructional designers that the instructional content be seen as practical and worthwhile. In developing learning goals, although we specifically created content that would be useful for their schoolwork, in each instance, we also asked the question, "How will this benefit students outside of school?" In addition, relevant examples and stories were used to engage our audience. We created interactive games and multimedia content using H5P, a free online tool that allows users to create HTML content without coding knowledge, to also increase engagement, but we also presented the information in static form for those who did not have time or want to play games.

Transparency in Learning and Teaching (TILT) is a strategy that has been shown to be effective in education to at-risk populations (Winkelmes et al., 2016). The TILT framework focuses on being transparent in learning tasks underscoring the how and why of a learning experience by making these aspects explicit to the learner. Utilizing these elements of the TILT framework that are centered on motivation, we prefaced each module with a section entitled "What this module is about?" and "Why this is important?" In addition, we provided a list of key takeaways describing how a learner could be successful in completing the module content.

Multiple Means of Representation

The UDL framework can be used to scaffold the pedagogical actions of a teacher until they are instinctively creating inclusive learning experiences. UDL helps keep them cognizant of what research has shown to be effective for most students. It helps the teacher make sure everyone is able to access instructional content by creating an environment that fosters what Meyer et al. (2014) term "expert learners"—purposeful motivated learners who are resourceful and goal-directed. Although the end goal of UDL is to create expert learners, instructors must start by making all content accessible, not as an afterthought, but built into the design.

Accessibility

Accessibility is a core value of academic librarians. It should be even more so when librarians create content for distance learners, who cannot receive technological or educational support as immediately and frequently as traditional students. Distance learners of Tseng College might have time and geographic constraints affecting their ability to seek help or accommodations during the course. It is therefore crucial to make instructional content understood by learners with different abilities as much as possible. As such, when we designed the information literacy module with Tseng College, we took into consideration accessibility practices from the beginning. As the college on campus that is most proactive about ensuring accessibility, our LMS team considers Tseng College an ideal partner with which to develop and disseminate examples of accessible curricular materials and practices. After consulting the instructional designers of Tseng College, we applied the following practices:

Creating the Modules

- Texts: We use the template, heading, and structure provided by the Canvas platform.

- Videos: We use only videos that include captioning. For our users who need more flexibility, we add a compressible section of transcripts for all videos and include a "key takeaway" section highlighting important skills taught in the video.

- Images: We include alt-text or descriptive texts for all images so it is easy for screen readers to convey the information to our users with visual impairment.

- Tools: When deciding on the tool to make our interactive content, we checked the website of different tools for their commitment to accessibility and decided to use H5P, an open-source content collaboration framework to create interactive tutorials.

Testing

- Files: This design project is an opportunity to investigate best practices of creating accessible information literacy content in Canvas using ALLY, a pilot tool that can be integrated into Canvas to automatically check course content according to ADA guidelines. In the spring of 2018, Tseng College was the only college at CSUN piloting ALLY. Therefore, throughout the design project, our LMS team examined all our information literacy materials according to ADA guidelines, as well as evaluating the effectiveness of using ALLY. For all file types, including images, screen shots, PDFs, etc., we utilized ALLY to identify those that might be difficult for students with disabilities to access the content.

- Pages: Canvas pages allow instructors to create content using the rich content editor. Although there are both manual and automatic testing tools such as WAVE, the Accessibility Checker in Word, and the Accessibility Audit in Chrome for web content, it is difficult to examine the accessibility of a Canvas page using the traditional web accessibility testing tools. Fortunately,

Instructure, the company that owns Canvas, released an accessibility checker for Canvas toward the end of 2017, and we were able to learn and apply it with the help of instructional designers at Tseng College.

Recommendations and Lessons Learned

Our LMS team did not create many textual files on our own. Instead, we utilized files from reputable websites, such as the American Psychological Association (2019), but it is still much more reliable to create our own files to ensure the ease of access for students with varied abilities. Because of their strong commitment to accessibility, Microsoft products and H5P became our tools to generate all textual documents. We understand that it's the content creator who makes the content accessible, not the tool. Thus, aside from using ALLY, we manually examine all of our content following the guidance of the Universal Design Center at CSUN.

Not only is it important to ensure that all students can access the content, but that all students can interpret the content as well. Recognition helps students create meaning from content. It helps them recognize patterns that they then use to make sense of the content. As we have seen, learning is highly varied, and if a student is unable to recognize a pattern, they will have trouble making sense of the content. For example, a teacher might assume that using word problems tests only students' knowledge of mathematical computations, but any number of learners can have difficulty understanding a word problem, even though they are able to do the mathematical computation, including students with poor verbal reasoning or reading comprehension, or learners whose native language is not English. To provide more recognizable patterns irrespective of the learners' background, abilities, or experiences, it is important to include multiple means of representation.

Each module created for Tseng College included both textual information and multimedia formats, such as images, videos, and interactive content. As students' interest levels differ, the information could be accessed in multiple ways. Key takeaways were provided for students as a means of determining how much time and to what extent they needed to access the content, as well as links to supplementary material for those desiring to learn more or needing additional support. We also sought to give students a multitude of tools for those parts of information literacy that are difficult to grasp and take up a lot of time, but are not as beneficial after graduation (e.g., links and reviews of plagiarism checkers, templates for papers, Boolean search generators).

Multiple Means of Action and Expression

Assessment often fails to account for the varied strengths, abilities, and intelligences of different learners, and it frequently takes the form of testing, which can be problematic for many groups of learners (Gay, 2018; Meyer et al., 2014). UDL considers instances of formative assessment to be more beneficial than summative assessment as it allows for educators to gauge students understanding and revise instructional methods accordingly. Creating expert self-directed learners requires educators to create opportunities for students to develop the ability to monitor their own comprehension. Therefore, we provided multiple self-check opportunities in each of our modules, including a checklist of key takeaways on each content page and interactive games and quizzes created using H5P, with the aim of providing immediate feedback for students to use to assess their progress.

Checking for Student Success

Pilot Course

We piloted the information literacy module in one of the instructional designers' own courses, which enabled us to work closely with the instructor and gain insights into the module. Instead of being included in the course itself, the module was introduced to the students in a separate pilot course as an external, optional resource. To best serve the distance learner population who are emerging professionals with different responsibilities in life, we deemed it important to design the course in a way that offers them greater flexibility and enables them to achieve learning outcomes in the most efficient manner. Therefore, our information literacy module had been provided at the orientation without a deadline so students could refer back to resources and guidance as they engage in different research assignments. Knowles (1984) and scholars later on emphasized the crucial role of self-direction and integration for adult learners. This means that these nontraditional adults learn the best when both flexibility and mentorship are provided and when learning has immediate application in their lives.

The Application of the Module

The pilot course is one of the required courses for a Master of Science program that trains future professionals serving those who rely on assistive technology devices. Unlike most other courses provided through Tseng College, this pilot course has an embedded librarian who created a LibGuide for the course that includes specific information on borrowing privileges and domain knowledge. However, there is no designed information literacy session on the specific research assignment. Although the module created by our LMS is not customized for the course itself, the interactive activities are meant to engage distance learners to learn how best to find, evaluate, and use online information. One of the goals for the course is to provide these emerging professionals with an opportunity to conduct contemporary literature analysis on assistive technology. The information literacy module, therefore, is crucial for them to conduct the literature analysis so as to understand current trends of the field and become well versed with finding and evaluating information that inform their future evidence-based practices.

Feedback from the Instructor/Instructional Designer

The instructor of the pilot course was enthusiastic to have a module to improve the information literacy skills of her students. There are two students with visual impairments in the course, so we worked with the instructional designer to ensure all Canvas pages and uploaded files are accessible by screen readers. There are 21 students in the class. From Canvas analytics, we can see that students accessed the page throughout the first two weeks of class (January 22–February 3, 2018) had a few views among the 21 students. After revisiting the modules, we realized it might be better to make a condensed but mandatory module with a quiz component directly linked in the course itself. Going forward, our LMS team will assess the impact of the module on student learning outcomes based on their performance of the research assignment toward the end of the semester.

Conclusion

As a course focusing on assistive technology, the pilot course is unique in that students in the course have very clear professional goals. Our LMS team will assess their improvement on information literacy skills, but more importantly, more actionable feedback on the benefits of these skills to their professional development. To create a more inclusive library information literacy support system that provides all graduate students, including distance learners, the access to the information and education Oviatt Library has to offer, our LMS team will continue partnering with instructional designers at Tseng College to incorporate the online information literacy module into various courses in other disciplines targeted at different populations of distance learners.

References

American Psychological Association. (2019). *Related resources.* Retrieved from https://www.apastyle.org/manual/related

Association of College and Research Libraries. (2000). *Information literacy competency standards for higher education.* Retrieved from http://www.acrl.org/ala/mgrps/divs/acrl/standards/standards.pdf

Association of College and Research Libraries. (2016). *Framework for information literacy for higher education*. Retrieved from http://www.ala.org/acrl/standards /ilframework

Caravello, P. (2001). Library instruction and information literacy for the adult learner: A course and its lessons for reference work. *The Reference Librarian, 33*(69–70), 259–269.

Finch, J., & Jefferson, R. N. (2013). Designing authentic learning tasks for online library instruction. *Journal of Academic Librarianship, 39*(2), 181–188.

Fletcher, J., & Stewart, D. (2001). The library: An active partner in online learning and teaching. *Australian Academic & Research Libraries, 32*(3), 213–221.

Fox, A. (2001). The after-five syndrome: Library hours and services for the adult learner. *The Reference Librarian, 33*(69–70), 119–126.

Gay, G. (2018). *Culturally responsive teaching: Theory, research, and practice* (3rd ed.). New York, NY: Teachers College Press.

Gold, H. (2005). Engaging the adult learner: Creating effective library instruction. *portal: Libraries and the Academy, 5*(4), 467–481.

Knowles, M. S. (1984). *Andragogy in action: Applying modern principles of adult learning*. San Francisco, CA: Jossey-Bass.

Lippincott, J. K. (2005). Where learners go: How to strengthen the library role in online learning. *Library Journal, 130*(16), 35–37.

Meyer, A., Rose, D. H., & Gordon, D. (2014). *Universal design for learning: Theory and practice*. Wakefield, MA: CAST Professional Publishing.

Shea, P. J., Fredericksen, E. E., Pickett, A. M., & Pelz, W. E. (2003). A preliminary investigation of "teaching presence" in the SUNY Learning Network. In J. Bourne & J. C. Moore (Eds.), *Elements of quality online education: Practice and direction* (pp. 279–312). Needham, MA: Sloan Center for Online Education.

Simmonds, P. (2001). Providing quality library service to the adult learner: Views of students, faculty, and administrators. *The Reference Librarian, 33*(69–70), 395–406.

Turcotte, K. (2015). Helping the adult learner succeed: How community college libraries in Massachusetts are serving this growing population. *Library Philosophy and Practice*, 1–13. Retrieved from https://digitalcommons.unl .edu/libphilprac/1264

Winkelmes, M. A., Bernacki, M., Butler, J., Zochowski, M., Golanics, J., & Weavil, K. H. (2016). A teaching intervention that increases underserved college students' success. *Peer Review, 16*(1/2), 31–36.

CHAPTER ELEVEN

Supporting the Whole Person: Structuring Graduate Student Work to Be Meaningful and Empowering

Bridget Farrell

Introduction

The relationship between academic libraries and their student employees is often portrayed as symbiotic, with the underlying idea that when libraries provide student employment opportunities, both parties benefit; libraries receive cost-effective labor, while students receive a source of income and gain knowledge about library services that will aid them in their studies. In practice, the benefits derived from the library-student employee relationship can vary greatly depending on the student supervisor's commitment to providing opportunities for students' growth and learning, as well as variables in individual students' engagement in their work. To create a truly mutual beneficial relationship requires continued commitment and open, honest communication between student employees and their supervisors.

There is a long history of academic libraries' reliance on student labor that continues to today (Gregory, 1995). In 2011, student employees accounted for 20.7% of staff in ARL University Libraries (Kyrillidou, Morris, Roebuck, &

Association of Research Libraries, 2012). With academic librarians' dependence on student employees, and students serving as our primary patron group, libraries have the unique responsibility of nurturing and supporting this important population as they navigate the stress of their degrees.

Graduate student employees in particular are often stretched between competing obligations. They work late nights, on weekends, and carry out the vital and mostly unglamorous task of keeping the day-to-day operations of the library running while balancing the demands of their studies and nonwork life. They do this without health benefits, sick leave, or vacation time. This sort of schedule takes a toll—mentally, physically, and emotionally. Though librarians can and should join graduate students in their fight for equitable work environments that fully compensate them for their skills and knowledge (Kroeger, McNicholas, Wilpert, & Wolfe, 2018), we should also consider ways to restructure graduate students' work so it can provide meaningful experience and empower them to succeed personally, academically, and professionally.

As librarians seek to create rewarding workplaces for graduate student employees within the library, attention should be given to supporting students' career and educational goals. This is particularly true for graduate students in Library and Information Science programs who plan to pursue librarianship as their career, but it is also relevant to graduate student employees who will choose careers that require high-level research skills, as the library is uniquely qualified to help students develop those skills. These graduate students may go on to be future academic faculty, international relations researchers, health care providers, counselors, or educators. Regardless of program, employment at the library could and should provide an extension of the information literacy skills students develop in their courses.

Supervisors of graduate student employees are also in the unique position of being able to assist their student employees as they navigate the mentally and emotionally draining work of pursuing their graduate degrees. As the graduate student and supervisor build trust, this support can evolve from simple questions and answers about university procedures and policies to whole-person mentoring on interpersonal relationships and challenges the students face, both in their graduate programs and in their day-to-day lives.

In my position as a supervisor for graduate students at two different institutions' reference desks, I have sought to make library work meaningful for the graduate students I supervise by using mentoring principles, offering opportunities for learning and professional growth, tying what students do at the reference desk with their academic and career pursuits, and endeavoring to create an inclusive environment for all employees.

This chapter will share case studies from two academic libraries where graduate students serve as the frontline support at the libraries' reference desks. One library is staffed primarily by LIS students, while the other library is comprised of graduate students pursuing other professional and academic degrees. Through the course of the chapter, I will share ways in which I have supported the graduate student employees' career goals and educational pursuits, as well as provided emotional support through mentoring for other challenges employees face while navigating their graduate degree programs.

Literature Review

There is a large body of literature in library and information science focused on student employment in academic libraries, with topics ranging from hiring and training to management and motivating student employees. This review is centered on three main themes: (1) students' perceptions of the benefits of library employment; (2) how libraries have endeavored to structure student positions in such a way as to support the learning and growth of their student employees; and (3) the realities of the psychosocial issues, such as impostor syndrome or microaggressions, that graduate student employees might experience while working in a library. These thematic areas provide valuable insight into how library work is meaningful to students and details ways libraries have sought to create positive environments for their student employees, while acknowledging the social and emotional challenges that graduate students may face while employed in a library.

Student employment in the library has not always been perceived as valuable as it is today. Some authors have chronicled how the perception of the usefulness of student employment in the library has changed over time. An older article by White (1985) explored the increasing reliance on student employees in academic libraries and how this reliance is a shift from previous attitudes toward student employees. The initial negative attitude of librarians toward student employees was explored in-depth by Gregory (1995) as he chronicled the cold and dismissive portrayals of the quality of student library employees in the early 20th century, before sharing more current, positive perspectives on the benefits of students working in a library. Recent articles have noted this shift in attitude toward student employment in the library and have explored the value of student employees in the provision of library services (Logan, 2012; Maxey-Harris, Cross, & McFarland, 2010).

Many articles have reported on undergraduate students' perceptions of library employment, or share undergraduate and graduate students' perceptions collectively, without differentiating education level. Though there are sometimes differences in the orientation undergraduate and graduate students take to their work, reviewing the literature on undergraduate student experiences of library employment can still provide insight into what benefits library jobs might provide to graduate students as well. With this in mind, the following section will cover both undergraduate and graduate students' general perceptions of the benefits of working in academic libraries.

Several articles have shared that schedule flexibility is one of the most desirable aspects of library work for student employees (Benjamin & McDevitt, 2018; Walker & Fliotsos, 1992). In other studies, students remarked that they felt working at the library helped them in their academic pursuits (Benjamin & McDevitt, 2018; Jacobson & Shuyler, 2013; McCoy, 2011; Weston, 2008; Zink, Medaille, Mundt, Colegrove, & Aldrich, 2010). Outside of the academic benefits of library employment, students have also described how their library jobs increased their confidence in social situations (Jacobson & Shuyler, 2013; Weston, 2008) and helped them develop general workplace skills, such as knowledge of professional expectations (Benjamin & McDevitt, 2018; Jacobson & Shuyler, 2013; Zink et al., 2010).

Fewer articles discuss how library work should be structured to ensure students receive benefits from their employment. One article stated that librarians have the "obligation to offer learning opportunities to aspiring candidates who in the future may very likely become their colleagues in a broad or narrow sense" (Wu, 2003, p. 144). Although librarians felt the obligation to develop the skills of their future colleagues, the level of responsibility given to these graduate students did not necessarily equate to what you might expect of a future colleague, saying students could help out with library instruction by "doing the 'clicking' while librarians talk" (Wu, 2003, p. 147), or assist with rote questions while understanding, "rigorous in-depth research for patrons . . . is the librarian's job" (Wu, 2003, p. 144).

A systematic review of the last 20 years of the literature investigated the link between student employment in academic libraries and the Association of American Colleges and Universities' High-Impact Practices (Mitola, Rinto, & Pattni, 2018). These High-Impact Practices are correlated with increasing student success in the areas of engagement and retention through six practices: providing opportunities for professional development, creation of relationships with faculty and peers, diversity, sharing feedback, transferability of knowledge to other contexts, and creating connection with students' communities. This study found that student employment in libraries is aligned with these practices, particularly in the areas of faculty and peer relationships as well as professional development. However, the authors noted that libraries need to work more intentionally to foster student success saying, "If libraries really want to contribute to the success of our student employees, we have to view their role as more than transactional and instead intentionally consider how to make their experiences transferable to other contexts" (Mitola et al., 2018, p. 362).

Meyer and Torreano (2017) share how a focus on empowering library student employees at Grand Valley State University (GVSU) gives students a skill set they can take with them to future jobs. Students at GVSU serve as peer research consultants for their fellow students, providing support and guidance through the research process. Beyond the soft skills they could develop through any part-time job, working at the library allows students to "develop transferable skill sets in addition to professional poise" (Meyer & Torreano, 2017, p. 50).

Several libraries have attempted to structure student work in such a way that students receive a variety of experience and greater responsibility over time. For example, at the University of Nevada, Las Vegas, the library provided professional development opportunities to students through workshops taught by librarians and campus partners. These workshops allowed students to develop additional academic, technological, and professional skills outside of what they would learn through the course of their student position (Melilli, Mitola, & Hunsaker, 2016). In another example, at the University of Illinois at Urbana-Champaign, after making changes to student staffing that allowed students to carry out their work independently, students remarked favorably about the greater amount of autonomy and trust placed in them (Mestre & LeCrone, 2015). The University of Illinois Springfield has implemented several strategies to improve training and increase responsibility for their student employees. One such effort is the creation of student manager positions that allow experienced students to take the lead in training new employees (Hoag & Sagmoen, 2017). Finally, at Kent State, student employees played important roles in both organizing and participating in focus groups designed to identify ways the library could better serve students on campus (Seeholzer, 2013).

Most articles that investigate how to improve the work experience of graduate students employed in the library focus on students enrolled in Library and Information Science (LIS) programs. Leuzinger, Rowe, and Brannon (2016) discussed the value of mentoring LIS graduate student employees when considering succession planning. Denda and Hunter (2016) shared how mentoring is an underlying principle in librarians' work with LIS interns at Rutgers University Libraries. Other libraries have provided internships with the ultimate goal of recruiting students to choose librarianship as a potential career path (Knowlton & Imamoto, 2006). If libraries encourage the growth of their student employees, this can have a positive effect on recruitment to the profession. Maxey-Harris et al.'s (2010) study of employees at two academic libraries discovered that 65% of library faculty surveyed at those two institutions were employed in a library as students, demonstrating a link between student employment in the libraries and eventual pursuit of a professional library position. Campbell-Meier and Hussey (2016) have expanded on this research with a survey of LIS students that, in part, has explored how the role student employment in a library played in their decision to pursue librarianship as a career path.

Though there are many benefits to library employment for students, academic libraries can also be a source of psychosocial distress in the form of racial microaggressions and imposter feelings for the people that work there. Racist practices such as microaggressions, defined as "subtle insults (verbal, nonverbal, and/or visual) directed toward people of color, often automatically or unconsciously" (Solórzano, Ceja, & Yosso, 2000, p. 60), are pervasive in libraries. Alabi (2015) surveyed academic librarians to explore experiences of microaggressions and found that while librarians of color are experiencing racial microaggressions from their colleagues, white librarians are less likely than minority librarians to report observing a microaggression between colleagues in the workplace. A study of undergraduate students by Nadal, Wong, Giffin, and Davidoff (2014) has also shed light on how racial microaggressions negatively affect students' self-esteem.

In addition to the negative impact of racial microaggressions, a study by Clark, Vardeman, and Barba (2014) indicated that people that work in libraries, especially those new to the field, are susceptible to experiencing imposter feelings. Imposter syndrome, also known as the imposter phenomenon, can be defined as feelings of intellectual fraudulence among high-achieving people, characterized by the mistaken belief that their success was achieved through luck, charm, or trickery instead of skills and knowledge (Parkman, 2016).

Though there are many identified benefits for students to working in academic libraries, and some libraries are endeavoring to structure their student positions to increase the positive impact of library employment, there is still more that libraries can do. In their systematic review of the literature on student employment in academic libraries, Mitola, et al. (2018) call for more discussion in library literature of how employment in libraries benefits student learning. This chapter aims to add to the growing literature in this area through case studies at two different institutions.

Institutional Background

At both my previous role at Auburn University and in my current position at the University of Denver (DU), I have been responsible for hiring, orienting, and training reference graduate assistants. Though there were certainly similarities in my roles at both institutions, there are some significant differences in the graduate students' programs of study and how work was structured that are important to clarify and contextualize.

Auburn University is a public university classified by the Carnegie Foundation as an R1 institution with the highest level of research activity. Its 2018 enrollment included 30,440 students: 24,628 undergraduates, 4,707 graduate students, and 1,105 enrolled in professional programs. Auburn is a predominately white institution, with white students accounting for 75.9% of total enrollment. Students of color, including black (5.9%), Hispanic (3.3%), and Asian and Asian American students (2.3%), make up less than a fourth of the entire student population. In regards to gender, the student body is evenly split between male and female students with no available data on the number of students with other gender identities (Auburn University, 2019). Auburn University operates on the semester system with two 15-week semesters and two minisemesters over the summer.

In contrast, the University of Denver is a private, nonprofit university with a Carnegie Classification of High Research Activity. Its 2018 enrollment was comprised of 11,952 students including 5,801 undergraduates and 6,151 graduate students. It is also a predominantly white institution with 65.3% of the student body identifying as white and 22.7% of total enrollment comprised of students of color including 11.3% Hispanic students, 3.7% Asian and Asian American students, and 3.3% black students. In terms of gender diversity, a slightly higher percentage of DU's student population is female (57.8%) compared to men (41.9%). No information was available that indicated the number of students with other gender identities (University of Denver, 2019). DU operates on the quarter system with three 10-week quarters and a 9-week summer session.

Structuring Graduate Student Work

The aim of the following sections is to add to the literature on how libraries have structured positions to support the learning and growth of their student employees. This includes sharing different ways this objective was pursued at two different institutions, with an emphasis on creating a positive and inclusive workplace. In the following sections, I will share institutional differences I have experienced when supervising graduate student employees, how mentoring principles influence my leadership style, ways I have created opportunities to learn in line with students' career goals, and librarians' roles as allies to graduate students of color.

Institutional Differences

During my time at Auburn University from 2012 to 2017, I hired four graduate students who worked at our reference desk predominately in the evenings and on weekends. These students worked 20 hours a week, and their employment included a tuition waiver. Librarians regularly staffed the reference desk during normal business hours (9:00 a.m.–5:00 p.m.), with some evening and weekend shifts shared with the graduate student assistants. There was no Library and Information Science program at Auburn, so we sought to hire graduate students who were pursing degrees from a variety of disciplines— with several students from the counseling psychology program and College of Engineering. We felt that by hiring students from different programs, we would have the benefit of students' interdisciplinary knowledge. Though the students' ultimate supervisor was the associate dean of public services, I was responsible for hiring, training, and onboarding all new graduate assistants. Because of this, I was often the person students would contact if they had any questions or concerns when working at the desk.

At the University of Denver (DU), where I have worked since 2017, I am the direct supervisor for the nine graduate students who staff our Research Center's front desk. These students are hourly employees who do not receive a tuition waiver and work an average of 8 to 11 hours per week, throughout the day, evening, and on weekends. As DU has a Library Science program, the vast majority of our student staff is made up of graduate students pursuing their master's degree in Library and Information Science, with the occasional graduate student from other programs, such as religious studies or international studies.

At DU, librarians do not have regular shifts on the desk, but we have set hours in our consultation room where we offer one-hour consultations with researchers. The consultation room is staffed by full-time librarians during normal business hours, with evenings and weekends covered by our part-time nights and weekend librarian and second-year graduate student assistants. Since librarians do not regularly work at the desk, and our graduate students are often alone at the desk on evenings and weekends, it is vital that the graduate students receive thorough training to prepare them for the questions they will receive from students, faculty, and staff that visit the Research Center. We provide an intense, quarter-long training program to increase graduate students' confidence and comfort with our library resources.

I feel it is important to provide this background as the differences in compensation, my supervisory relationship, desk staffing, and the educational interests of the students have a great effect on how I went about connecting with these students and building an engaging and empowering work environment. My relationship with the graduate student assistants at Auburn was very different because I was not their direct supervisor, while I have more control over the structure of students' jobs in my position at DU. I am hopeful that these differences might help other librarians see how they can mentor the graduate students who work in their department, whether or not they directly supervise student employees.

Leading through Mentorship

My leadership style is influenced by mentoring principles—I want to help the graduate students I supervise to grow in experience and confidence through their work at the library. This means as a supervisor I need to be vulnerable and open to sharing my experiences with them, be someone they can trust, and become familiar with their career goals and actively help them work toward those goals. Though I am sure not all of the graduate students I work with see me as a mentor, I still try my best to offer a listening ear and provide advice and support when they approach me with questions or concerns.

One way I endeavor to build mentoring relationships with the graduate students I supervise is by being open about my failings and areas where I do not have expertise. By being vulnerable and acknowledging my limitations and failings, I try to create an environment where students feel comfortable sharing their own worries and troubles. Early in my career I often felt like an imposter—believing that others would find out that I did not know as much as I pretended to know (Farrell, 2013). One thing that helped me in that situation was talking with my more experienced colleagues about their own struggles with imposter syndrome. Through those discussions I was able to see that I was not alone—that my colleagues who I perceived as more experienced sometimes felt like they were "faking it until they made it" as well. Though some graduate students do not experience these feelings, the environment of higher education and working in libraries can ignite imposter insecurities, which can be alleviated by mentoring (Clark et al., 2014; Farrell, Alabi, Whaley, & Jenda, 2017; Parkman, 2016; Zorn, 2005).

I have been lucky enough to build strong relationships with some of the students I have supervised, to the point they feel comfortable talking to me about challenges they are facing in their lives outside of work. I always try to respect the trust they place in me by listening and only offering advice when requested. This can at times be difficult to balance, but sometimes the best support you can offer is to listen without judgment or advice. I feel grateful that some of my students feel safe discussing their problems with me—whether it is issues with roommates and family, or conflicts and challenges they are facing in their program of study—and I want to honor that trust by respecting their boundaries.

One goal I have for the graduate students that work with me is that they ultimately feel they can take on the role of mentor themselves. Learning about the library should empower students and give them a sense of agency. When the graduate student employees with whom I work share their knowledge with other students in their programs, I see that as the true marker of success. I am always thrilled when students tell me how they took the lead in a group literature review paper, or when they share how they helped a classmate navigate library services like interlibrary loan. For me, instilling the confidence to teach others about the library is one real indicator that students' work has been structured in such a way as to be an empowering force in that student's life. This sort of peer mentoring between students cannot be coerced, but offers the chance for building authentic relationships between students and the library that otherwise would not exist.

Opportunities for Learning

Since the primary mission of librarians and libraries is the support of student learning, this mission should underlie how we conceptualize and structure work for graduate student employees. For graduate students who work at libraries' research centers and reference desks, the search skills and comfort they develop with the library's databases can benefit them in their academic pursuits. But that is only skimming the surface of the many ways library work can be structured to foster student growth and learning. If librarians design training in a way that scaffolds on students' preexisting knowledge, then both libraries and students stand to benefit.

At Auburn University, one way I tried to demonstrate the value of the information and skills graduate student employees brought to their work at the library was through a training program based on flashcards. I worked with other librarians and graduate students to identify core concepts, vocabulary, and services within the library that graduate student employees should know and then wrote those individual pieces of information on flashcards. Throughout two weeks of training, I would quiz new student assistants with the flashcards, asking them to sort the cards into three stacks: I know it, I may know it, and I don't know it.

On the first day of reference training we would conduct a "pretest" where we worked through the entire stack of flashcards together. I made sure to emphasize that they were not expected to know everything yet, and that this exercise was designed to help me understand what information they already knew about the library and to use that to structure what we would cover over the course of the rest of our training hours together. If students were already familiar with some information about the library from their previous experiences, I would put those items in the "know it" pile and not quiz students on those topics anymore. I took pictures of how the flashcard stacks shifted over time to mark the students' progress, and, at the end training, I showed the students the pictures to emphasize how much we covered over such a short time.

Another way I tried to acknowledge and build on prior learning was by asking students to reflect and connect what we were discussing in training to what they were learning in their courses. At Auburn, we had great success hiring graduate students from the counseling psychology program due to the skills they had developed through their counseling courses, such as reflective listening and the ability to ask thoughtful questions. Through the course of training, I made sure to highlight how the skills they developed for counseling clients were transferable to the reference interviews they would conduct when working with patrons at the desk. Similarly, I would remind students that the content knowledge they brought from previous bachelor's or master's program would be invaluable when helping patrons navigate their disciplinary research questions at the desk.

I take a different approach when supervising the LIS students who work at the Research Center at DU. We offer many opportunities for the LIS students to participate in projects that allow them to build on what they have learned in their library science courses. Some students work on updating or creating LibGuides, allowing them to get hands-on experience with that software. Librarians sometimes ask for help with collection development work, such as reviewing gift book lists or cross-checking faculty requests with items we already have in the library's collection. There is also a seemingly never-ending amount of data gathering and analysis for students interested in assessment.

For those entering their second year as employees at the Research Center, we offer additional opportunities for them to lead and learn in their job. All new Research Center employees must shadow returning students during their first week on the job. This allows incoming students to learn from and meet their peers while also giving returning students a chance to share their knowledge and gain leadership experience. For second-year students who are interested in instruction or more in-depth reference work, I offer the chance for graduate students to teach stand-alone workshops as part of our quarterly workshop series, or to be trained to carry out consultations in the consultation room. This allows students to expand on the knowledge they have gained in their courses and brings more depth of experience to the work that they carry out at the reference desk.

Finally, one other way I allow graduate students the opportunity to learn is by encouraging them to take ownership of what we do at the Research Center. In our quarterly staff meetings, I ask students to take the lead on agenda items and share any issues or concerns they have encountered while working at the desk or in the consultation room. By doing this, I hope to create a sense of community around our work, so students know they are not only accountable to me as their supervisor, but that their colleagues depend on them as well. I have noticed that students are more likely to send reminders out to their colleagues when they encounter new issues or challenges while working the desk. They are also more comfortable sharing ideas with me about how the Research Center could be improved.

One change we will be making in the coming academic year in response to students' feedback is to increase the number of hours a week available to work at the Research Center. Currently our graduate assistant positions are capped at 8 to 10 hours per week. Several students have shared with me the stress they face when juggling more than one job with the demands of a full course load. By offering additional hours a week at the Research Center, I hope that will help some students who would prefer to have more hours at one job instead of fewer hours at several different workplaces. Though I am hopeful this change will be beneficial to the graduate students I supervise, I will ask for feedback next year after this policy goes into effect to gauge how impactful it was and to look for other ways I can adjust how we structure work at the Research Center to create a more flexible and equitable work environment.

Career Goals

I have found that graduate students sometimes struggle with translating the work they do at the library to other employment opportunities they might pursue after graduation. This is true, of course, for students in disciplinary programs outside of library science, but also surprisingly relevant for library science students as well. In an effort to help students see the transferability of the knowledge and skills they develop at the reference desk, I have started to be more explicit in how the projects or other work they carry out as part of their job could be referenced in their CVs, cover letters, or job interviews.

The first step in this process, however, is making sure I understand what career goals they would like to pursue. If an LIS student tells me they are interested in pursuing a career in an academic library after graduation, the projects and framing for their work would be very different from a student who hopes to eventually have a career in a public library. As graduate students, I know part of the journey through their program is being open to changes in career paths, so I try to touch base with my students regularly to understand how their goals might have shifted or evolved as they take courses covering different aspects of librarianship. Then I try to keep an eye out for projects they can complete while working at the Research Center that will allow them to get the experience they need.

For non-LIS students at Auburn University, I helped students translate the work they did at the library in order to demonstrate its value to their future employers. For counseling psychology students, I would ask them to reflect on the experience they gained when helping students who were anxious or stressed about an assignment and to think about how their reference interview skills might be helpful in a clinical setting. For the student pursing a doctorate in engineering, who hoped to one day work as a professor, I asked them to think about how their experience assisting patrons at the desk might be transferable in a larger classroom environment, and to consider how their research expertise might prove useful when writing articles for publication as a faculty member in engineering.

For LIS students at DU, I remind them that the projects they complete while employed at the Research Center should be included in their curriculum vitae and chat with them about how they can describe their experience at the Research Center when answering questions in a job interview. For students who choose to pursue careers in technical services in academic libraries after graduation, I try to assign them projects that they can point to when highlighting their data management or assessment skills. For LIS students interested in public services, we have many projects that can directly translate to the sorts of skills and experience employers look for in reference and instruction librarian positions. Many of those students choose to teach workshops, create or update LibGuides, and carry out consultations in their second year working at the Research Center.

Students who are approaching graduation sometimes struggle with anxiety about searching for a job. Though it is impossible to completely alleviate this anxiety, I do my best to provide support and encouragement to them in every step of the search process. I share the CVs and cover letters I wrote for my current job as well as the materials I used when applying for my first professional position. I talk with them about how to create CVs and cover letters that engage with the required and desired skills that are listed on job advertisements. Most importantly, I encourage these students to ask other librarians to share their application materials and their experiences of the job search with them. When I know my experience is limited in an area, I am quick to refer students to others who can speak to them about application materials and what potential employers might be looking for in a candidate for a specific type of position.

Allyship

Academic libraries can be fraught with microaggressions and other racist practices that can create an environment where people of color and other marginalized groups are not valued and are excluded (Alabi, 2015, 2018). It should be the work of every person in the library to create a more inclusive and welcoming workplace. Moreover, when student employees of color experience microaggressions or comment on exclusionary practices in libraries, as colleagues and supervisors we must listen to their experiences and let them know we believe them, amplifying their voices so that they can be heard and working with them to change inequitable systems within libraries. We must identify exclusionary practices in our own departments and endeavor to make libraries a safe and equitable environment for all employees.

This is not a simple task and requires continued commitment. For white supervisors, the first step down this path is self-education and listening, reflectively and deeply, to the experiences our employees share with us. The next step is to not break the trust our employees place in us. Clarify how you can best help while avoiding jumping in to "save" the student—an insincere corruption of allyship that does not ultimately help overturn oppressive systems (Spanierman & Smith, 2017). Work with the student to identify a way forward that feels right and authentic to them, offering to step in if that is what they need. It is vitally important that supervisors and colleagues listen to and validate the experiences of our students of color and avoid committing microaggressions by questioning students' experiences. As white librarians, we must also remember that allyship is an active state that requires us to acknowledge our privilege and use that privilege to work with people of color to fight oppressive systems. We are not allies simply because we declare ourselves to be so, but rather because our actions are continually aligned with and support the needs of marginalized groups.

Examining how the structure of student work in the library might uphold unjust systems can be difficult without reflection and listening. It is not enough to simply hire students of color to work in the library. Recruitment without retention is a hollow commitment to diversity in libraries and creates workplaces that are at best unwelcoming and at worst hostile (Alabi, 2018). Supervisors must continuously listen and make changes to create systems that are more inclusive, keeping in mind that there is no perfect, utopian workplace and that change and growth is a natural part of the process.

At DU, we have provided training for all of our student employees to help them when navigating hostile interactions with patrons such as gaslighting, aggressive behavior, inappropriate advances, and boundary pushers. This training emphasizes the importance of self-care after these interactions. I acknowledge that there is more that I can do as a supervisor to provide training and support not only for my students of color, but also for my white students, to help them be more cognizant of how they might be committing microaggressions against their colleagues. Though the library has provided training on microaggressions in the past, few of my employees were able to attend due to scheduling restraints. In the future, I would like to expand this training to allow more students to attend and to focus on the systems and oppression present in our own library, not just interactions with patrons.

Oppression and the exclusionary practices prevalent in libraries cannot be fixed with simple policy changes, but small changes can have big impacts on employees' quality of life. By listening and acting on what we learn, supervisors can work with our student employees to partner in creating workplaces where every person feels valued and respected.

Conclusion

As institutions of learning with the mission of supporting student success and growth, academic libraries have the responsibility of creating a meaningful environment for all of their student employees. There are many ways supervisors can structure student work in such a way as to provide career, academic, and social support through a mentoring orientation to supervision. Though there are many paths to pursue in creating a more meaningful work environment for graduate students, it takes a great deal of time, thoughtfulness, and energy to structure work in ways that best support students. This emotional labor can sometimes be invisible to colleagues and administration within the library, but the effects of this work can be incredibly impactful for the students whose supervisors pursue this path. Though the work is hard, it is worth doing.

References

Alabi, J. (2015). "This actually happened": An analysis of librarians' responses to a survey about racial microaggressions. *Journal of Library Administration, 55*(3), 179–191.

Alabi, J. (2018). From hostile to inclusive: Strategies for improving the racial climate of academic libraries. *Library Trends, 67*(1), 131–146.

Auburn University. (2019, April 19). *Factbook—Total enrollment*. Retrieved from http://auburn.edu/administration/ir/factbook

Benjamin, M., & McDevitt, T. (2018). The benefits and challenges of working in an academic library: A study of student library assistant experience. *Journal of Academic Librarianship, 44*(2), 256–262.

Campbell-Meier, J., & Hussey, L. K. (2016). Learning outcomes for student workers? Perceived mentoring and the gap between training and educating library student workers. *The Journal of Academic Librarianship, 42*(6), 745–749. https://doi.org/10.1016/j.acalib.2016.06.007

Clark, M., Vardeman, K., & Barba, S. (2014). Perceived inadequacy: A study of the imposter phenomenon among college and research librarians. *College & Research Libraries, 75*(3), 255–271. https://doi.org/10.5860/crl12 -423

Denda, K., & Hunter, J. (2016). Building 21st century skills and creating communities: A team-based engagement framework for student employment in academic libraries. *Journal of Library Administration, 56*(3), 251–265.

Farrell, B. (2013). New kid on the block: The troubles and triumphs of being a new business librarian. *Journal of Business & Finance Librarianship, 18*(3), 251–258. https://doi.org/10.1080/08963568.2013.795786

Farrell, B., Alabi, J., Whaley, P., & Jenda, C. (2017). Addressing psychosocial factors with library mentoring. *portal: Libraries and the Academy, 17*(1), 51–69.

Gregory, D. (1995). The evolving role of student employees in academic libraries. *Journal of Library Administration, 21*(3–4), 3–27.

Hoag, B., & Sagmoen, S. (2017). Leading, learning, and earning: Creating a meaningful student employment program. In S. Arnold-Garza & C. Tomlinson (Eds.), *Students lead the library: The importance of student contributions to the academic library* (pp. 1–20). Chicago, IL: Association of College and Research Libraries.

Jacobson, H. A., & Shuyler, K. S. (2013). Student perceptions of academic and social effects of working in a university library. *Reference Services Review, 41*(3), 547–565. https://doi.org/10.1108/RSR-11-2012-0075

Knowlton, S. P., & Imamoto, B. (2006). Recruiting non-MLIS graduate students to academic librarianship. *College & Research Libraries*, 67(6), 561–570. https://doi.org/10.5860/crl.67.6.561

Kroeger, T., McNicholas, C., Wilpert, M. von, & Wolfe, J. (2018). *The state of graduate student employee unions: Momentum to organize among graduate student workers is growing despite opposition*. Retrieved from https://www.epi.org

Kyrillidou, M., Morris, S., Roebuck, G., & Association of Research Libraries. (2012). *ARL Statistics 2010–2011*. Washington, DC: Association of Research Libraries. Retrieved from http://publications.arl.org/ARL-Statistics-2010-2011

Leuzinger, J., Rowe, J., & Brannon, S. (2016). Mentoring library students for career development & succession planning. *Texas Library Journal*, 46–47.

Logan, F. (2012). Student workers: Essential partners in the twenty-first century academic library. *Public Services Quarterly*, 8(4), 316–325.

Maxey-Harris, C., Cross, J., & McFarland, T. (2010). Student workers: The untapped resource for library professions. *Library Trends*, 59(1/2), 147–165, 374, 377.

McCoy, E. H. (2011). Academic performance among student library employees: How library employment impacts grade point average and perception of success. *The Christian Librarian*, 54(1), 3–12.

Melilli, A., Mitola, R., & Hunsaker, A. (2016). Contributing to the library student employee experience: Perceptions of a student development program. *The Journal of Academic Librarianship*, 42(4), 430–437.

Mestre, L. S., & LeCrone, J. M. (2015). Elevating the student assistant: An integrated development program for student library assistants. *College & Undergraduate Libraries*, 22(1), 1–20.

Meyer, K., & Torreano, J. (2017). The front face of library services: How student employees lead the library at Grand Valley State University. In S. Arnold-Garza & C. Tomlinson (Eds.), *Students lead the library: The importance of student contributions to the academic library* (pp. 39–55). Chicago, IL: Association of College and Research Libraries.

Mitola, R., Rinto, E., & Pattni, E. (2018). Student employment as a high-impact practice in academic libraries: A systematic review. *The Journal of Academic Librarianship*, 44(3), 352–373.

Nadal, K. L., Wong, Y., Griffin, K. E., Davidoff, K., & Sriken, J. (2014). The adverse impact of racial microaggressions on college students' self-esteem. *Journal of College Student Development*, 55(5), 461–474.

Parkman, A. (2016). The imposter phenomenon in higher education: Incidence and impact. *Journal of Higher Education Theory and Practice*, 16(1), 51–60.

Seeholzer, J. (2013). Making it their own: Creating meaningful opportunities for student employees in academic library services. *College & Undergraduate Libraries*, 20(2), 215–223.

Solórzano, D., Ceja, M., & Yosso, T. (2000). Critical race theory, racial microaggressions, and campus racial climate: The experiences of African American college students. *Journal of Negro Education*, 69(1), 60–73.

Spanierman, L. B., & Smith, L. (2017). Roles and responsibilities of white allies: Implications for research, teaching, and practice. *The Counseling Psychologist, 45*(5), 606–617.

University of Denver. (2019). *Institutional research & analysis: Factbook.* https://www.du.edu/ir/factbook/enrollment.html

Walker, L., & Fliotsos, A. (1992). Student assistants and their expectations. *The Southeastern Librarian, 42,* 69–71.

Weston, C. (2008). *Understanding the integrative role of an academic library for undergraduate student workers.* University of New Orleans Theses and Dissertations. Retrieved from https://scholarworks.uno.edu/td/700

White, E. C. (1985). Student assistants in academic libraries: From reluctance to reliance. *Journal of Academic Librarianship, 11*(2), 93–97.

Wu, Q. (2003). Win-win strategy for the employment of reference graduate assistants in academic libraries. *Reference Services Review, 31*(2), 141–153.

Zink, S. D., Medaille, A., Mundt, M., Colegrove, P. T., & Aldrich, D. (2010). The @One service environment: Information services for and by the millennial generation. *Reference Services Review, 38*(1), 108–124. https://doi.org/10.1108/00907321011020761

Zorn, D. (2005). Academic culture feeds the imposter phenomenon. *Academic Leader, 21*(8), 1, 8.

CHAPTER TWELVE

Digital Badge Programs: Unifying Graduate Student Learning across Campus

Victor Baeza and Cinthya Ippoliti

Introduction

Library service for graduate students is not a new concept, and much has been written regarding library services and resources geared toward this user population over the past few years. From research on medical libraries supporting the use of mobile technology (Boruff & Storie, 2014), to how first-year international students transition to U.S. academic libraries (Cooper & Hughes, 2017), or the effectiveness of a thesis consultation with a librarian prior to submission (Robinson, Nelson, & Lewis, 2018), ways to help graduate students have been of growing interest. There has been particular attention in recent years dedicated to the needs of this group beyond academics, such as the research by Zhou, Zhang, and Stodolska (2018) on the use of leisure activities to alleviate acculturation stress of international students, or the stress mothers face in deciding between their graduate studies and their families (Prikhidko & Haynes, 2018). Libraries are attempting to tackle more than the typical student information-seeking tasks, and are looking to address the obligations of family life, and the preparation for a career within a specific field that entails research, teaching, and writing.

To address the different aspects of a graduate student's life, the Oklahoma State University (OSU) Library began a graduate student 360° workshop program. Based on a model developed at Western University in Canada, the emphasis was to build programming that would create opportunities for students to gain skills that would help them in all aspects of their life (i.e., finance, stress, family care, job seeking). Almost simultaneously, the Graduate College at OSU began looking for a means to recognize the learning students were doing outside of the class setting. Digital badges, or micro-credentials, started gaining popularity because it paved the way for institutions to formally recognize and authenticate learning achievement through various avenues. For academic institutions, micro-credentialing has given institutions a way to recognize "soft" skills learned.

Background

OSU, a land-grant university, was founded in 1890 as Oklahoma Agricultural and Mechanical College. Renamed Oklahoma State University in 1957, OSU offers bachelor's, master's, and doctoral degrees to approximately 23,800 students, with roughly 16% (3,701) students admitted to graduate programs. According to the 2018 student profile, 906 (24%) of the graduate students were listed as being international students, 1,782 (48%) identified as female, and 1,013 (27%) were out-of-state students. The graduate student population is distributed among seven different colleges with 66% (2,441) being part-time (see Table 12.1) (Oklahoma State University, Institutional Research and Information Management, 2018).

In 2005, the OSU Library conducted a survey of graduate students to discover their impressions of library services. In general, the students felt the library favored undergraduate services and lacked attention toward graduate students. As a result, the position of director of library graduate and research services was established to coordinate efforts in support of graduate students and faculty. In 2014, the position title was shortened to director of library graduate services to better illustrate the growing importance of services and resources specifically for graduates.

Prior to 2015, many OSU support service departments on campus provided presentations and learning opportunities for graduate students, but sometimes these support offices lacked the ability (i.e., public speaking, teaching experience) or facilities to conduct workshops. Often these departments would conduct short 10- to 15-minute presentations at orientation sessions, or at graduate student organization meetings, and were not experienced at conducting one-hour workshops. To reach out to students, they would send notices to be included in mass messages, like a weekly e-mail newsletter from the graduate college. Although there was a lot of support for targeted areas of a

Table 12.1   OSU Graduate Student Enrollment by College, Fall 2018

College	Part-Time	Full-Time
Agricultural Sciences and Natural Resources	271	117
Arts and Sciences	523	288
School of Business	429	322
Education, Health and Aviation	509	288
Engineering, Architecture and Technology	405	132
Human Sciences	111	75
Center for Veterinary Health Sciences	0	374
Graduate College	193	38

Source: OSU Student Profile 2018. Retrieved from https://irim.okstate.edu/SPdownload#2018

graduate student's life, there was no one central location for graduate students to gain awareness of the various opportunities available. Like the library, most campus support offices believed the graduate college had the best chance to reach the entire graduate student population, but they depended heavily on the students reading a weekly e-mail newsletter, the *Monday Memo*. Unfortunately, the *Monday Memo* also listed meetings, deadlines, announcements, and other general information, so the workshops were not a focus. The graduate college also used the bi weekly meetings of the Graduate and Professional Student Government Association (GPSGA) meetings as a method for disseminating information, but it was up to the graduate student representatives to share announcements with their departments. Students could have benefited from taking related workshops offered by various support service offices, but since there was no coordinated effort to promote them, students often were unaware of these opportunities.

Within this context, in the spring of 2015, the OSU Library started the 360° program for graduate learning through the Edmon Low Library. Using the Western University's (Ontario, Canada) 360° Graduate Student Professional Development Initiative as a guide, as well as other programs discussed in the Association of Research Libraries (ARL) special report, *New Roles for New Times: Research Library Services for Graduate Students* (Covert-Vail & Collard, 2012), the OSU Library began to develop campus partnerships. During 2015–2016, various support departments began participating, including the Writing Center and Career Services. When the library started developing the digital badge program in 2016, the Institute for Teaching and Learning Excellence (ITLE), the Wellness Center, and the High Performance Computing Center (HPCC) were also invited.

Literature Review

Graduate Student Challenges

Debra W. Stewart, president, Council of Graduate Schools, writes, "In June 2012, the National Academy of Sciences released a congressionally requested report, *Research Universities and the Future of America*, which called directly for universities to strengthen the preparation of graduates for careers both within and beyond the academy" (Stewart, 2013, p. 13). She goes on to discuss that subjects, such as planning, resilience, engagement, and professionalism, are either being offered by graduate schools outside of the curriculum, or in some cases, they are being integrated within it, but the results are often mixed, and there is great variety in how these opportunities are implemented across departments, programs, and organizations.

Furthermore, Pontius and Harper (2006) argue that "graduate students have specific needs and face developmental challenges that may differ from, but are as important as, those experienced by undergraduates" (p. 48). They go on to explain that departments often lack the resources to adequately address issues such as housing, counseling/wellness, and career development, all of which have profound effects on student success. They outline several best practices to engage graduate students:

1. Eradicate marginalization among underrepresented students;
2. Provide meaningful orientation to the institution beyond academics;
3. Invest resources in communicating with graduate students;
4. Facilitate opportunities for community building;
5. Provide engagement opportunities beyond the classroom;
6. Enhance career and professional development; and
7. Systematically assess satisfaction and needs.

Nesheim, Guentzel, Gansemer-Topf, Ross, and Turrentine (2006) summarize various studies that reveal the challenges graduate students face, such as difficulty in meeting the various professional and personal demands on their time, lack of accommodation for the various roles they fill, concerns about their career plans, lack of opportunities to meaningfully interact with other graduate students, inconsistent relationships with faculty, and better awareness regarding institutional resources. Ducheny, Alletzhauser, Crandell, and Schneider (1997) also discuss study results from a survey distributed at the Chicago School of Professional Psychology, which indicate that students wanted more in way of supervisory skills, encouragement to explore multidisciplinary relationships, mentorship opportunities, and awareness of the different aspects of professional development.

Springer, Parker, and Leviten-Reid (2008) discuss how female graduate students experience the tensions of motherhood and entering their professional careers at the same time, causing significant work-life balance struggles. They also discuss the lack of campus child care options, the indifference shown for parents in terms of departmental support, and lack of systematic peer interaction. Their solutions, which range from flexible scheduling, training for department chairs, child care stipends, and paid parental leave, although admirable, entail engaging the institution at a high administrative level and the allocation of significant resources that may not be feasible, especially from a library perspective. Additionally, Renfro and Stiles (2018) states that "the literature reveals that one of the most significant demographic markers for graduate students is academic department. Departmental differences manifest as disparate work space needs, differing knowledge, and differing use of the library" (p. 5).

Social and Psychological Motivators

It is clear from all of these examples that there is much work to be done in sustaining graduate students outside the classroom. But the role of the library is a limited one, insofar as we rely on graduate students coming to us and being aware of our services, no matter how well marketed. We must, therefore, look to other approaches, and it is within this environment that libraries can act as catalysts for learning outside the classroom where most of the challenges for graduate students exist. Part of the answer rests with graduate students themselves. Self-determination theory discusses three main aspects—feeling competent, having meaningful choices and experiencing freedom, and connecting to other individuals—as the linchpins that nurture growth and movement toward well-being. Ryan and Deci (2000) discuss the fact that choice, acknowledgment of feelings, and opportunities for self-direction enable the necessary conditions for that motivation to propel the individual forward toward achieving a desired goal. They also state that "despite the fact that humans are liberally endowed with intrinsic motivational tendencies, the evidence is now clear that the maintenance and enhancement of this inherent propensity requires supportive conditions" (p. 70).

In essence, libraries can create an environment where students feel like they can safely and regularly address their self-identified necessities. "Self-regulated learning (SRL) takes place when individuals plan, monitor and evaluate their own learning experiences" (Cucchiara, Giglio, Persico, & Raffaghelli, 2014, p. 133) and makes them take an active role in earning and promoting their learning and the skills they've accumulated.

Digital Badges

Digital badges, in this instance, can act as a powerful combination of the elements discussed above. For a comprehensive look at digital badges,

Foundation of Digital Badges and Micro- Credentials: Demonstrating and Recognizing Knowledge and Competencies offers a wonderful introduction. Fanfarelli, Vie, and McDaniel (2015) state that badges can "encourage users to enact certain behaviors or meet particular goals" (p. 57). Badges also offer constructive opportunities to help improve the learning process via built-in assessment mechanisms (p. 57). Badges can also help frame an accomplishment "within the context of a larger environment" (p. 58), thereby allowing recipients to create their own narratives about the knowledge or skills gained and what they mean for their academic, professional, or even personal journeys of development. To accommodate all of these elements, a digital badge program would have to establish the "credibility and accountability" and the "authenticity of the acquired skills the badges" would represent (Hurst, 2015, p. 184). Badges allow for a high degree of personalization through different pathways and scaffolding mechanisms that allow them to be combined. Harkening back to the assertions of Ryan and Deci, Devedžić and Jovanović (2015) indicate that badges "combine motivational mechanisms and assessments into a single construct" (p. 607). This is significant because badges support both of the intrinsic motivational elements to emerge and manifest themselves according to an individual's goals and desires.

Building on this, Kehoe and Goudzwaard (2015) discuss how badges are tied to students' identities by empowering them to see themselves as authors of their learning experiences which, in turn, validates ownership of that process by encouraging independence, internal incentives, and, ultimately, a greater sense of accomplishment that goes beyond the simple acquisition of skills or knowledge. Campbell, Silver, Sherbino, Cate, and Holmboe (2010) discuss how competency-based professional development is a process that focuses on self-directed learning that allows students to "sustain and expand their capabilities and to acquire new knowledge and skills over time" (p. 658). This process entails several domains, all of which have more specific competencies associated with them. Some of these competencies range from identifying learning priorities, ability to access information sources, and using tools to assess competence. As a final point, Campbell et al. (2010) emphasize that this type of learning can occur in many instances, and is not simply relegated to the classroom, something which is also a strength of digital badges. Similarly, Antin and Churchill (2011) articulate the notion that digital badges serve as psychological motivators via five primary psychological functions for achievement: goal setting, instruction, reputation, status/affirmation, and group identification. McDaniel and Fanfarelli (2016) also argue that the functions that shape the user experience of badging are further mediated by cognitive, social, and affective forces, more specifically:

> The cognitive dimension is important for understanding phenomena such as learning, self-regulation, and goal orientation. The affective dimension is critical for evaluating players' feelings of motivation, arousal, and curiosity,

feelings often targeted by badge designers. The social dimension is important because digital badges are mechanisms for reputation and credentialing. (p. 80)

Another area of importance is therefore the focus on the environment, resources, and circumstances that allow these tendencies to flourish. It is here that institutions have fallen short in nurturing graduate students' motivation and ability to connect with one another in a context that allows them to develop their own set of professional competencies beyond an introductory level. In a 2016 report titled *Promoting Inclusion and Identity Safety to Support College Success*, Murphy and Destin (2016) list practices institutions can implement to help low-income, first-generation, and racial/ethnic minority students. Many of the practices match those discussed earlier for graduate students (i.e., eradicating marginalization, investing resources, and facilitating opportunities), but one a digital badge program can facilitate is in building a community of students where they can discover they are not alone in their struggles. No matter how well constructed, badges do not exist in a vacuum, and they are only as useful and meaningful as the larger program of which they are part. Scaffolding, progression, and institutional endorsement all play an important role in what the badges mean once the student leaves the institution. But how can these rather abstract elements support graduate students in a way that becomes more tangible, and more importantly, what can the library do about it?

In this instance, the OSU Library played a central role in bringing these various units to the table and setting a vision for how this program would work, not only from an operational standpoint, but from a strategic one. These efforts entailed gaining an understanding of the types of training opportunities students were seeking, as well as ways we could raise awareness regarding the resources they already had available on campus. In collaboration with the graduate college and partners such as Career Services, the Writing Center, and the High Performance Computing Center, we embarked on an ambitious digital badge program to offer, capture, and assess the impact of having a centralized professional development program on graduate student learning and professional development.

Implementation of Digital Badges at Oklahoma State University

360° Program Prior to Digital Badges

To initiate the Edmon Low Library 360° workshop program, with the intention of aiding graduate students on both their academic and personal paths, a basic outline of broad areas to address was created. The identified areas revolved around Communication (writing, speaking, reading), Leadership (team building, negotiation, inclusiveness), Life Skills (self-care, personal finance, family dynamics), and Teaching (assessment, best practices, learning models). In reviewing the outline, it was determined that the easiest place to begin would be within Communication.

Early in 2015, collaborating with the Writing Center was the first step in coordinating campus workshops for graduate students. The first programming the director of the Writing Center implemented was a Wednesday lunch writing workshop series, "How to Write a Lot," to be held on four consecutive Wednesdays during the summer. She developed a four-part, one-hour series from the book *How to Write a Lot: A Practical Guide to Productive Academic Writing* by Paul J. Silva. She had lacked a place, with computers and writing space, where she could conduct the workshops for students. The OSU Library was able to provide an updated computer-training lab in the main building. The dearth of places for support service offices to hold workshops became the cornerstone of our development of the 360° program. From the beginning, the program intended to support the personal, professional, and educational aspects of the student's life. So, with the success and popularity of the workshop series, the Writing Center followed with a literature review, and the library began hosting Career Services workshops later in the year, which covered the creation of résumés/CVs and interviewing techniques.

As planning continued, we decided to provide workshops in support of graduate students' financial, leadership, and teaching needs as well, but we also wanted to increase workshop attendance. We decided to ask the graduate college not only to help advertise the workshops, but also to endorse them. As it turned out, the dean of the graduate college had been looking for a way to recognize graduate students' "soft skills" acquired from various sources outside of the classroom. The new associate dean of research and learning services at the library promoted the idea of a digital badge program, which the graduate college dean enthusiastically endorsed. Unfortunately, the graduate college could not invest the resources to develop an unproven digital badge program, so the library resolved to create a "proof of concept" digital badge program.

The 360° Program and Digital Badges

We believed a digital badge program would allow the library and its partners to better reach students, while also improving the promotion of the coordinated workshops to other potential partners. But switching to a digital badge program required considerably more work than just adding badges and workshops, which the library didn't take lightly. By adding digital badges to the 360° program, the project had to be changed from simply offering spaces and assessing the learning opportunities to managing a heavily administered self-regulated learning (SLR) environment. Since the graduate college wanted the badge program to assist graduate students to differentiate themselves from students at other institutions, a lot of research was done to investigate various ways digital badges could be acknowledged beyond the campus environment. In general, we discovered the more we want the badges to be recognized, or respected, the more work has to be done both on the front end and back end. Work on the front end would include workshop design, development, and assessment, and on the back end with metadata creation for the badge and registration/recognition by external entities (i.e., Credly, Badgr, or Accredible).

Due to the amount of work to develop the badge program at the level the graduate college desired (18 badges), the OSU Library would not have been able to maintain the digital badge program had the plan not been from the beginning to transfer the administrative responsibilities to the graduate college, once the viability had been proven. This would allow the library to concentrate on developing and conducting workshops. If library resources could have been found, or staffing could have been reassigned to coordinate a digital badge program, the program would have been worthwhile for further development. Many of the benefits sought by the library, like greater support for students and increased awareness of library services, could have been garnered by a local-level digital badge program. The graduate college's desire for badges recognized by organizations, such as Credly or Accredible, simply required more resources than the library could dedicate.

One of the advantages of the 360° program, and then the digital badge program, is the increased contact with graduate students. Part of the appeal to other support services on campus is that the library would deliver a training lab and the Springshare suite of products (i.e., LibGuides, LibCal, and Lib-Wizard) to handle all the registrations, communication, and assessment. Although the library only conducted about a third of the workshops, a library employee took attendance at all workshops to track no-shows, and also used the 5 to 15 minutes before the workshop to speak with the students about their impressions of the workshop program. For example, through these conversations we learned about workshops offered in the international students' campus living communities. In some cases, the activities identified by the students led to new workshop partners. In other instances, the increased knowledge of additional services available on campus allowed us to direct graduate students to those services. Over the years, because someone from the library was present at all of the workshops, students began to recognize us as a source of information on services across campus. In addition, because most of the workshops were offered in the library training lab, students began to associate the library with graduate workshops.

According to many instructors, another unintended benefit of the workshop design was that the opening conversations seemed to "warm up" the audiences, leading to greater interactions during the sessions. We made a concerted effort to ask the students during this warm-up period to please fill out the evaluation survey they would receive from the registration system. Once this personal appeal began, the participation rate jumped from below 5% up to 20%. Although that is only one in five participants, this was by far the highest survey participation the graduate workshops had ever reached. The higher survey rate boosted the assessment of workshops, which allowed the program to better address the challenges identified by the graduate students.

In the fall of 2016, the first semester of the digital badge program, 12 different workshops were offered with a total of 180 attendees. Two years later in the spring of 2018, the last semester administered by the library, the program had grown to 28 workshops with 315 attendees. In that final semester before the graduate college took over administrative responsibilities, 24 students attended three different workshops, and 35 attended two workshops. Of those repeat attendees, 20 of them (34%) requested digital badge credit for the workshops. The remaining 39 were contacted through e-mail, and the 27 who replied said they did not request digital badge credit because they were only attending the workshops because of the topic matter. Fifteen of the 27 who replied also stated that they weren't completely sure what the purpose was for the digital badge program. We took this to mean that the program was useful for many of the attendees, but that clearer communication and material would help promote the existence and benefits of the digital badge aspect of the program.

Conclusion/Recommendations

Unifying graduate student learning across campus has many advantages for libraries, program partners, and graduate students. By offering a single location for graduate students to discover learning opportunities on campus, libraries can increase the possibility of students finding the workshops or presentations they need. Also, organizing one registration system, a standard communication channel, and opportunities to offer sessions throughout the year, instead of only at the beginning of the academic year, can help students from underrepresented populations identify beneficial workshops and services on campus by simplifying these elements that can become barriers to workshop participation. In addition, unifying and standardizing the campus workshops, including listing the workshops on a single webpage, can help expose underserved populations, as well as all graduate students, to the numerous workshops available when advertising a specific workshop designed for these populations (i.e., Introduction to American Libraries for International Students).

Libraries are in a rare situation in that they typically have contact with students, staff, and faculty from all areas of the campus. By attempting to coordinate learning opportunities, librarians can help increase exposure of support service "have nots," which are departments that don't have access to an adequate training facility or to a suite of products (i.e., Springshare), which can handle registration, communication, and assessment. This increased exposure can aid the students in easily encountering opportunities to address issues they may disregard because they feel they don't have the time to investigate. In deciding to organize or coordinate learning opportunities for graduate students, an organization must be clear about overall goals and what resources can and are available to be dedicated to the endeavor. This will determine the level to which you can begin the program and help to plan a timeline of how the program can grow if certain objectives are met. In order to determine if goals are being met, a clear and easily quantifiable method of how to collect statistics should be planned prior to program initiation.

Recommendations for Campus Partnerships

Whether building an entire badge program or attempting to coordinate a single location for students to find workshops, there are elements that will greatly increase the chances of success. As with most programs, those built on solid foundations are typically much stronger. In this case, the group of partners, or collaborators, forms the foundation that will help build and grow the program. Whether they are providing funding, content, personnel, or facilities, program partners will have the greatest influence on whether the program truly identifies and addresses the needs of the graduate student populations. Communication among this group is key and can be greatly facilitated through a workshop training group or an advisory board with a representative from all the primary partner groups. This representative group must also agree on what will define success for the program, so that all the partners have the same aim. This doesn't mean the different groups can't have different goals they are trying to accomplish, but that the smaller goals will all be leading to the overall definition of success for the group.

Another thing to consider, which is sometimes considered unnecessary, is the creation of a memorandum of understanding (MOU) between the parties. Although it may sound overly official, like a contract, it is not. For one, MOUs are not legally binding, although they can be as detailed or brief as you want, but they should clearly state what each partner expects and is responsible for with the project. An MOU was not used at the beginning of the 360° and digital badge programs, mainly because all participants were supportive and enthusiastic about the project. But as with many academic institutions, people change positions or leave the institution and their replacements may not have a clear understanding of what is expected and why. An MOU can help with the transitions of employees and department priorities.

Feedback from Students

Assessment and feedback is an important element of this service model. Students consistently mentioned that the small number of workshop locations was extremely helpful. Although it seems like something very simple, not having to search for or figure out where the training is taking place does influence student's choices to register for and attend workshops. So, limiting workshops to a few locations requires agreements between the partner offices. Along with a few physical locations for workshops, students have identified having one location for finding information on available workshops as important. Creating a programming calendar or online schedule helps in the discovery aspect for students, but also allows the workshop providers to know when events take place. The schedule not only helps to avoid workshops being offered at the same time, but it can also be used to benefit student learning, by promoting scaffolding of the workshops in an order that enables sessions to build on each other.

Of even greater importance are the changes and improvements suggested through both the formal and informal feedback channels. The workshops are small representations of what the different support offices provide, and many times feedback from the students cannot only be used to enhance the workshops themselves, but to improve or offer new services to meet student's needs. As an example, feedback on a literature review workshop resulted in a new workshop to specifically address U.S. academic standards of citing material and avoiding plagiarism.

How Unified Workshops Help Different Graduate Student Populations

Finally, it generally is not good to follow the axiom of "build it and they will come." Promotion is key to the usefulness of the program to students, which is a major measure of success. Removing barriers is important whether targeting underserved populations, such as international, first-generation, or non traditional students, or hoping to reach those from large programs with an abundance of resources. First, a central and easily discoverable calendar of events with registration links is a must. Informal channels like word of mouth, or viral marketing, of the workshops will be among the largest determinants of success. This is especially true of the international graduate student population, who tend to do more socializing across departmental lines than others. Many international students, and some domestic, mentioned their belief that the workshops provided an avenue to ask questions they were unwilling to ask their faculty for fear of damaging their reputation.

Groups that can benefit greatly from a consistent workshop program are departments with small numbers of graduate students, and colleges that have a large population of part-time students. These groups typically either don't have a lot of departmental resources dedicated to them or have time constraints that serve as barriers to them discovering and attending workshops. Similar barriers also exist for distance/online students and those who have parental or family obligations. Workshops that are repeated each semester, or that can be recorded for later viewing, will not only be more accessible to underserved populations but to all students.

As academic institutions support students and their learning experiences using digital badges, librarians can leverage the micro-credentialing (digital badge) movement as an opportunity to become campus leaders in developing, offering, and coordinating student learning to address the diverse needs of graduate students. Librarians can also utilize the digital badge model to enhance the development and coordination of workshops offered across campus that promote student well-being and provide aid to underrepresented groups. In doing so, libraries can organize and host training activities for all graduate students.

References

Antin, J., & Churchill, E. F. (2011). *Badges in social media: A social psychological perspective.* Paper presented at the CHI 2011 Gamification Workshop Proceedings.

Boruff, J. T., & Storie, D. (2014). Mobile devices in medicine: A survey of how medical students, residents, and faculty use smartphones and other mobile devices to find information. *Journal of the Medical Library Association, 102*(1), 22–30. doi:10.3163/1536-5050.102.1.006

Campbell, C., Silver, I., Sherbino, J., Cate, O. T., & Holmboe, E. S. (2010). Competency-based continuing professional development. *Med Teach, 32*(8), 657–662. doi:10.3109/0142159X.2010.500708

Cooper, L., & Hughes, H. (2017). First-year international graduate students' transition to using a United States university library. *IFLA Journal, 43*(4), 361–378. doi:10.1177/0340035217723355

Covert-Vail, L., & Collard, S. (2012). *New Roles for New Times: Research Library Services for Graduate Students.* Washington, DC: Association of Research Libraries. Retrieved from https://arl.org/resource/nrnt-graduate-roles

Cucchiara, S., Giglio, A., Persico, D., & Raffaghelli, J. E. (2014). *Supporting self-regulated learning through digital dadges: A case study.* Paper presented at the International Conference on Web-Based Learning.

Devedžić, V., & Jovanović, J. (2015). Developing open badges: A comprehensive approach. *Educational Technology Research & Development, 63*(4), 603–620. doi:10.1007/s11423-015-9388-3

Ducheny, K., Alletzhauser, H. L., Crandell, D., & Schneider, T. R. (1997). Graduate student professional development. *Professional Psychology: Research and Practice, 28*(1), 87–91. doi:10.1037/0735-7028.28.1.87

Fanfarelli, J., Vie, S., & McDaniel, R. (2015). Understanding digital badges through feedback, reward, and narrative: A multidisciplinary approach to building better badges in social environments. *Communication Design Quarterly Review, 3*(3), 56–60. doi:10.1145/2792989.2792998

Hurst, E. J. (2015). Digital badges: Beyond learning incentives. *Journal of Electronic Resources in Medical Libraries, 12*(3), 182–189. doi:10.1080/1542406 5.2015.1065661

Kehoe, A., & Goudzwaard, M. (2015). ePortfolios, badges, and the whole digital self: How evidence-based learning pedagogies and technologies can support integrative learning and identity development. *Theory into Practice, 54*(4), 343–351. doi:10.1080/00405841.2015.1077628

McDaniel, R., & Fanfarelli, J. (2016). Building better digital badges. *Simulation & Gaming, 47*(1), 73–102. doi:10.1177/1046878115627138

Murphy, M., & Destin, M. (2016). *Promoting inclusion and identity safety to support college success.* Retrieved from https://vtechworks.lib.vt.edu/bitstream /handle/10919/83635/InclusionIdentityCollegeSuccess.pdf?sequence =1&isAllowed=y

Nesheim, B. E., Guentzel, M. J., Gansemer-Topf, A. M., Ross, L. E., & Turrentine, C. G. (2006). If you want to know, ask: Assessing the needs and experiences of graduate students. *New Directions for Student Services, 2006*(115), 5–17. doi:10.1002/ss.212

Oklahoma State University, Institutional Research and Information Management. (2018). *OSU student profile 2018.* Stillwater, OK. Retrieved from https:// irim.okstate.edu/SPdownload#2018

Pontius, J. L., & Harper, S. R. (2006). Principles for good practice in graduate and professional student engagement. *New Directions for Student Services, 2006*(115), 47–58. doi:10.1002/ss.215

Prikhidko, A., & Haynes, C. (2018). Balancing graduate school and mothering: Is there a choice? *International Journal of Doctoral Studies, 13*, 313–326. doi:10.28945/4109

Renfro, C., & Stiles, C. (2018). *Transforming libraries to serve graduate students.* Chicago, IL: Association of College and Research Libraries.

Robinson, K. P., Nelson, K. S., & Lewis, J. C. (2018). Thesis consultation: A review. *Reference Services Review, 46*(1), 16–28. doi:10.1108/RSR-04-2017-0009

Ryan, R. M., & Deci, E. L. (2000). Self-determination theory and the facilitation of intrinsic motivation, social development, and well-being. *American Psychologist, 55*(1), 68–78. doi:10.1037/0003-066x.55.1.68

Springer, K. W., Parker, B. K., & Leviten-Reid, C. (2008). Making space for graduate student parents. *Journal of Family Issues, 30*(4), 435–457. doi:10.1177/ 0192513x08329293

Stewart, D. W. (2013). Professional development for graduate students: Reflections on the demands, the resources, and the skills. *GradEdge: Insights on*

Graduate Education and Research, 2(7), 1–3. Retrieved from https://cgsnet .org/sites/default/files/AugSept_2013_GradEdge_1.pdf

Zhou, Y., Zhang, H., & Stodolska, M. (2018). Acculturative stress and leisure among Chinese international graduate students. *Leisure Sciences, 40*(6), 557–577. doi:10.1080/01490400.2017.1306466

PART 4

Rethinking Library Spaces for Graduate Populations: Collaborative Design for Academic and Affective Needs

The Grad Commons and the Scholars' Commons: Reimagining Collaborative Learning Spaces and Services for Graduate Students

Angela Courtney and Michael Courtney

Introduction

During the fall 2013 semester, the Indiana University Libraries (Bloomington, Indiana) officially launched the Grad Commons, a flexible, multipurpose space in the heart of the Herman B Wells Library's research collection stacks, to provide graduate and professional students easy access to the information resources and subject librarian expertise vital to their research. As part of a much larger vision that has sought to fulfill user needs by reimagining conjoined library spaces, such as the Learning Commons—a 24/7 technology-infused learning center where students work on class assignments from start to finish—the Scholars' Commons was designed to stimulate scholarly conversation, interdisciplinary exchange, and intellectual discovery within a space that supports the journey from curiosity to discovery to publication.

Further, the Grad Commons was fully realized through several years of inclusive, participatory design and assessment. This chapter will discuss the realization of the Grad Commons and Scholars' Commons, from the collection of assessment data using ethnographic methods to how the findings were applied to the design and improvement of library technologies, spaces, and services for graduate and professional students.

The inclusion of graduate students in all facets of a participatory design and implementation process has shaped the Grad Commons' potential for future programming and growth opportunities. Additional discussion will encompass innovative approaches to involving graduate and professional students in strategic planning for library spaces. The overarching vision to enjoin complementary spaces at the Indiana University Libraries' Herman B Wells Library, such as the Scholars' Commons and the Learning Commons, was an intentional effort to support current and emerging modes of graduate student research and publication, as well as extending the array of academic support services delivered by the library. Finally, we will also discuss the development of the Scholars' Commons, an academic service hub that offers easy access to experts and technology for every stage of graduate student scholarship, as well as workshops and consultations from campus partner units ranging from the Office of the Vice Provost for Research, College of Arts and Sciences, Institute for Digital Arts and Humanities, and more.

Background

Indiana University Bloomington (IUB) is the flagship campus of a multicampus, public research institution, whose mission comprises providing broad access to education for graduate and professional students. IUB strives to create an inclusive and multicultural educational environment through the retention and recruitment of a diverse student body, and to maintain a strong commitment to academic freedom. According to the IUB University Graduate School (2019), there are over 8,500 graduate students enrolled on the Bloomington campus, 405 of which were enrolled in doctoral coursework. Fifty-six percent of the graduate student population is male, with female students comprising 44% of the overall graduate student body. The international students make up 27.68%, and while over half of all graduate students at IUB are white (54%), the remaining domestic graduate students are broadly diverse: African American (4.36%), American Indian/Native Alaskan (0.12%), Asian American (5.79%), Hispanic/Latino (4.22%), Pacific Islander (0.10%), and two or more races (2.01%). Supporting those graduate students' research needs, the Indiana University Libraries' Herman B Wells Library is the visual center of a multilibrary system, and its 4.6 million volumes principally support the humanities and social sciences disciplines, with collections that bolster IUB's international and area studies, encompassing interdisciplinary research collections developed in the areas of African Studies, Russian and East European Studies, Uralic and Altaic Studies, East Asian Studies, and West European Studies. Throughout the Herman B Wells Library are specially designed student research spaces that consist of the Learning Commons, Scholars' Commons, and Grad Commons. Although the Learning Commons has a particular focus on undergraduate student research, it does offer a host of services that also pertain to graduate students, boasting 24/7 technology help, as well as collaborative work and research space.

All three of these spaces work together to form a vision of an academic environment where graduate students can conduct high-level research and make use of an array of information and technology resources. Although there are many tools that the library provides, graduate students may be unaware of the resources that exist. Also, they could feel the resources are not relevant, or they could be aware of, but not take advantage of the resources. It is important for library staff to know which resources and services are beneficial to students and which are not, as well as the reasons why. Further, it is helpful to learn what resources the library does not have, but that graduate students would like to see. This information can aid staff in adjusting and improving their services to best meet the needs of these patrons, which will encourage greater use of the library.

Literature Review

In our new, rapidly evolving environment of higher education, graduate students are increasingly expected to create knowledge, rather than just consume it. In this environment, they must understand not just how to find and evaluate information, but also how to employ it correctly and ethically. Working with local, campus, and community partners, 21st-century librarians also face new and ongoing challenges of adapting to these changing research paradigms in order to better empower graduate students to think more critically about where knowledge originates. Librarians are well situated to enable students to think about information as something communities create in conversation within a greater societal context. They have the ability to devote more time, resources, and ingenuity into supporting localized creativity and discovery via spaces and services, empowering graduate students at all levels to become active participants in the direction of their research and learning.

As researchers have discovered (Dewey, 2008; Steiner & Holley, 2009), graduate students, in particular, express continuous need for quiet, inspirationally designed places to conduct research. Additionally, scholars have found that graduate student learning is increasingly collaborative and original. Green (2014) offers that graduate student scholars "take advantage of digital tools and research resources not only to expand their access to materials but also to transform the very scholarly work flows that they operate within" (p. 219). Indeed, as both Posner (2013) and Sula (2013) found, if libraries wish to support new and emerging modes of graduate student research output, they must provide the space, support, and funding to create an arena within which such scholarly pursuits are possible. Through deep and meaningful liaison work with faculty to integrate information literacy into the campus curriculum, librarians can capitalize on changing and evolving library spaces and services to enable students to add their own voices to the scholarly conversation.

Responding to the *Survey on Graduate Student and Faculty Spaces and Services* conducted by the Association of Research Libraries (2008), librarians overwhelmingly reported that "the single biggest motivator [for introducing services and spaces to graduate students] was requests from graduate students" (Lewis & Moulder, 2008, p. 11). Many scholars also correctly point out the need for a variety of services to support graduate student research, including information literacy workshops and training sessions; librarian subject specialists; online resources and services; and generic orientation sessions (Allan, 2010; Matthews & Walton, 2013; Rempel, 2010). Increasingly, though, a greater emphasis is being placed on exploring space requirements for student research (Kinsley et al., 2015; Primary Research Group Inc., 2015; Rempel, Hussong-Christian, & Mellinger, 2011). Webb (2018) suggests, "academic libraries choosing to devote space and services to supporting creativity on campus are usually responding to a need that has been articulated by campus administration, a vocal group of faculty, student requests, or their own library strategic planning process" (p. 10). The importance of such user-generated library space assessment cannot be understated:

> New library learning space has the potential to excite and inspire those who use it and to become their place of choice for a wide range of learning activities from private study to group-based project work. The factors that enable the development of a successful space are not just 'soft' and 'intangible' but also often combine in unexpected ways to produce their overall impact. (Watson, 2013, p. xxv)

The research demands of graduate students differ from other groups on the university campus (e.g., undergraduates, faculty). Typically, graduate student utilization of the library tends to be more focused on ongoing research. True, too, is the notion that graduate student needs for library spaces also differ from their campus counterparts: "perhaps the most telling example is the widely corroborated desire of graduate students for study and work spaces free of undergraduates, who are perceived as noisy, inconsiderate, or not serious enough" (Rod-Welch, 2018, p. 4).

The Grad Commons at IUB

In the late fall of 2008, a Graduate Student Library Satisfaction Study was carried out by the Reference Department of the Wells Library. Graduate students had access to the online survey from the IUB Libraries' webpage. In addition, links to the survey were e-mailed to graduate students through list-servs of individual departments. The study aimed to measure graduate student library usage, as graduate students are some of the primary and most in-depth patrons of the library. We were curious to find out the ways in which graduate students engage with the library to gain valuable ideas about potential areas of improvement for services and spaces. The 96 respondents' disciplinary homes ranged from anthropology, linguistics, English literature, folklore, comparative literature, education, public and environmental affairs, history, music, information science, and beyond. Although the response rate seemed low, we were encouraged by the diversity of majors and departments included as it enabled a broad view of graduate student desires. Of the students surveyed, approximately 75% had consulted with a librarian on a research project at some point in their student career. But the majority of respondents had not taken advantage of other spaces, services, or workshops. Lack of awareness of these services and resources was a major factor cited in these responses. Not surprisingly, though, 80.5% of graduate student respondents stated they would desire and/or use a dedicated graduate student center in the library.

The overall results received varied from student to student, but an overwhelming majority of students mentioned the need for more resources and services specifically for graduate students. When asked to suggest new services the library should offer to graduate students, students showed strong opinions on a wide array of topics. The comments listed ranged from separate, dedicated graduate students' areas to a better food court. As the results demonstrated, graduate students believed the IUB Libraries could broadly provide better resources and services for graduate students. Although a majority of the graduate student respondents thought there were several aspects of the library that could and should be improved, one particular idea mentioned repeatedly was a dedicated graduate student research center. Put simply, students expressed a common sentiment: "We just need a quiet place to study."

One immediate result of the graduate student study was a renewed interest in convening a group of graduate students who would meet regularly with library staff to share concerns of and feedback from students as related to research and library use. In the spring of 2009, the Graduate Student Library Committee was formed in earnest with seven graduate and professional students from the humanities, sciences, and social sciences disciplines. The inaugural meeting of this committee was held on March 6, 2009, where the results of the graduate student survey were reported. There was also an initial discussion on what a graduate student only space in the library might look like. In the fall of 2009, given an expressed need and interest in developing new spaces specifically for graduate students, the IUB Libraries' head of reference services and the head of public services met with the activities director of the Graduate and Professional Student Organization (later renamed Graduate and Professional Student Government (GPSG). For more than 35 years, the GPSG has been the official university-sponsored student government for graduate and professional students across all IUB schools and departments. Entirely student-run and student-driven, the GPSG serves students at IUB by championing advocacy, academic support, community building, and access to resources. The purpose of the initial meeting between the Libraries and the GPSG was to discuss the possibility of moving the "Grad Pad" from the student union to the Wells Library. The GPSG "Grad Pad" was, essentially, an informal lounge for graduate students housed in a room in the student union that had been rented by the GPSG each academic year since 2006. Throughout the following academic year, the GPSG Library Committee continued to meet regularly to provide input to the Libraries about student needs, as well as generating ideas to facilitate new and emerging modes of graduate student research in the library.

On May 19, 2011, a "Grad Summit" was held for library staff. Departmental representatives from each of the Libraries' Public Services departments got together to brainstorm ideas for library services for graduate students. The librarians came up with lots of ideas, some of which they felt were feasible to accomplish that year. For example, a workshop, developed specifically for librarians, was arranged in order to discuss services and resources that could be promoted to graduate students. Information presented during the librarian-focused workshop included details on circulation assistance; a refresher on how to use the Libraries' online catalog and submit interlibrary loan requests; documentation on supporting graduate students as teachers; news updates from librarians who were piloting initiatives, such as online office hours; the schedule for graduate student workshops; and more. Building on these ideas, in the summer of 2011 the Libraries worked with the GPSG to organize an information resource fair event in the Wells Library for new and returning graduate students. It was further determined that, over the next year, we would investigate (through pilot programs, testing, focus groups, and user surveys) identifying and packaging library support for dissertations, including workshops and ongoing outreach efforts, and to continue to develop a new curriculum for research workshops—all with general interest in working toward developing a space and suite of services for graduate and professional students.

Following quickly on the heels of the work that had begun as a result of the Grad Summit, the librarians drafted an official proposal to create dedicated graduate student study space in the Wells Library. Its purpose centered on providing a quiet, secure space for graduate students to study and store materials in close proximity to library resources; creating a break room for socializing and for conducting research consultations with librarians; and designing a space to building community among graduate students within and across disciplines. The proposed new space would feature a dozen or more computer workstations, a dedicated printer, lighting conducive to study space, task lighting on tables, abundant wireless Internet access, individual study carrels and tables with power for laptops and peripherals, adjustable chairs, movable and/or wall-mounted white boards, and new carpet and painted walls. The break room would consist of lounge seating, tables and chairs, and lockers to store personal and interlibrary loan materials (fixed or movable). Although the proposal established some specific understandings and features of the space, the librarians were keen to engage the members of the GPSG Library Committee in participatory design, an approach to design the imagined graduate study space by actively involving all stakeholders in the process to help ensure the result would be both functional and meet their research needs.

To that end, the GPSG Library Committee was charged with creating a survey on the creation of a dedicated graduate student study space in the Herman B Wells Library. The survey, which included multiple questions specific to space and design, was distributed to graduate and professional students via the GPSG newsletter, as well as through individual departmental e-mail lists, at the beginning of the spring 2012 semester. The survey ran for two weeks in January 2012, with 154 respondents completing the survey; roughly one-third of respondents added additional commentary. Interestingly, other than access to workstations (very important) and the idea of the graduate student study space itself (extremely important), most everything else (scanner, task lighting, etc.) was deemed either moderately important or slightly important. Students were mostly concerned with power outlets, Internet connectivity, comfortable chairs, and table space, and not at all interested in mobile lockers or storage space.

Following the energy and enthusiasm that surrounded the conceived project and survey, the Libraries made a firm commitment to renovate a 2,500-square-foot space on the eighth floor of the East Tower of the Wells Library. The space allotted was both convenient for the Libraries (an area that needed renovation anyway) and ideal for students (located in the heart of the research collection's stacks and proximate to library resources and service points). In the fall of 2012, architectural renderings were made that provided some insight into how the finished project would appear. Additionally, some initial decisions were made regarding the space's name and its governance. Input directly from the GPSG determined the name, the Grad Commons, and a combined effort between Libraries' administration and the GPSG Library

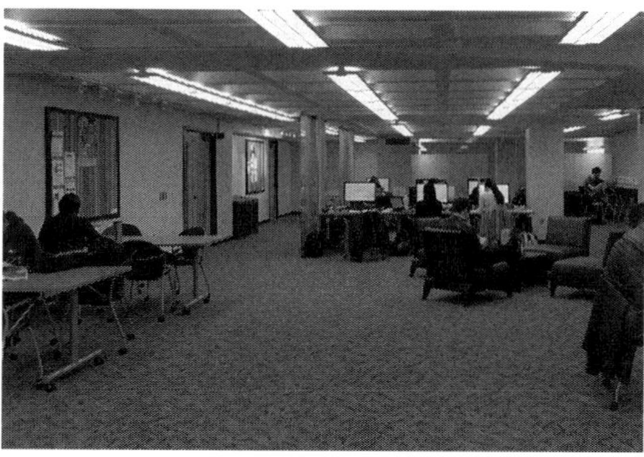

Figure 13.1   Grad Commons, Wells Library, Indiana University. This photograph is a wide-angle view of the Grad Commons space

Figure 13.2   Grad Commons, Wells Library, Indiana University. This photograph is of the card swipe entrance to the Grad Commons

Committee led to the drafting of general space policies and governance (see Appendix 13.1). Construction began in the first half of 2013, and the Grad Commons officially opened on October 7, 2013 (see Figures 13.1 and 13.2). Boasting an impressive array of flexible, movable furniture, a variety of study spaces (tables, reconfigurable alcove furniture, and glass partitions for privacy), requested technology (PC and Mac workstations with a dedicated printer and Wi-Fi enabled throughout the space), and campus identification card entry to limit access to graduate and professional students only, the fully realized space gave graduate students easy access to resources, collections, and experts vital to their research.

Unfortunately, the idea of a break room with kitchen facilities was not carried out as other elements of the space were given greater priority.

Scholars' Commons at IUB

It is important to note the realization of the Grad Commons is only one piece of a larger approach to aligning library spaces and services with new modes of research and scholarship. A discussion of the Grad Commons would not be complete without mentioning the complementary space in the Wells Library, the Scholars' Commons. Opened in 2014 in the Wells Library, the Scholars' Commons was initially focused on strengthening digital humanities skills. With an overarching goal of supporting teaching, learning, and research amid the constantly changing landscape of libraries and higher education, it serves to address the many and widely differing expectations of our graduate students, as well as those of the teaching and research faculty. The Scholars' Commons space was a renovation of a previous reference department area originally built in 1969. This undertaking started from the bottom up when the frontline librarians began to notice that there were research needs that graduate students and faculty were voicing that were going unanswered. The librarians felt we had to address the research demands or we would risk being left out of new modes of scholarship, such as digital humanities.

Working with colleagues and Libraries' administration, we submitted a successful grant request in support of holding a symposium designed to help the Libraries determine the level of interest in digital scholarship space on campus, as well as explore the possibilities of how the library could become an active participant with students and faculty. The symposium featured a variety of campus attendees, from disciplinary experts to librarians and graduate students working in the digital humanities. Soon after, we began initial planning for the space renovation that would become the Scholars' Commons, which opened one year after the Grad Commons, on October 30, 2014 (see Figure 13.3). In addition to the traditional library resources and services, it features a range of teaching and research support services from campus partners including the Office of Research Administration, Digital Humanities Cyber Infrastructure, the Center for Survey Research, the Institutional Review Board, and more.

Currently, the Scholars' Commons is a sought-after location for conferences and a wide range of programming. We have been able to use our exhibit spaces to showcase student research with evening events in which students are invited to discuss their research projects with peers, professors, and librarians. We have offered mock presentation forums for graduate students presenting at conferences for the first time, within a space that approximates a real conference setting. In addition to teaching, the space has been utilized for a reception for incoming graduate students, an event that was conceived to be an introduction not only to the Libraries' resources, but also an event that conveys the library as a welcoming space for informal networking opportunities. This reception is held after the library is closed, and the graduate

Figure 13.3 Scholars' Commons, Wells Library, Indiana University. This photograph is of the computer workstation area in the Scholars' Commons

students, librarians, and a few partners are the only attendees. Our subject specialists are expected to greet the new students in their areas of expertise. This ongoing event has had long-lasting results and has forged strong librarian-graduate student partnerships that continue to evolve. In the end, the goal of the Scholars' Commons has been realized—it's a busy place with shared work spaces that encourage collaborative initiatives.

Conclusion/Recommendations

Reaffirming the importance of the Grad Commons, as well as the Scholars' Commons, is an ongoing task. In order to hold onto their relevance, we must continuously reach out to the user population to remind them of our principal focus on teaching, learning, and research, which comprises everything that we do as librarians, from reference to teaching to collections to data management to special collections, access services, archives, outreach, administration, liaisons, technology, and more. As the Wells Library has been a part of change at Indiana University for over 50 years, we have empowered our students at all levels to become active participants in their research and learning.

Moving forward with future space considerations and work to improve on the Commons' spaces already in place, we continually assess space management and graduate student requirements through a variety of means. Card swipe entry data and other helpful tools, such as heat maps, allow us to know when and how the spaces are being utilized, which in turn serves to inform our policies and governance. It is important, too, to never lose the direct line of communication with the graduate and professional student population. We have had several advisory boards and library committees over time that have served to inform what we do and how we do it. It is crucial to hear directly from library patrons about what is successful and what is simply not working. The library collection is not static (collections ebb and flow with time), nor is library space. There is much we can do to change and alter the space without a large budget or construction. Even small, incremental changes can dramatically improve the user experience. We have relied heavily on the input of faculty and campus administrators to inform policy and collections decisions; so, too, should we rely on the invaluable input of our future professoriate and align our work with the ever-changing needs of the graduate student researcher.

References

Allan, B. (2010). *Supporting research students*. London, England: Facet Publishing.

Dewey, B. (2008). Social, intellectual, and cultural spaces: Creating compelling library environments for the digital age. *Journal of Library Administration, 48*(1), 85–94.

Green, H. (2014). Facilitating communities of practice in digital humanities: Librarian collaborations for research and training in text encoding. *Library Quarterly: Information, Community, Policy, 84*(2), 219–234.

Kinsley, K., Besara, R., Scheel, A., Colvin, G., Brady, J., & Burel, M. (2015). Graduate conversations: Assessing the space needs of graduate students. *College & Research Libraries, 76*(6), 756–770.

Lewis, V., & Moulder, C. (2008). *Graduate student and faculty spaces and services* (SPEC Kit 308). Washington, DC: Association of Research Libraries.

Matthews, G., & Walton, G. (Eds.). (2013). *University libraries and space in the digital world.* Farnham, UK: Ashgate Publishing.

Posner, M. (2013). No half measures: Overcoming common challenges to doing digital humanities in the library. *Journal of Library Administration, 53*(1), 43–52.

Primary Research Group Inc. (2015). *Survey of academic library plans for group work rooms and spaces.* Middletown, DE: Author.

Rempel, H. G. (2010). A longitudinal assessment of graduate student research behavior and the impact of attending a library literature review workshop. *College & Research Libraries, 71*(6), 532–547.

Rempel, H. G., Hussong-Christian, U., & Mellinger, M. (2011). Graduate student space and service needs: A recommendation for a cross-campus solution. *The Journal of Academic Librarianship, 37*(6), 480–487.

Rod-Welch, L. J. (2018). Understanding graduate students: Examining the nature of their distinct library needs. In C. Renfro & C. Stiles (Eds.), *Transforming libraries to serve graduate students* (pp. 3–15). Chicago, IL: Association of College and Research Libraries.

Steiner, H. M., & Holley, R. P. (2009). The past, present, and possibilities of commons in the academic library. *The Reference Librarian, 50*(4), 309–332.

Sula, C. A. (2013). Digital humanities and libraries: A conceptual model. *Journal of Library Administration, 53*(1), 10–26.

The University Graduate School. (2019). *About: The University Graduate School.* Retrieved June 6, 2019, from https://graduate.indiana.edu/about/index .html

Watson, L. (Ed.). (2013). *Better library and learning space: Projects, trends and ideas.* London, England: Facet Publishing.

Webb, K. K. (2018). *Development of creative spaces in academic libraries: A decision maker's guide.* Cambridge, MA: Chandos Publishing.

Appendix 13.1: Grad Commons—Policies and Procedures

A space dedicated to graduate students, the Grad Commons occupies 2,500 square feet on the eighth floor of Wells Library and was designed as a flexible, multipurpose space in the heart of the stacks to provide graduate students easy access to resources and experts vital to their research.

Conduct and Environment

The primary purpose of the Grad Commons (GC) is to provide an environment for graduate students to be productive and work. Students using the GC should work quietly, refrain from talking, and avoid disrupting their colleagues. Please seek alternative spaces for discussion-based group work (Consultation Rooms in the Scholars' Commons are available for graduate students). The Grad Commons is self-monitored, and anyone disrupting the work of others may be asked by their colleagues to cease activity or leave. Those who wish to file a complaint must do so via e-mail (see Governance).

Emergency and Personal Safety

Do not leave personal belongings unattended. Report any threatening behavior to Circulation/Security (812-855-4673). Call 911 for all emergencies. When the fire alarm is activated, occupants must leave the building. During severe weather events, follow directives of library staff.

Access

The GC is for graduate student use and entry requires a valid IU Bloomington graduate student ID. Exceptions to access include guest speakers, scheduled event participants, librarians, and staff. Those using the space must not provide access to unauthorized users. The GC is open for use when the library stacks are open. The library stacks and the GC close 15 minutes prior to building closing.

Technology

The workstations are first come, first served, and cannot be reserved. The large display monitor is reserved when events are scheduled. If there is a problem with a computer, printer, or monitor, please e-mail libref@indiana.edu to report the problem and place one of the out-of-order signs on the machine.

Governance

The GPSG Library Committee meets regularly with an IUB Libraries representative during the academic year to review policies, use of the space, review special requests, review and respond to complaints, and address any issues related to the Grad Commons. To contact the GPSG Library Committee about the Grad Commons, e-mail gradcom@indiana.edu.

Events

GPSG and other IU-sanctioned graduate student groups may request to reserve the GC for an event. Fridays are the only day of the week that events will be scheduled, and the schedule will be posted in advance on the bulletin board. Appropriate events are relevant to the academic life of graduate students, examples of which include organizational meetings, group discussions, lectures, presentations, workshops, and consultation sessions. Requests should be submitted to the GPSG Library Committee (gradcom@indiana.edu). Requests should be submitted for consideration a minimum of 14 days in advance. The individual who submits the request for the event is responsible for setting up the furniture for the event and returning it to its regular configuration. Those who fail to return the furniture to its normal configuration will lose the privilege of reserving the space.

Food

Group meals and food delivery to the GC are prohibited except for GPSO Library Committee approved events. Food and drink are permitted but are subject to the policy on disruption (see Conduct and Environment). All GC users must clean up after themselves. Do not discard food waste in Grad Commons trash receptacles.

Bulletin Boards

The bulletin boards located in the GC are intended to share information of relevance to the academic life of graduate students. Do not post fliers for sales, housing needs or opportunities, giveaways, coupons, tear tab sheets, or commercial fliers. Boards are cleared every Tuesday.

Rev. 04/05/2015

CHAPTER FOURTEEN

Supporting Graduate Student Success: Social Networking and Family Spaces

Marie Paiva and Lis Pankl

Introduction

Graduate students face many challenges and obstacles in their pursuit of advanced degrees. With a significant dropout rate, graduate students know the road ahead will be tough (Creighton, Creighton, & Parks, 2010). Although the academic workload is often heavy for graduate students, many of their difficulties come in the form of nonacademic pressures, including family responsibilities, social isolation, housing, and financial issues. With increasing pressures on faculty, academic libraries are stepping up to help students by offering more pertinent services. Renfro and Shields (2017) note that, "When faculty have little time to work with students on these issues, libraries may find new ways to help students transition into the graduate student role" (p. 202). Although the library has traditionally been a place for help with the academic side of the graduate student experience, increasingly libraries are also responding to the affective needs of graduate students.

At the J. Willard Marriott Library at the University of Utah, tailored services to graduate students have grown steadily in the past seven to eight years. Although these services do involve academic assistance, they also include opportunities to network and socialize and study spaces that can accommodate families with young children, as well as quiet areas for individual work. As a result of this shift in service focus, librarians at Marriott now have increased contact with graduate students, and consequently have been able to impact student success at the University of Utah more than ever before.

Many of the existing studies on graduate students focus almost solely on their research needs (Gibbs, Boettcher, Hollingsworth, & Slania, 2012; Kayongo & Helm, 2010); however, this chapter will describe our library's efforts at meeting the affective needs of graduate students, including their family responsibilities, socialization desires, and needs related to productive work space. In fact, one of the key concentrations in this study is the impact of space on both the emotional and practical lives of graduate students. With a Graduate Reading Room (GRR) and a Family Reading Room (FRR), the Marriott Library has dedicated significant space and resources to graduate students and, in the case of the FRR, all students (or library users) with children.

Our chapter will describe the ways in which Marriott Library has improved the social and family lives of graduate students at the University of Utah. Our research includes data from two focus groups held in 2018 that concentrated on the element of affective space, as well as observational and anecdotal evidence from our two major graduate student events each semester, the Graduate Student Social and the Dissertation/Thesis Writing Boot Camp.

Background

The University of Utah (UU or simply the "U") enrolls approximately 33,000 students, which includes over 8,250 graduate students, and is considered an urban campus. The ethnic composition of the graduates is 63% white; 7% Hispanic/Latino; 15% international, 5% Asian; 1% African American; and 0% for both Native Hawaiian/Pacific Islander and Native American/Alaska Native (University of Utah, Office of Budget and Institutional Analysis, 2018). The graduate students are enrolled in 212 different degree programs. The U has a national and international reputation for STEM graduate programs, in particular Chemistry, Mathematics, and Physics, which draw students from all over the world. According to Grigg, Jeong, and Exner (2018), graduate students in STEM disciplines face all the challenges of other graduate students with increased discipline-specific hurdles.

Located in Salt Lake City, Utah, flanked by the Wasatch Mountains in the western part of the United States, the U is a commuter campus, with many students traveling by car, train, or bus from as far as 40 miles away to attend class. In recent years, the real estate and rental market around the U has exploded and has increased the need for students to live at a distance from campus. Given its location and history in Utah, the U has a large population of Church of Jesus Christ of Latter-Day Saints (LDS) students, which creates a unique situation for the U in that some students go on church missions (one and a half to two years in length) and/or get married and start having children while they are in school. Because of these additional family responsibilities, many students work long hours and have part-time or even full-time employment. However, this is not necessarily unique to the U. At other institutions, students also take long breaks for personal reasons or gap years and then return to school, such as Portland State University (Petit, 2014). As higher education becomes increasingly expensive, it is difficult for students to go straight through in a traditional four-year timeframe. All of these factors do mean that University of Utah students often take extended time to finish their degrees, with most students taking six to eight years to finish a first bachelor's degree. In some ways, the adult responsibilities of undergraduates at the U makes them more like graduate students, and consequently, services like the FRR can provide needed relief for both populations (Godfrey et al., 2017).

The J. Willard Marriott Library is an imposing structure that occupies a central location on campus, and it is the most trafficked building on campus. As a member of the Association of Research Libraries, the Marriott Library holds over four and a half million print and electronic volumes with a total operating budget of over $18 million. The library offers an extensive suite of user services, including poster printing, scanner use, 3D printing, a café, research consultations, classes and workshops, interlibrary loan, technology checkout, exercise workstations, extensive software options, online research guides, a graduate student reading room, and a family reading room. The Marriott Library also offers extensive programing, including a regular film series, graduate student socials, a campus-wide reading group, first-generation student outreach, high school student outreach, finals week activities, a start of the academic year fair, and opportunities for students to communicate directly with the dean.

Literature Review

Although student demographics, in general, are changing rapidly, graduate students have always been different in that they are often faced with competing responsibilities, including the care of children, work, and spousal relationships and, consequently, they deserve special attention and consideration. In reviewing the literature, and from our own experiences, it is clear that graduate students' needs vary and many of those needs can fall outside of the traditional categories of scholarly help. Research shows that graduate students are a growing population at universities around the country (Gibbs et al., 2012). Thus, institutional success will increasingly depend significantly on graduate student success. One of the stumbling blocks to graduate student success is that faculty often make incorrect assumptions about the research skill level of graduate students (Rempel, Hussong-Christian, & Mellinger, 2011; Renfro & Shields, 2017). Ince (2018) states that, "Some [graduate students] are recent graduates while others might be returning students after many years in the workforce" (p. 426). Because of the library's expertise in teaching research skills, this situation provides an ideal entry point into improving the lives of graduate students.

Research suggests that library spaces can have a significant impact on the affective well-being of graduate students. For example, Ellis and Goodyear (2016) contend that "there is compelling logic in the idea that the design, management and use of learning space should be a shared concern for all members of a university: a collective responsibility, the discharge of which can benefit all participants" (p. 150). They also assert that the use of the physical environment at universities is the least understood part of research and learning. Research shows that graduate students use library space much differently than undergraduates. For example, Rempel et al. (2011) found that graduate students "visited the library for specific tasks, such as carrying out research or using specific resources, and that fewer students used the library for extended study periods" (p. 481). This might be true due to the fact that graduate students often have their own offices or cubicles in their home departments. They also found that graduate students wanted the ability to use the library for both social and private spaces. Additionally, Forbes, Schlesselman-Tarango, and Keeran (2017) found through their study that "graduate students really enjoyed talking to each other and wanted more opportunities to meet other students outside their departments" (p. 306). Unexpected needs or desires such as this are what fuel many of the Marriott Library's graduate student events, such as the Graduate Student Social and the Dissertation/Thesis Writing Boot Camp.

Unlike undergraduates, graduate students may not be given the distinction "traditional" vs. "nontraditional"; however, it can be assumed, because of their age, that they might hold many of the same responsibilities as nontraditional undergraduate students, including the responsibility of being a parent. At institutions like the University of Utah, which have a high rate of student-parents (both graduate and undergraduate), resources can be combined to create family-friendly policies that boost retention rates (Brown & Nichols, 2012). It is clear that students who are also parents need extra support to successfully complete their studies (Godfrey et al., 2017).

Issues of diversity, equity, and inclusion continue to shape and influence the success of graduate students at research institutions. Although many strides have been made in higher education, the environment is still often perceived as hostile by students of color, in particular female students of color (Shavers & Moore, 2014). Libraries can play an important role in addressing campus climate issues. As a central place on most campuses, libraries have the opportunity to bring disparate groups and unheard voices together. For example, in the spring of 2019, the Marriott Library held its inaugural First-Generation Student Conference. Although the conference was attended primarily by undergraduates, about one-third of the participants were graduate students. Libraries can take advantage of their space and their extensive outreach networks to create events that not only reach underserved populations, but also events that create community. Ignoring elements of diversity, equity, and inclusion will only hamper graduate student success in the long term.

Graduate Student Spaces at the University of Utah

Graduate Reading Room

After the last library renovation in 1996, there was an unused space on the first floor, which was reconfigured to be the new Graduate Reading Room (GRR). It is an "L" shaped room, 2,600 square feet in size, which seats 45, and has a library classroom outside of it. It has an assortment of cubicle spaces, lounge chairs with a coffee table, additional library tables and seating, as well as a standing adjustable height desk. There were about 14 house plants of various sizes on a counter, which students said they liked seeing as the room has no windows, but due to water leaks, the plants have been temporarily removed. The room is fully carpeted, has some artwork, and one wall is painted sweet pea green as an accent. There are also four large-framed posters that advertise upcoming library events or services. To promote awareness of other events around campus, there is a bulletin board on which the library staff, the graduate school staff, and graduate students can post relevant flyers pertaining to upcoming workshops, events, or funding opportunities. Finally, technology is also available in the room and includes four PCs and Macs and a scanner.

To gain entry to the space through one of three controlled entrances, UU graduate students need to fill out an entry form, which then allows them swipe card access for the academic year. The room also has surveillance cameras and, a few times an hour, library security walks through the space on their rounds ensuring safety. The room is designated as being a quiet workspace, as requested by the graduate students, but food and drink are allowed, which is also true for most other spaces in Marriott Library. Additionally, inside the GRR is the Graduate Writing Center, which is run by the Writing Center on campus. Students can make appointments ahead of time online, or drop by, to utilize the services of writing peers for proofreading and editing term papers, dissertations, CVs, cover letters, or professional publications. As an example of usage, the Graduate Reading Room had 144 student visitors in February and 199 in April 2019. The peak time for use is around the lunch hour with the majority of use occurring during the hours of 10 a.m. to 7 p.m., Monday through Friday.

Family Reading Room

Another space frequently used by graduate students is the Family Reading Room (FRR) on the third floor of Marriott Library. Similar to the GRR, access is through swiped ID entry to all University of Utah faculty, students, and staff. At 1,900 square feet in size, it has plenty of space to accommodate different activities, and the large floor-to-ceiling windows on one side provide lots of natural light. The FRR has two group study rooms, some cubicle space, two computer terminals, a scanner, a printer, a set of children's books, several toy sets, and some colorful artwork on the wall. The back room has a few private breast-feeding/lactation cubicles, a small refrigerator, and a microwave oven. There are surveillance cameras, and library security walks through this area when they do their rounds each hour the building is open. There is a Security/Circulation desk at the entrance nearby, as well as bathrooms and drinking fountains directly outside. Finally, the FRR space is adjacent to the Marriott Library's Juvenile Collection, so parents have easy access to these materials while using the space. The number of users varies each month. In February 2019 the FRR had 164 users, and in April 2019 it had 194 users.

Graduate Student Social and Dissertation/Thesis Writing Boot Camp

In addition to targeted spaces, twice a year, during the fall and spring semesters, a Graduate Student Social has been offered to the graduate student community at the University of Utah. The event is held in the Graduate Reading Room and is coordinated by the library's Graduate Student Services Committee (GSSC). We advertise ahead of time that there will be a social with refreshments, in the usually quiet GRR, for a two-hour time slot in the middle of the week. The GRR location was chosen as a way to introduce this library space to graduate students. We also invite librarian subject selectors to attend at any time during the two-hour social. They meet with graduate students in their assigned disciplines and introduce users to library services and resources. In the past two years, we also have asked Marriott Library administrators and staff from the University of Utah Graduate School to attend the social, so they can meet graduate students and learn about their needs.

Our library administration pays for the event's refreshments, which include coffee, tea, hot chocolate, assorted bagels, and veggie trays. Although the event has traditionally been for graduate students to socialize, in recent years, we have also advertised library services and had library staff at the event to answer questions. The GSSC also invite staff who work in specific areas of the library to talk about additional services and resources, such as tools for virtual reality, zines, on-demand acquisitions, 3D printing, the Audio and Video Studio, and interlibrary loan.

In the beginning years, 2011 to 2018, only about 25 to 35 students attended this event. To increase attendance, the food offerings have been tweaked to include vegetarian sushi and wraps, which has brought in crowds of 120 to 130. To keep better statistics on attendance, we now also ask graduate students to sign in so we can see what departments are represented. Recently, we met with the library's graphics department staff to seek their input for creating visually appealing artwork for our posters and announcements of the event. In the past, we have had two large framed posters hung up in the library, easel posters at the two library entrances, smaller flyers posted on some campus boards, and also on the library's webpage. Our events are also posted on social media and promoted at information tabling events.

Based on these changes in promotional methods, between the fall of 2017 and the spring of 2019, we have seen students flocking into the Graduate Reading Room for almost the whole two hours of the social, making it quite a spirited and busy place. It is a lively atmosphere, and students often walk in with their peers from their discipline, but also meet graduate students from other departments. It is not unusual to run out of food after the first 90 minutes, but we try to at least maintain the hot beverage service.

Since 2011, the Marriott Library has been offering a Dissertation/Thesis Writing Boot Camp to graduate students during the fall and spring breaks. This four-day boot camp spans all disciplines, even those in the STEM fields as our extensive health sciences programs. The focus of the boot camp is for participants to spend time writing either in the library or wherever is most productive. For this event, students register in advance through an online form that is maintained by the library. Roughly 50 to 80 students participate each day of the boot camp. Brief workshops and sessions include citation management, formatting, and research-based software.

This event is a collaboration between the graduate school and the Marriott Library. The graduate school provides the majority of the funding for the hot breakfast that is served each day. We provide nutritious items by working with the library's food services coordinator who arranges with several professional catering companies. The food choices include vegetarian options as well as hot beverages and snacks, and these are available from 8:30 a.m. to 1 p.m. daily. The Marriott Library supplements the budget and also provides the expertise for the workshops and sessions as well as the dedicated space for the event. Graduate school administrators and staff drop in the first half-hour of the boot camp, which is devoted to networking with peers, librarians, and library staff.

For the past six years, the University of Utah's Graduate School Diversity Office has also offered a social for underrepresented graduate students. It is held every fall semester as a welcome to new and returning underrepresented graduate students and draws about 100 students of color. The J. Willard Marriott Library pays for the catered meal, and a librarian from the Graduate

Student Services Committee is invited to attend in order to meet students, to introduce them to library services, and to answer questions. After the meal, a drawing is sometimes held for prizes, including items like iPads. This informal event is quite successful as underrepresented students are introduced to each other via an ice breaker, can meet staff from units across campus, and can chat with their peers while enjoying dinner with their family members and colleagues. The venues have changed from time to time, and in recent years, have been held on campus early in the semester.

Focus Group Assessment

In addition to observation and anecdotal evidence from our graduate student events, we collected data from focus groups with University of Utah graduate students held in the spring of 2018. Following approval from the university's Institutional Review Board (IRB), we conducted focus groups in an attempt to dig deeper into how graduate student affective needs are impacted by space.

We directed two focus group sessions, each consisting of five graduate students in April 2018. At each focus group, we asked a series of 10 questions (see Appendix 14.1). As an incentive to attend the focus groups, we provided pizza and drinks, as well as an opportunity to win a $20 gift card (at each focus group) and a $50 gift card (overall).

Findings

Following our analysis of the focus group responses, we noted general themes and then made recommendations for improvements related to space and support for graduate students' emotional needs.

- Some students love the Graduate Student Reading Room as is (bare, closed in), but mentioned it is not well advertised. Some students avoid the reading room because it has no windows and feels claustrophobic. However, other students will need to use the reading room often because their departments are losing their offices for graduate students when they move to new buildings. Students would like to see standing desks in the reading room and more double-monitor computer stations with large work areas. Also, others noted that the room needs more color and better art.

- The James E. Faust Law Library, not a part of Marriott Library, was mentioned as a preferred place to study (by non-law students) because of its natural light and quiet atmosphere with no undergraduate students.

- There was a suggestion to have more social writing times, like the Dissertation/Thesis Boot Camp. These could include something like mini-writing workshops—for instance, a challenge to write 100 words in 100 minutes.

- Students noted that they are not able to leave materials unattended in the library to use the restroom or get food and asked about possibilities for graduate students to have locked, reserved carrels.

- Students like the Graduate Student Social and Dissertation/Thesis Writing Boot Camp; however, students would like to see a boot camp in the summer due to hectic semester schedules.

- Social media, departmental listservs, and flyers in buildings are great ways to get messages out about events and services as well as build community among graduate students.

- The Family Reading Room is not well publicized and books in the room are not well organized. There is a need to promote the availability of the room to graduate students and also to better organize the space.

Overall, the results of the focus groups indicated a need for increased social interaction among graduate students, better space utilization to meet student needs, and increased marketing of the resources and spaces available for graduate students. Although we feel that the Graduate Student Social and the dedicated spaces of the GRR and FRR are the best current avenues to meet these needs, we are continuing to work on changes to better meet student needs.

Recommendations and Future Directions

Our connections with graduate students have been strengthened due to our event collaborations with the graduate school and the Office for Equity and Diversity. We will continue to work with the Office for Equity and Diversity to reach out to new and returning underrepresented students of color so that they feel comfortable using the library's services and collections. We definitely want to see the numbers of underrepresented participants grow in attendance at the socials and other events we offer. The University of Utah is currently striving to increase underrepresented students, international students, and graduate students, so we hope to see a shift for more interactions with the Marriott Library. Along with the library Graduate Student Social and the GRR and FRR space, the Dissertation/Thesis Writing Bootcamp has also seen increased usage in recent semesters, perhaps because of improved partnerships, and better promotion and advertising—online, in person, in print, and on social media.

Due to the availability of some endowment funds, we hope to revive the GRR space and give it a more polished look. Future plans include a modest renovation in stages to update the furniture offerings, and to remove the long countertop, old chairs, and houseplants. We hope to add more seating space where the countertop was previously located and have larger, more attractive plants in the room. The larger plants might serve as a buffer in between workstations and brighten up the space for users, since there are no windows present. We are also planning on repainting a wall in an appealing and pleasant color and adding contemporary furniture and individual lighting to make users feel more comfortable and productive when working in the space. Finally, regarding the Family Reading Room space, we recently heard that some grants have been received to build a bathroom inside this area. This will make the space much more convenient for parents who may want to wash out their feeding supplies and take their small ones to the restroom.

Conclusion

From both our observations and our data from the focus groups, we realize that graduate students are significantly impacted by their environment and their need for community. Social interaction and flexible spaces are crucial for graduate student success, and we will continue to improve current spaces and continue current events. Although graduate students are generally pleased with our services, the focus group data and continuing observations have helped us realize where we can improve resources and what services students might make use of in the near future. For example, we continually have requests for more electrical outlets, which we hope to add gradually in the GRR.

Acknowledgments

We would like to thank and acknowledge the following individuals for their interest and/or providing funds for graduate students at the University of Utah. Associate Dean Katie Ullmann from the graduate school, Danny Nelson from the graduate school, Araceli Frias from the Office for Equity and Diversity, Alberta Comer, dean of the Marriott Library, Catherine Soehner, associate dean of Research and User Services, Rick Anderson, associate dean for Collections and Scholarly Communications, and Ian Godfrey, director of Library Facilities.

References

Brown, V., & Nichols, T. (2012). Pregnant and parenting students on campus: Policy and program implications for a growing population. *Educational Policy, 27*(3), 499–530.

Creighton, L., Creighton, T., & Parks, D. (2010). Mentoring to degree completion: Expanding the horizons of doctoral protégés. *Mentoring & Tutoring: Partnership in Learning, 18*(1), 39–52.

Ellis, R. A., & Goodyear, P. (2016). Models of learning space: Integrating research on space, place and learning in higher education. *Review of Education, 4*(2), 149–191.

Forbes, C., Schlesselman-Tarango, G., & Keeran, P. (2017). Expanding support for graduate students: Library workshops on research funding opportunities. *College & Research Libraries, 78*(3), 297–313.

Gibbs, D., Boettcher, J., Hollingsworth, J., & Slania, H. (2012). Assessing the research needs of graduate students at Georgetown University. *The Journal of Academic Librarianship, 38*(5), 268–276.

Godfrey, I., Rutledge, L., Mowdood, A., Reed, J., Bigler, S., & Soehner, C. (2017). Supporting student retention and success: Including family areas in an academic library. *portal: Libraries and the Academy, 17*(2), 375–388.

Grigg, S. G., Jeong, S. H., & Exner, N. (2018). Providing innovative library services to STEM graduate students. In C. Renfro & C. Stiles (Eds.), *Transforming libraries to serve graduate students* (pp. 139–154). Chicago, IL: Association of College and Research Libraries.

Ince, S. (2018). Trends in academic libraries graduate student services: A case study. *The Journal of Academic Librarianship, 44*(3), 426–429.

Kayongo, J., & Helm, C. (2010). Graduate students and the library: A survey of research practices and library use at the University of Notre Dame. *Reference & User Services Quarterly, 49*(4), 341–349.

Petit, J. (2014). A family-friendly study room for student-parents and their children at Portland State University Library. *OLA Quarterly, 20*(1), 36–39.

Rempel, H. G., Hussong-Christian, U., & Mellinger, M. (2011). Graduate student space and service needs: A recommendation for a cross-campus solution. *The Journal of Academic Librarianship, 37*(6), 480–487.

Renfro, C., & Shields, E. (2017). Transforming libraries to serve graduate students: Trends and issues from a new conference. *College & Research Libraries News, 78*(4), 202–205.

Shavers, M., & Moore, J. (2014). Black female voices: Self-presentation strategies in doctoral programs at predominately white institutions. *Journal of College Student Development, 55*(4), 391–407.

University of Utah, Office of Budget and Institutional Analysis. (2018). *University of Utah fast facts*. Retrieved from https://www.obia.utah.edu/wp-content/uploads/2017/08/fastFacts.pdf

Appendix 14.1: Graduate Student Focus Groups

Thank you all for agreeing to be a part of a focus group to help us improve our understanding of how you use library spaces and services. When we contacted you to be a part of this focus group, we sent you a copy of the consent form to read over. Here is a print copy for you to sign and date if you still wish to participate in this focus group. As a reminder, you are free to stop participating at any point if you need to. Once you have signed that copy, please hand it back to us. Thank you.

1. Which library space do you find the most conducive to conducting your work?
2. Are there additional library services you'd like to see?
3. Do you use the Graduate Student Reading Room? Why or why not?
4. Have you met with your liaison librarian? Why or why not?
5. What frustrates you most about doing library research?
6. What do you find lacking about the library spaces and services?
7. Do you attend the Social and/or the Boot Camp this year?
8. What types of resources do you use most for your work? Can you list specific resources?
9. What should the library stop doing?
10. Would you be interested in a journal club or writing group organized by the library?

CHAPTER FIFTEEN

The Library as Client: Immersive Professional Experiences in the Library

Kristen Elizabeth Cardoso

Introduction

Immersive projects where the library becomes a client of an individual student or team of students within a particular course not only provide students with hands-on experience in a "real- world" environment, but they also offer students a chance to learn more about the library from a new perspective, to become more invested in the library as a place of their own while they are here, and to personally improve the library for future students. Librarians and library staff also get a hands-on chance to learn new problem-solving approaches, such as design thinking and action research, and forge new relationships with students where student and librarian get to be both teacher and learner together.

In this chapter, I will share three small examples of immersive professional experiences in my library as case studies for other librarians who would like to offer something similar for their graduate students. The first case involved hiring a student who was already employed with the library to focus on our new student orientation design over the summer of 2015, with an emphasis on international students and more interactive activities. Her redesign with the library was implemented during the following fall semester, and she was able to submit her deliverables in partial fulfillment of her practicum requirement for her dual degree in International Education Management and Public Administration.

The last two case studies involved collaborating with teams of students in specific courses throughout the semester on projects for which they received course credit. One group of students applied the design thinking process to our reference area study space, which resulted in small, immediate changes that they were able to see as the semester progressed, as well as more substantial changes such as new furniture and the installation of additional wall outlets that continued after they had graduated. I attended classes with the students and participated directly in the design thinking process alongside them. Using action research principles, the second group of students redesigned the new student orientation in order to create an alternative, shorter session for students unable to attend or intimidated by the larger orientations. I met with this team throughout the semester and was able to involve the larger staff at certain stages throughout the process. These shorter orientations continue to be offered each semester. This chapter will show how immersive professional experiences can be offered for low to no-cost with long-lasting value to both students and the library.

Background

The Middlebury Institute of International Studies (MIIS) in Monterey, California, is a small, professional graduate school, with approximately 800 students—63% female and 32% male. The majority of students pursue master's degrees in fields such as international policy and development, international education management, translation and interpretation, and language teaching education. The student body is quite diverse with 30% of the population coming from 53 different countries (MIIS, n.d.). The institute strives to provide immersive experiences such as practicums, semesters abroad, and client projects to students in preparation for their professional careers after graduation. In partnership with our parent institution, Middlebury College in Vermont, undergraduate students are given the opportunity to take courses with graduate students at the institute and even to earn an accelerated master's degree. Although few of our students go on to become professional librarians, the library has collaborated with instructors to offer immersive professional experiences relevant to the future careers of our students.

The William Tell Coleman Library at the Middlebury Institute houses a collection of approximately 100,000 volumes with about a third of the materials in a language other than English to support the curriculum's international focus. The space is divided into two floors with the upstairs reserved for quiet study and the downstairs allowing for group work, discussions, and socializing. A team of graduate assistants provide services for students, faculty, staff, alumni, and community members at the library year-round, in addition to the library's seven staff members. In an effort to become more student-centered, the library created a new user experience librarian position in January 2016 dedicated to improving library policies, services, and spaces for the Middlebury Institute community. As the staff member in this new role, I was able to work directly with students and instructors in new ways that created professional development opportunities for them and myself while also enhancing the user experience of the library.

Literature Review

Much of the literature about experiential learning in academic libraries focuses on undergraduate students. In their recent systematic literature review on student employment as a high-impact practice, as defined by Kuh (2008), graduate students were only mentioned in relation to LIS programs and developing future librarians (Mitola, Rinto, & Pattni, 2018). Kuh's (2008) Association of American Colleges & Universities publication does, however, include experiential learning with community partners as a high-impact practice. Not much has been written with regards to graduate students and experiential learning, but the existing body of literature on undergraduate students and experiential learning can offer insight into how these types of experiences can be beneficial for graduate students.

Experiential learning is defined by the Association of Experiential Education (n.d.) as "a philosophy that informs many methodologies in which educators purposefully engage with learners in direct experience and focused reflection in order to increase knowledge, develop skills, clarify values, and develop people's capacity to contribute to their communities" (para 1). As noted by Sanders and Balius (2015) in their annotated bibliography on experiential learning and academic libraries, experiential learning and active learning are often used synonymously, but active learning is better understood as one part of the entire experiential learning process (pp. 51–52). In Kolb's (1984) foundational work on learning styles, he describes his experiential learning style theory as a four-stage cycle: concrete experience, reflective observation, abstract conceptualization, and active experimentation. According to his theory, learning "is the process whereby knowledge is created through the transformation of experience" (Kolb, 1984, p. 38). McDonnell (2017) argues in the conclusion to his edited volume on experiential learning in academic libraries that engaging in these types of learning experiences with students can reposition the academic library as collaborators in "active knowledge generation, rather than passive assimilation of information" and thus "can heighten libraries' visibility in and engagement with their parent institution's mission" (p. 204).

The library as client is one form of experiential learning with the potential for high impact on the learning and professional development of graduate students. The use of client-based language is perhaps most familiar in a business context; for example, one article uses this language to describe working with two advanced undergraduate-level marketing research classes (Chestnut, 2011). However, the concept is not limited to a specific discipline. A first-year English instruction librarian at Georgia Tech used the idea for a Communications course (Brown, 2014). Library as client has been defined as "where the library hires students from a class to accomplish a related task" (Tomlinson & Arnold-Garza, 2017, p. 22) and more broadly as "student-based projects" where "students can reap the benefits of embedded librarianship while at the same time providing a service, product, or insight to the library in return" (Brown, 2014, p. 4). Published examples of academic libraries partnering with graduate students on library as client project-based experiential learning are lacking and would be a welcome addition to the literature.

Case Study 1: New Student Orientations

During the spring semester 2015, the library was asked to consider no longer requiring students to attend a new student library orientation. The mandatory status of library orientations meant that those students who did not attend would have a hold placed on their account barring them from registering for the next semester's courses. The argument against the mandatory status was that students were already overwhelmed with the amount of orientation sessions they were required to attend in addition to dealing with personal concerns such as trying to find housing in our high cost-of-living area. Although we understood these issues, we were not willing to lose the opportunity we had with the mandatory orientations to meet new students, introduce them to our spaces and services, and begin building relationships with them, whereby they would know we were people they could come ask for help.

That said, we also knew there were challenges with our current orientation design. Library orientations were hour-long sessions led by one librarian who often did as many as six in a day throughout orientation week. The design was not sustainable for the librarian responsible for orientations, and students did not get a chance to meet other staff members. We wanted orientations to be less intimidating, more fun, and more interactive. We also wanted to reassess our content and address any assumptions about skill levels or previous knowledge; although we are a graduate school, our students come from a variety of backgrounds. Some of our students are returning to school after years in the field, while some are coming right from their undergraduate studies. Many are new to the United States, while others are returning after many years abroad. When one of our graduate assistants who was pursuing a dual degree in International Education Management and Public Administration began asking us about local practicum opportunities, we realized our orientation redesign project might have potential as a practicum project. She had skills and knowledge we did not have as librarians, and we were able to offer her a hands-on experience working in an international education setting on a real-life project.

She and her advisor agreed to the collaboration, as did library leadership. As this student's supervisor, I increased her pay grade by one level and gave her a desk with a computer that was unoccupied in the library's Public Services office. Although she had her own desk, the Public Services office is shared between two people and is located behind the busy front desk, so she was fully immersed not only in the project but the library's organizational environment during her time with us. She worked part-time over the summer of 2015 and began by meeting with each member of the staff to hear their thoughts, wishes, and goals, and to share reflections on her own new student orientation experience the year prior. Throughout the summer we also met together as a team to brainstorm, assign tasks, and assess progress. At the end of the project, she passed on all her documentation to us on a flash drive, in a shared Google Drive folder, and on our departmental shared drive.

During the summer, she created new signage using brightly colored card stock to help students navigate the space, as well as visually map out the orientation path. Since we knew students often felt overwhelmed by the amount of information delivered in the orientations, but also often wished they had been introduced to key resources earlier in their program, we created program-specific lists of helpful databases and journal titles. The librarians selected the content, and she added the design and formatting. She also created a handout in the form of a passport that had a general outline of the orientation, a page for each station with key points to help with content memory, a list of all the staff members, and a map of each floor. These passports especially were very well received by students and fit the overall international culture of the campus. Created in Google Docs, they were inexpensively printed on a color printer and stapled with a long-reach stapler in-house. As I was to observe after we ran the orientations, many students would return to the library with these handouts as a reference for something they wanted help using.

What was once an hour-long session by one librarian became a series of stations at which students would spend 2 to 15 minutes with different members of the staff. The station design allowed for students to meet more members of the library staff and also built in variation to help reduce overwhelm and increase engagement. Two stations consisted of short videos with music for students to watch, while in the middle of the orientation students had a chance to sit down together in a group study room. The last activity was optional, but offered students an opportunity to explore the quiet study floor upstairs through a self-guided scavenger hunt using the floor maps in the passport booklet. Short, three-question feedback forms were developed to give to students at the end of each session to help us assess our new design's effectiveness. Before implementing the new orientation design, the practicum student coordinated rehearsal runs with the staff so we could become comfortable with the arrangement and timing and make changes if needed. Throughout the project, she helped us keep the student perspective first and foremost, resulting in a week of successfully running orientations for over 300 students. Her resulting portfolio was submitted in partial fulfillment of her practicum requirements, and she gained firsthand experience working in a team environment in an academic, international education setting similar to that of her current position after earning her degree.

Case Study 2: Design Thinking and Library Space

Shortly after my position became user experience librarian, I was invited to give a presentation to a class studying social innovations in the public sector. They were going to be learning design thinking techniques, and the instructor wanted the students to partner with clients on real-life projects. I visited the class and presented three "How Might We" questions framing potential projects in the library suitable for a design thinking approach. Two of the questions focused on physical spaces in the library, and the third looked at promoting digital resources. A week or so following the class visit, five students interested in pursuing improvements to the library's space joined together, named themselves Team Library, and wrote to me accepting the library as their client for the course.

I began regularly attending the class sessions and participating actively in the design thinking process alongside the students. The instructor kindly gave me access to all the course materials on the shared class drive. I also made myself available outside of class when the team had questions or ideas to share, although some of the steps, such as interviewing students and conducting observations, were done by the students without me. Since the library was their client, they were also required to write a final report to be shared with the entire library staff of their findings and recommendations, which they did at the end of the semester. The team's responsiveness and accountability to the staff impressed everyone, and helped establish a new sense of trust and enthusiasm for bringing graduate students on board to actively participate in shaping the library in the future.

Using the model originally developed by the Hasso-Plattner Institute of Design at Stanford University (also known as the d.school), the five stages of design thinking we followed are empathize, define, ideate, prototype, and test (Stanford, 2010). We went through each stage, except testing, throughout the course of the semester. We began by refining the original challenge I had presented, coming up with the framing question: "How might we improve functionality of the library's first floor?" The second floor is reserved for quiet study, but the first floor allows for a reasonable amount of noise for collaboration, group study, and socializing. However, the arrangement and type of furniture in the space was not the most conducive for those purposes. In class we brainstormed ideas using Post-it notes on a large white board, and then the team went out into the library to observe students using the space and selecting a few to interview about their use of the space and their needs. We brainstormed again after reviewing the results and were also able to get feedback from the instructor along the way.

The team began prototyping new arrangements by creating space visualizations in Adobe Photoshop and designing signage that could potentially be used to communicate the space's permissible noise levels. I began prototyping myself as well; for example, we learned that there were not enough electrical outlets near two specific tables, so I added power strips. We were then able to use what we had learned with the demonstrated usage of the power strips to justify Facilities installing additional electrical outlets in the space. Based on their Photoshop images, I borrowed a rolling white board from another office on campus and had it placed into the space for a few weeks to see how people would use it. As they designed new signage, I had old and outdated signage removed from the space. The team appreciated knowing I was taking their proposals seriously, and they were encouraged to see their work coming to life in the space.

Of the three case studies presented here, the project with Team Library took the most of my time; however, the impact was significant and well worth the level of involvement required. The team not only acquired hands-on experience with design thinking, but they also witnessed firsthand some of the changes that were made to the library's space based on the recommendations they developed through the project. As library users themselves, they discovered a new sense of pride and investment in the library as their space. As a young professional, I also profited from the opportunity to learn more about design thinking and how it could apply to my user experience practice in the library, as well as the chance to engage with graduate students in a new way. We were equals on the project in that we were all learning and building something new together. Future graduate students also benefited from the improvements made through this project. Long after the course was over, I continued working with colleagues and students to transform this particular space to better meet the changing needs of our users.

Case Study 3: Action Research and Orientation Options

Having heard about students teaming with me on a project for course credit, a group of students in a class on sustainability in social change organizations contacted me and asked if the library could be their client. The instructor and I both approved the idea of the students applying the action research methodology they were learning in class to our new student orientation design. Although our redesign, described in the first case study, had been successful, we had lost our mandatory status and knew we were no longer reaching everyone. In particular, we knew international students often were not on campus for orientation week and were thus behind from the start. Often, they had arrived but were struggling to find a stable housing situation or employment on campus and could not sacrifice valuable free time to attend a nonmandatory, hour-long library orientation, no matter how much they would have liked to or found it useful in the long run. Although we were happy to meet with individual students one-on-one as their schedule allowed, we could not provide individual orientations in this way for every single student. We charged the student team with trying to find ways we could offer alternative orientations that were sustainable for our organization while being accessible to all our students.

The students began by diagnosing the current state of our organization. They interviewed two library staff members, conducted a focus group with 10 students about their orientation experiences and expectations, and reviewed materials from previous orientations. When they finished mapping out our current situation and structure, they began benchmarking our practices with other libraries of a similar size and even reached out to a local academic library to discuss with a reference librarian what they did for their new student orientations. Unlike with Team Library, I did not attend classes with these students, nor did I participate in the process alongside them. They met with me periodically throughout the semester to share progress and ideas, and I coordinated for them when they wanted to meet with the entire library staff, which we did twice. In the first meeting the group led an identity collage exercise, and during the second meeting they presented their findings and recommendations.

For the identity collage exercise, they asked us all to select words that come to mind when thinking of certain concepts such as "library" and "research" within the context of our specific community. Using our computer projection screen, they would then do a Google image search of the word and ask us to select the image that best represented the word. These images were posted in a Word document, and the result was a visual diagram of our hopes and dreams for the library and the students we serve. The library staff especially enjoyed participating in this activity. After finishing their data gathering, they began generating and testing ideas. They solicited volunteers and I gave a mock orientation to a group of students who then spent 15–20 minutes discussing their feedback with us. Several of the volunteer students had not attended a library orientation, which gave us some further insights into why students may choose not to or not be able to attend and how we can help address those challenges. We found the two most significant reasons behind choosing not to attend included trying to navigate feeling overwhelmed with information at the start of their first semester when orientations are typically held and preferring to only attend sessions focused on their specific program rather than general library orientations.

The second and last meeting with the group and the whole staff was for their final presentation of their work over the semester and their recommendations. They presented three tiered recommendations, with the idea being that we start small with the first recommendation and then build up to the second and third over time. Following the presentation, they submitted a final report as well as a copy of their slides to both the library staff and the instructor.

Since we had found students were deterred from attending orientations due to competition for their attention during orientation, the group's first recommendation was to offer miniorientations they called "411 Tours." These tours would only be 15 minutes each, would not require any prior sign-up, and would be offered not only during the campus orientation week but one or two weeks into the semester as well. These tours would be general in nature, but would provide an easy platform for marketing program-specific workshops and resources available through the library. Requiring the work of only one staff member at a time with multiple staff capable of giving the tours, these miniorientations are still offered by the library as of this writing. The second recommendation was to leverage technology to create digital library orientations available 24/7 that would highlight not only the library, but our staff as well, in an effort to build relationships with students we might not otherwise meet. The third recommendation involved collaborating with faculty to offer faculty-sponsored, program-specific orientations. These orientations may be required for students to attend and would expand on the work being done by librarians who visit classes for instruction sessions.

The "411 Tours" were implemented immediately upon their recommendation. Students have appreciated the chance to meet with someone in a way that fits their overloaded orientation schedule, and the students who helped us create this alternative option knew their research made a difference. A digital library tour was created approximately a year following the recommendation, and the third recommendation is still in progress. It is worth noting that our willingness to foster not only these types of immersive, professional learning experiences, but also to then enact the results produced by the students helped build the reputation of the library to other students and instructors. We provided students with concrete experience and tangible deliverables they could showcase in portfolios or include on résumés, became references after students graduated, and in some cases even became colleagues we could call on for help and inspiration long after students started their professional careers.

Conclusion/Recommendations

I learned something new each time I partnered with students on immersive projects in the library and found it energizing to work with graduate students as fellow professionals. I felt better equipped to assist other students learning action research in their classes, and I integrated design thinking principles into my own professional practice as well. Generally speaking, it was not possible to pay students for their labor as I was able to do in the first case study. However, the model of students receiving course credit at the conclusion of the project was a successful arrangement for everyone involved. In both cases shared in this chapter, the instructors of each class spoke with me afterward about the value to their students of being able to experiment firsthand with a real project in the library and for my availability to them along them the way. The library staff also gave positive feedback and appreciated being invited to be involved. Whether it is feasible for other staff members to be involved or not, I recommend at least sharing regular updates and any materials produced by the students so that staff feel included and have the opportunity to share feedback or ideas if they wish. It can also be inspiring for everyone to see what students are coming up with for the library.

A key takeaway from these library-as-client relationships with students over the years is being open-minded and open-ended; don't start from a place of restrictions or a specific end goal. Asking students to keep a limited budget in mind from the beginning inhibits creative thinking unnecessarily, as does responding to ideas defensively by saying something has already been tried in the past and did not succeed, even if it is true. Let creativity flow from both them and yourself and see what happens. Even small changes to library services or spaces can have a big impact both on the students doing the work and on everyone who uses the library now and in the future. If you have the opportunity to collaborate with an individual student or a team of students on a real-life project in the library, it will be well worth your time. It not only helps the students grow and shape their identity as professionals, but it helps you and the library grow as well.

References

Association of Experiential Education. (n.d.). *What is experiential education?* Retrieved from https://www.aee.org/what-is-ee

Brown, S. (2014). A symbiotic relationship: The library as client in undergraduate courses. *LOEX Quarterly, 41*(1), 3–5.

Chestnut, M. T. (2011). Recession-friendly library market research: Service learning with benefits. *Journal of Library Innovation, 2*(1), 61–71.

Kolb, D. A. (1984). *Experiential learning: Experience as the source of learning and development* (Vol. 1). Englewood Cliffs, NJ: Prentice-Hall.

Kuh, G. (2008). *High-impact education practices: What they are, who has access to them, and why they matter.* Washington, DC: Association of American Colleges & Universities.

McDonnell, P. (2017). Conclusion: An experiential librarian's creed. In P. McDonnell (Ed.), *The experiential library: Transforming academic and research libraries through the power of experiential learning* (pp. 203–208). Cambridge, MA: Chandos Publishing.

Middlebury Institute of International Studies (MIIS). (n.d.). *About the institute.* Retrieved from https://www.middlebury.edu/institute/about

Mitola, R., Rinto, E., & Pattni, E. (2018). Student employment as a high-impact practice in academic libraries: A systematic review. *The Journal of Academic Librarianship, 44*(3), 352–373. doi:10.1016/j.acalib.2018.03.005

Sanders, E., & Balius, A. (2015). Experiential learning and academic libraries: An annotated bibliography. *Codex, 3*(3), 49–52.

Stanford d.school. (2010). *An introduction to the design thinking process guide.* Retrieved from https://dschool.old.stanford.edu/sandbox/groups/designresources /wiki/36873/attachments/74b3d/ModeGuideBOOTCAMP2010L.pdf

Tomlinson, C., & Arnold-Garza, S. (2017). The library as leadership incubator: A case study of Towson University's A-LIST program. In S. Arnold-Garza & C. Tomlinson (Eds.), *Students lead the library: The importance of student contributions to the academic library* (pp. 21–38). Chicago, IL: Association of College and Research Libraries.

About the Editors and Contributors

Editors

Carrie Forbes, MLS, MA, is a professor and the associate dean for student and scholar services at the University of Denver. She is the coeditor, with Peggy Keeran, of *Successful Campus Outreach for Academic Libraries: Building Community through Collaboration*. She has written several articles and book chapters on information literacy pedagogy, graduate student support, and assessment of public services in libraries, including a coauthored article, "Expanding Support for Graduate Students: Library Workshops on Research Funding Opportunities," in *College & Research Libraries*.

Peggy Keeran, professor, is the arts & humanities librarian at the University of Denver. She is the coeditor, with Carrie Forbes, of *Successful Campus Outreach for Academic Libraries: Building Community through Collaboration* and, with Forbes and Gina Schlesselman-Tarango, coauthored "Expanding Support for Graduate Students: Library Workshops on Research Funding Opportunities" in *College & Research Libraries*. Keeran's research interests include library services for graduate students, integrating digital and physical primary source research into the curriculum, and visual literacy for students in non-arts disciplines.

Contributors

Tarida Anantachai is the lead librarian of the Learning Commons at the Syracuse University Libraries, where she serves as the liaison to her campus's international student services center, English language institute, and multicultural affairs office. Her research interests include diversity and inclusion, early career development and mentoring, and outreach programming. Tarida was an ALA Emerging Leader, a participant in the Minnesota

Institute for Early Career Librarians, and stays connected to the library profession as an active contributor and officer on several national and regional library association committees, including those within ALA, ACRL, APALA, and the Eastern NY Chapter of ACRL. She received her MS in library and information science from the University of Illinois at Urbana-Champaign.

Victor Baeza is the director of library graduate services for Oklahoma State University—Stillwater. He provides leadership and direction for the OSU Library in the areas of services and resources for graduate students. He has continuously worked to develop new outreach opportunities and collaborations across campus, including the development of the campus-wide graduate digital badge program. His 24 years of involvement in library instruction has given him diverse experience in designing, directing and delivering workshops, training sessions, and seminars to the academic community. Victor has a BS in communication from Eastern New Mexico University. He earned his MLS from the University of North Texas and received his MBA from Texas Christian University.

Lisa Becksford is the online & graduate engagement librarian at the University Libraries at Virginia Tech in Blacksburg, Virginia. She received an MA in English from North Carolina State University and an MSLS from the University of North Carolina at Chapel Hill. Becksford is the author of research articles and presentations about online learning, information literacy instruction, and usability testing. She is active in the education committee of ACRL's Education and Behavioral Sciences Section and has held leadership positions in the Virginia Library Association's New Members Round Table Forum.

Greta Boers is the librarian for classical studies and linguistics at Duke University Libraries, Durham, North Carolina. She is a good, solid, in-the-weeds reference librarian with the conviction that the best research support and teaching are necessarily imaginative, eclectic, and multidisciplinary, and this wide-ranging engagement across disciplines is reflected in her writings. They range from the cultural assimilation of Gypsies, book reviews on paddle-stamping (a decorative technique in pottery) in the pre-Columbian South East, and civil rights activists in Birmingham before Martin Luther King Jr., as well as an in-depth encyclopedia article on the history and science of twin studies. Of the awards that she has received, the most transforming was "Greatest Improvement in Spelling."

Jennifer Bowers, professor, is the social sciences librarian at the University of Denver, Colorado. She is coeditor, with Peggy Keeran, of the 15-volume Rowman and Littlefield series, Literary Research: Strategies and Sources, and the coauthor of three volumes in the series. She is also the coeditor, with Carrie Forbes, of *Rethinking Reference for Academic Libraries: Innovative Developments and Future Trends* and coauthor of the *Information Research* article, "Emotional Silos: A Review of Doctoral Candidates' Isolating Experiences and the Role for Academic Librarians in Campus-Wide Support Networks." Bowers's current research focuses on visual literacy and critical approaches to teaching with archival materials in the social sciences, collaborative research consultations, and popular press reception of the pioneering archaeologist, Harriet Boyd Hawes.

Steve Brantley is a professor of library services and the head of research, engagement and scholarship at Booth Library, Eastern Illinois University. Brantley is the librarian for Communication Studies, Political Science, and media collections. He has an MLS and an MA in media and cultural studies, both from Indiana University.

Kristen Elizabeth Cardoso is the circulation coordinator at the University of California, Santa Cruz, and was previously the user experience librarian at the Middlebury Institute of International Studies. She received her MLIS as well as an MA in English literature from McGill University, Canada. She is an active committee member of the Monterey Bay Area Cooperative Library System (MOBAC).

Jill Cirasella is an associate professor at the Graduate Center of the City University of New York, where she leads the Mina Rees Library's scholarly communication and digital scholarship services. Her research focus is scholarly communication, broadly construed, and she is committed to advancing open scholarship at CUNY and beyond. She currently serves as chair of the editorial board of the *Journal of Librarianship and Scholarly Communication*.

Ellen K. Corrigan is associate professor of library services at Eastern Illinois University, Charleston, Illinois, where she specializes in cataloging and metadata services. She is the liaison librarian for Art and Design. Ellen has an MLS and MA in art history, both from the University of Maryland.

Angela Courtney is the head of the arts and humanities department at the Indiana University Bloomington Libraries, where she is also the librarian for literatures in English and theatre and drama. Courtney is the author of several books, including *Literary Research and the Era of American Nationalism and Romanticism* and *Literary Research and Postcolonial Literatures in English*.

Michael Courtney is the outreach and engagement librarian at Indiana University Bloomington, where he connects the Libraries' resources and services to the academic priorities of various campus communities and student audiences, including first-year students, distance learners, international students, and others. Courtney is also an associate professor in the Department of Information and Library Science at Indiana University where he teaches the core pedagogy and praxis course in the effective design and teaching of information literacy education for the Master of Library Science program.

Kyrille DeBose is an associate professor at Virginia Tech, Blacksburg, Virginia. She originally served as the college librarian for Natural Resources & Environment and Animal Sciences from 2005 to 2017. As of July 2017, she became the head of the Veterinary Medicine Library & Liaison to Animal Sciences. As a liaison librarian for over a decade, she has extensive experience conducting in-person and online instructional sessions related to several facets of information literacy for disciplines within the life sciences. She has presented at multiple conferences and has written several publications related to her work in information literacy.

Heather De Forest is a librarian at Simon Fraser University. She leads the Community Scholars Program, a unique program that connects 500 individuals working in nonprofits and charities in British Columbia, Canada, with access to approximately 20,000 e-journals and e-books, and librarian support. De Forest's research and professional interests cluster around human-centered design, knowledge exchange, and engagement processes.

Yi Ding is online instructional design librarian and the affordable learning solutions co-coordinator at California State University Northridge. She is a 2019 Academic Library Impact Research Grant recipient, and her research and librarianship activities aim to bring affordability and accessibility to higher education.

Rebecca Dowson is a digital scholarship librarian in the Research Commons at Simon Fraser University, where she supports researchers who are engaged with the digital humanities (DH) and coordinates the development and hosting of DH projects through the library's Digital Humanities Innovation Lab. Dowson is responsible for project consultations and digital scholarship skill development training. Her research interests include the intersection of libraries and digital humanities, with a particular interest in digital cultural heritage projects, digital skill building, and new forms of scholarly publishing.

Kirstin I. Duffin is a research, engagement, and scholarship librarian and liaison to the sciences and math at Eastern Illinois University, Charleston,

Illinois. She holds an MLS from the University of Wisconsin at Madison and an MS in biological sciences from EIU. With coauthors Steve Brantley and Ellen Corrigan, she is the recipient of EIU's Graduate School Leadership Award in 2017 for development of the "Thesis Research 101" series.

Bridget Farrell is an associate professor and coordinator of library instruction & reference services at the University of Denver, Denver, Colorado. She has written articles for *portal: Libraries and the Academy*, *Reference Services Review*, and the *Journal of Library Administration*.

Emily K. Hart is the science and engineering librarian and research impact lead at Syracuse University, Syracuse, New York. She is a subject librarian who provides research support, instruction, and outreach services to several science-related departments within the College of Arts and Sciences. Emily has specialized in supporting science research for over 12 years. She also leads a team of librarians focused on improving research reputation and supporting the research enterprise at the university. Additionally, Emily has a background in web and electronic resources and chairs the libraries' discovery services team. She completed her BA in English with a minor in education at St. Bonaventure University, and her Masters of Library Science (MLS) and an Advanced Certificate in Educational Technology at the University at Buffalo. She has presented at local and national conferences, most recently on topics related to assessment and graduate programming. Her research interests include research reputation, systematic reviews, assessment, scholarly communications, and graduate student outreach. Emily is an active member of the ASEE Engineering Libraries Division, Eastern NY Chapter of ACRL, and NY Science Librarians group (NYSCILIB).

Julia Hon, MLIS, is a data services specialist at the Institute for Health Metrics and Evaluation at the University of Washington in Seattle, where she supports research teams with their data management and acquisition, and contributes to the Global Health Data Exchange (GHDx), a catalog of global health data. Prior to working as a librarian, she managed international education programs for international scholars, students, and administrators in Washington, DC.

Cinthya Ippoliti is the university librarian and director of the Auraria Library, which serves three institutions: Community College of Denver, Metropolitan State University of Denver, and the University of Colorado, Denver. Previously, she was the associate dean for research and learning services at Oklahoma State University where she provided administrative leadership for the library's academic liaison program, as well as services for undergraduate and graduate students and community outreach. Other past work includes head of teaching and learning services at the University of Maryland where she was in charge of the spaces, services, and programming offered by the Terrapin Learning Commons in addition to coordinating the libraries' first-year instruction program.

Edward F. Lener is an associate director of collection management in the University Libraries at Virginia Tech in Blacksburg, Virginia, and college librarian for the Sciences. He received his MLS degree from State University of New York at Albany. Lener is the university's representative to the Collections Committee of the VIVA library consortium and a coauthor of the book *Graduate Research: A Guide for Students in the Sciences* (4th ed., 2016). He is an active member of both the ACRL Science and Technology Section and the ALCTS Collection Management Section and currently serves on the STS Government Information Committee.

Rochelle Lundy is the scholarly communication officer at Seattle University in Seattle, Washington. She provides guidance on copyright, publishing, and digital scholarship in addition to managing the university's institutional repository. Prior to her career in libraries, she worked as an attorney specializing in copyright and media litigation. She received her JD from Columbia University and her MLIS from the University of Washington.

Heidi Madden serves as the librarian for Western European and Medieval/Renaissance Studies at Duke University Libraries, Durham, North Carolina. She is active in the European Studies Section (ESS) of the Association of College and Research Libraries (ACRL), formerly WESS, where she has convened the Classical, Medieval Renaissance Discussion Group, the Romance Languages Discussion Group, and the Germanist Discussion Group with programs on information literacy, research methods, digital humanities, and European fiction in translation. She served as vice chair and chair of WESS during 2011–2013 and is incoming chair of ESS for 2019–2020.

Liz Milewicz is the head of digital scholarship and publishing services at Duke University Libraries, Durham, North Carolina. Her department provides training and consulting in digital approaches to scholarship and partners with researchers and students on digital research, teaching, and publishing projects. Along with leading her department's interdisciplinary and often cross-institutional team of graduate students, she codirects Project Vox (http://projectvox.org), a digital publication and internationally engaged educational initiative that seeks to reform and diversify philosophy instruction. Currently, she serves on the steering committee for the Mellon Foundation–funded Triangle Scholarly Communication Institute (http://trianglesci.org). Before coming to Duke in 2011, Liz managed two NEH-funded digital humanities projects at Emory University (The Expanded Online Transatlantic Slave Trade Database, http://slavevoyages.org; and African Origins, http://african-origins.org) and worked with the Emory Libraries on a range of digital initiatives. She earned her doctorate at Emory as well, where she studied the evolving culture, role, and sound of academic libraries.

Alison J. Moore is a digital scholarship librarian in the Research Commons at Simon Fraser University, where she provides support for student and faculty researchers on the topics of scholarly communications, research impact, online presence, and data visualization. Moore's research interests include library assessment, knowledge mobilization, and scholarly publishing.

Marie Paiva is a social sciences librarian at the University of Utah working with students and faculty and serves as a liaison with Anthropology, Asian Studies, Economics, and Psychology. She serves on committees at the University of Utah such as the Marriott Library's Graduate Student Services Committee, and has recently served as chair of Faculty Review and Promotion, Retention and Tenure. Marie is a member of the American Library Association, Academic and College Research Libraries Association, and the Utah Library Association, and attends meetings and presents papers there and at international organizations as well. She has a volunteer library project training staff in Ethiopia at an academic institution.

Lis Pankl currently serves as the head of Graduate & Undergraduate Services (GUS) and holds the rank of associate librarian at the J. Willard Marriott Library at the University of Utah. Through diverse expertise and dynamic campus partnerships, GUS initiates innovation and leadership in teaching, learning, and assessment as well as promotes and enhances student engagement with the university and local communities. Lis holds a PhD in Geography from Kansas State University, a MSLS from the University of North Texas, a MA in English from Abilene Christian University, and a BA in English from Washington State University. Her areas of interest include critical and cultural geographies, 20th-century British and American literature, librarian identities, emerging pedagogies, student engagement, and higher education administration. Lis is currently completing a Master of Public Administration with a focus in higher education at the University of Utah.

Virginia Pannabecker is an associate professor and director, research collaboration and engagement at the University Libraries, Virginia Tech in

Blacksburg, Virginia. She is an author or coauthor of research articles and presentations on library instruction, online learning, and other topics. She serves on committees and in leadership roles in professional organizations such as the Association for College and Research Libraries (Science and Technology Section) and the Medical Library Association.

Melissa A. Rassibi is reference, instruction, and outreach services librarian at California State University Northridge. She is a Spectrum Scholar and dedicated educator. Her research interests include Universal Design for Learning and Student Success.

Jennifer Rosenstein, MLS, MA, is the director of the Henry Birnbaum Library on Pace University's New York City campus. Previously, she served as assistant university librarian for graduate services and first-year outreach services librarian at Pace. She has also worked as a secondary school librarian and high school English teacher. She holds degrees from Syracuse University, Teachers College Columbia University, and Brown University.

Kodi Saylor is the first-year teaching and learning librarian at Auraria Library serving University of Colorado Denver, Metropolitan State University of Denver, and Community Colleges of Denver in Denver, Colorado. She holds an MSLS from the University of North Carolina at Chapel Hill and an MFA in poetry from New York University.

Will Shaw is the digital humanities consultant at Duke University Libraries, Durham, North Carolina. As part of the Libraries' Digital Scholarship and Publishing Services department, he teaches about a range of topics in digital scholarship, provides consultation and technology leadership for numerous digital humanities projects, and mentors a team of graduate student interns. He studied English literature at Warren Wilson College and the University of North Carolina at Chapel Hill, where he also served as the technical editor of the William Blake Archive.

Roxanne Shirazi is an assistant professor and dissertation research librarian at The Graduate Center, City University of New York, and visiting assistant professor at Pratt Institute School of Information. Her work has appeared in *Journal of Librarianship and Scholarly Communication*, *Library Trends*, and *College & Research Libraries News*. Shirazi is an active participant in university faculty governance and the Professional Staff Congress of the City University of New York.

Nicole White is the head of the Research Commons at Simon Fraser University Library, an initiative that provides space and academic support for graduate students across the research life cycle. She participated in the development of SFU's award-winning Thesis Boot Camp alongside a team of writing facilitators, librarians, and other campus partners. White is interested in academic libraries' expanded support for emerging research software used for quantitative and qualitative data analysis, as well as services for research data management and data visualization. She leads a team responsible for tracking trends and issues in scholarly communication and increasing campus awareness of Open Access.

Index